# A Traveller's History of Spain

FOURTH EDITION

# Interlink's Bestselling Travel Publications

## The Traveller's History Series

| | |
|---|---|
| *A Traveller's History of Australia* | $14.95 pb |
| *A Traveller's History of the Caribbean* | $14.95 pb |
| *A Traveller's History of China* | $14.95 pb |
| *A Traveller's History of England* | $14.95 pb |
| *A Traveller's History of France* | $14.95 pb |
| *A Traveller's History of Greece* | $14.95 pb |
| *A Traveller's History of India* | $14.95 pb |
| *A Traveller's History of Ireland* | $14.95 pb |
| *A Traveller's History of Italy* | $14.95 pb |
| *A Traveller's History of Japan* | $14.95 pb |
| *A Traveller's History of London* | $14.95 pb |
| *A Traveller's History of North Africa* | $14.95 pb |
| *A Traveller's History of Paris* | $14.95 pb |
| *A Traveller's History of Russia* | $14.95 pb |
| *A Traveller's History of Scotland* | $14.95 pb |
| *A Traveller's History of Spain* | $14.95 pb |
| *A Traveller's History of Turkey* | $14.95 pb |

## The Traveller's Wine Guides

| | |
|---|---|
| *A Traveller's Wine Guide to France* | $17.95 pb |
| *A Traveller's Wine Guide to Germany* | $17.95 pb |
| *A Traveller's Wine Guide to Italy* | $17.95 pb |
| *A Traveller's Wine Guide to Spain* | $17.95 pb |

*Available at good bookstores everywhere.*
*We encourage you to support your local bookseller.*

To order or request our complete catalog,
please call us at **1-800-238-LINK** or write to:
**Interlink Publishing**
46 Crosby Street, Northampton, MA 01060

**THE AUTHOR** Dr Juan Lalaguna was born in Navarra in Spain and later graduated from the University of Zaragoza in History and Law. He came to London for his post-graduate studies at the LSE and has lived there ever since, teaching Spanish language, history and literature as head of Hispanic Studies at the University of North London. A new *Historia de España* which is being considered as a possible textbook for Spanish schools is near completion and the author is also researching for a history of monarchical power in Spain.

**SERIES EDITOR** Professor Denis Judd is a graduate of Oxford, a Fellow of the Royal Historical Society and Professor of History at the University of North London. He has published over 20 books including the biographies of Joseph Chamberlain, Prince Philip, George VI and Alison Uttley, historical and military subjects, stories for children and two novels. His most recent book is the highly praised *Empire: The British Imperial Experience from 1765 to the Present*. He has reviewed and written extensively in the national press and in journals, has written several radio programmes and is a regular contributor to British and overseas radio and television.

*Other titles in the series*

A Traveller's History of France
A Traveller's History of Paris
A Traveller's History of Greece
A Traveller's History of Turkey
A Traveller's History of Italy
A Traveller's History of Russia and the USSR
A Traveller's History of England
A Traveller's History of Scotland
A Traveller's History of London
A Traveller's History of Ireland
A Traveller's History of Japan
A Traveller's History of India
A Traveller's History of China
A Traveller's History of North Africa
A Traveller's History of the Caribbean
A Traveller's History of Australia

# A Traveller's History of Spain

**JUAN LALAGUNA**

Series Editor   DENIS JUDD
*Line drawings*   *JOHN HOSTE*

INTERLINK BOOKS
An Imprint of Interlink Publishing Group, Inc.
NEW YORK

First American edition published 1999 by
INTERLINK BOOKS
An imprint of Interlink Publishing Group, Inc.
99 Seventh Avenue • Brooklyn, New York 11215 and
46 Crosby Street • Northampton, Massachusetts 01060

Published simultaneously in Great Britain by The Windrush Press

**Library of Congress Cataloging-in-Publication Data**
    A traveller's history of Spain/by Juan Lalaguna; series editor, Denis Judd;
line drawings, John Hoste — 1st American ed.
        p. cm.
    Bibliography: p.
    Includes index.
    ISBN 1-56656-324-0
    1. Spain—History.   2. Historic sites—Spain.   I. Judd, Denis, 1938–.
II. Title.
    DP66.L25    1999
    946—dc20                                                        89-15344
                                                                        CIP

Printed and bound in Canada

To order or request our complete catalog,
please call us at **1-800-238-LINK** or write to:
**Interlink Publishing**
46 Crosby Street, Northampton, MA 01060
e-mail: interpg@aol.com • website: www.interlinkbooks.com

To my mother Isabel in memoriam

# *Table of Contents*

*Preface*                                                         xi

CHAPTER ONE: **The Iberian Peninsula**                              1

CHAPTER TWO: **Islamic Invaders**                                 22

CHAPTER THREE: **The Making of Castilla**                         47

CHAPTER FOUR: **Imperial Spain**                                  76

CHAPTER FIVE: **The End of the Spanish Colonial Empire**         112

CHAPTER SIX: **Growth without Stability**                        149

CHAPTER SEVEN: **The Civil War and its Sequels**                 183

CHAPTER EIGHT: **Contemporary Spain**                            213

**Rulers and Monarchs**                                          245

**Chronology of Major Events**                                   253

**Further Reading**                                              263

**Historical Gazetteer**                                         265

*Index*                                                          283

MAPS    **Relief Map of Spain**                                    2

        **The Iberian Peninsula at the beginning
        of the ninth century**                                   31

        **The Iberian Peninsula in the thirteenth century**      48

        **The Spanish Empire**                                   86

**The liquidation of Spanish supremacy in Europe**   100

**The Provinces of Spain**   130

**Autonomous communities of Spain**   226

# Preface

Spain's popular contemporary image provides few clues to the magnificence and potency of her past. To have been the pioneer recipient of the post-war cheap package holiday trade bestows a distinction of a sort, so does the production of sherry, the spectacle of the bull fight, and the international successes of great football teams like Real Madrid and Barcelona. But Spanish power and influence was once exercised on a global scale. The overthrow of the ancient American empires of the Aztec and the Inca were merely early triumphs in the assertion of Spain's military, commercial and cultural supremacy in the New World as well as further afield. With the conquistadors went the crusading zeal of the Holy Church, the Spanish language and Spanish customs. During her 'golden age' Spain was a political giant, bestriding the world from Germany to the western Pacific, and, rich on American gold and silver, able to send the Armada against England, defeat the Turks at Lepanto and challenge France for the hegemony of Europe.

For many modern travellers, Spain's history remains an enigma, or at best a progress only dimly and fitfully perceived. The Roman province of Hispania is a clear enough concept. But then? How exactly did the Moorish conquest occur – and, in any case, who were the Moors? Did the Middle Ages somehow pass Spain by? 'In fourteen hundred and ninety two Columbus sailed the ocean blue.' How many who at least know that jingle also know that in 1492 the last Moorish stronghold of Granada surrendered to Castille and Aragon. We are on firmer ground with the spread of Spain's Latin American supremacy from California to Tierra del Fuego. But where do the Philippines, or the Netherlands, fit in? Then what happened to Spain in the nineteenth century or, indeed, for much of the twentieth? Anarchy, revolution, counter-revolution, brief triumphs of liberalism, fascist dictatorship, and democratic renaissance apparently succeed each other in a bewildering sequence. Hence, perhaps, the temptation to stick to what one is sure of: bull fights, flamenco dancers, the Alhambra, rioja, the Spanish Inquisition, the package holiday, paella.

It is one of the achievements of this well-researched and thorough book that no important part of Spain's history is neglected. From pre-history to the present democratically elected socialist government, the essentials of the Spanish experience are made plain. Nor is geography neglected, for it is central to Spain's evolution. Cut off from the rest of Europe by the Pyranees, which acted as both a defensive barrier and (more negatively) as a bulwark to new ideas, Spain was nonetheless a country facing both the Atlantic and the Mediterranean. Internal separatism is also much more than the function of ideology. Although it is the Basques who seize today's headlines, the provincial pride of Catalonia, Granada or Aragon has deep physical, as well as quasi-national, roots.

Above all, this book will serve an invaluable double function: for those who know little of Spain's past it will provide necessary illumination and entertainment; for those who think they know a good deal already it will provide further stimulation and, I suspect, many revelations. Both groups will have been well catered for with Juan Lalaguna's painstaking and perceptive text.

Denis Judd
London, 1989.

# CHAPTER ONE

# The Iberian Peninsula

In Spain, it is said, 'la geografía manda' (geography always has the last word), and so it would seem, for its historical development has largely been influenced by its dramatic and diverse geography. Iberia, the largest of the three peninsulas in the south-western corner of the Eurasian continent with some 580,000 square kilometres, occupies a unique position at the crossroads between the Mediterranean and the Atlantic, Europe and Africa; separated from the rest of Europe by the Pyrenees, a mountain system 440 kilometres long with peaks over 3000 metres above sea-level, and from Africa by the Straits of Gibraltar, a mere 13.4 kilometres wide at its narrowest point, at Tarifa, the southernmost town in Europe (latitude 36° 1° N).

The name of Iberia was first used by a Greek author in the sixth century BC to refer to the country of the Iberians, or dwellers along the Iberus (River Ebro), believed to have migrated there from Africa. A satellite view of this pentagonal landmass perched on the Punta de Tarifa and set slightly to the west substantiates Strabo's description of a bull's hide stretched out at the tail-end of Europe.

The most distinctive physical feature of the Iberian peninsula, occupying almost half its total surface, is the vast table-land of the northern and southern mesetas hoisted along the middle by the Central System, a range of snow-capped sierras like Guadarrama (visible from Madrid), also known as the *Cordillera cárpeto-vetónica*, the dorsal spine of the country. Like a turreted fortress these central plateaux are walled by the Cantabrian mountains to the north, the Iberian mountains to the north-east and the Sierra Morena to the south. The overwhelming reality of this solid landmass is therefore its altitude: at an average 660 metres it is second only to Switzerland in Western Europe. Only 18.4 per cent of the land surface of Spain lies below 200 metres, the upper limit for optimum agricultural production. More to the point, only 12 per cent, some 6 million hectares (14.8 million acres), lies steadily at a gradient of less than 1 in 20 (5 per cent).

Beyond this formidable line of defences, the River Ebro winds from the Cantabrian mountains in Fontibre (Reinosa) to its delta in Tortosa, draining along a triangular basin between the Iberian foothills and the Pyrenees. The Guadalquivir, the mighty river of the Arabs, flows in the opposite direction, from the Sierra de Cazorla to the Atlantic Ocean near San Lúcar de Barrameda, opening out as it flows south-east to

Spain's most fertile agricultural plains, bounded in the north by Sierra Morena and in the south by Sierra Nevada (Bética mountains), which contain Spain's highest peak, Mulhacén (3478 metres). The River Ebro, its exit to the Mediterranean forged through the narrow passes of a double range of mountains, has nevertheless provided access from the Mediterranean to north-western Iberia, and through its tributaries to the northern meseta and the foothills of the Pyrenees. The Guadalquivir discharges freely to the Atlantic Ocean and its regular course explains its good fortune as a major route of communication. The other, less abundant rivers flowing to the Mediterranean (Ter, Llobregat, Júcar, Segura) are notorious for their irregularity and torrential floods, causing devastation and a great deal of erosion in their precipitous careers to the sea. The main rivers of central Spain, all three initiating their long descent not far from the Mediterranean (Duero, Tajo and Guadiana), flow to the Atlantic following the gentle incline westwards of the two mesetas, and at times because of the nature of the terrain have to burrow their way through deep gorges and sharp escarpments.

Except for the Guadalquivir and the Ebro, Spanish rivers did not appear to offer much promise to Iberian settlers. Abundant rainfall in the north corrected this imbalance. There is a 'wet Spain' as well as a 'dry Spain', and, with a variety of climates ranging from a pluvious zone in the north-west with a moderate temperature and more than 800 mm of rainfall a year, to a desert, semi-arid Almería in the south-east. Even if Homo Sapiens had not yet started to ravish the land, the harsh physical features of the landscape, climatic conditions and the poor quality of the soil give a clear idea of the hostility of this Iberian land and the considerable amount of toil and ingenuity the early Spaniards would have had to invest to scratch a living out of it. The alluvial, rich soils of the Guadalquivir and Ebro basins, and the Mediterranean littoral were therefore the pole of attraction of generation after generation of migrants and settlers.

## Sources of Wealth

The coastal waters of the Iberian peninsula, with more than 4000 kilometres of shoreline, have always been extremely rich in marine life and their produce was commercialised throughout the Mediterranean from very early times. But it was the wealth in mineral resources that made Iberia legendary in the ancient Mediterranean world. It early became a large-scale producer and exporter of wine, olive oil and grain but it was the lure of precious and industrial metals that brought the first colonists to Gades (Cádiz) in the eighth century BC. Southern Iberia contained rich deposits of silver, lead, iron and copper in Carthago Nova (Cartagena), Sierra Morena, Río Tinto and Jaén, while in the north-west (Galicia and León) there was gold, copper and tin, for making bronze.

## EARLY EASTERN MEDITERRANEAN TRADERS AND LOCAL COMMUNITIES

In the early centuries of the first millennium BC, Phoenician merchants and Greek traders made their appearance among the native inhabitants of the peninsula, mainly along the coastal regions. The Phoenicians from Tyre (modern Lebanon) founded a chain of trading establishments from Onuba (Huelva), at the mouth of the Río Tinto, Gades and Malaca (Málaga), to Sexi (modern Almuñécar). Their first trading partner was Tartessos (Biblical Tarshish), a highly stratified and sophisticated society, according to classical sources, between the lower Guadalquivir and Guadiana rivers, and their parent colony at Carthage (modern Tunisia). These trading connections formed a very complex network of commercial exchanges filtering through to all parts of Iberia and beyond the Pillars of Hercules (the Straits of Gibraltar) along the coast of Portugal and the Bay of Biscay. This commercial interchange seems to have peaked by the seventh century BC.

The Greeks were interested in trade and the mineral wealth of the south and founded several commercial colonies. They introduced iron technology, the potter's wheel and a monetary economy to eastern Spain. They traded all kinds of Mediterranean goods: Etruscan ceramics, Phoenician amphorae, Greek pottery, which has been found as far inland as Zaragoza and Toledo. The Greek traders profited from the land resources of the Catalan coast, the Ebro valley and La Mancha, and iron mines in Jaén; and they also exercised a strong artistic influence in those regions.

The Greeks referred to the people of the eastern part of the peninsula as Iberians; the term covered a mixture of tribes. These lived in semi-urban settlements, large hill-forts in easily defensible positions which were clearly influenced by Greek military traditions. Years of excavations have brought to light a distinct civilisation defined by a common language, partly alphabetical, partly syllabic, ceramic painting, and small terracotta and bronze votive offerings. Also discovered were large stone sculptures and near-life-size statues of people and animals, such as the famous Dama de Elche (now in the Museo Arqueológico Nacional in Madrid), which seem to have belonged to the first phase of Iberian culture in the regions of Alicante, Murcia and Albacete. They show a strong eastern Mediterranean influence and perhaps animal-based cults.

The Lady of Elche: the first of four '*damas*' discovered in the area of Alicante which are important examples of pre-Roman, Iberian sculpture.

The local communities of the south and the south-east, whom Strabo, the Greek geographer writing in the first century AD, also described as Iberian, underwent a similar development, but retained different features as a result of their cultural and trading contact with Tartessian, Phoenician and Carthaginian influence. Strabo writes of 200 Turdetanian settlements in the lower Guadalquivir, which were like small city-states with their own agricultural hinterlands, most of which the Romans used as the basis for their own urban foundations. Recent finds of personal and ornamental objects in their sanctuaries and wealthy cemeteries bear witness to the richness and sophistication which brought Carthage and Rome into armed conflict at the end of the third century BC.

## THE CELTS

Developments in central, north and north-western territories were significantly different. The inhabitants of these regions were heirs to the Celtic world of south-eastern France and the Danube basin. They arrived in northern Spain in the year 1000 BC and by 700 had reached the River Tajo, bringing the technology of iron and the potter's wheel (as the Phoenicians and Greeks were also doing in eastern and southern Iberia). Our knowledge of these Celtic people is still largely based on accounts by Roman observers from their first contacts during the second century BC. Polybius, and Strabo after him, wrote of the several tribes such as the Lusitani. In the far north-west the rugged countryside and continued warfare moulded a habitat of heavily fortified structures with dry defensive walls, called *castros*. These northern tribes have come to epitomise the Celtic heritage, with their circular houses still standing in some remote mountain villages of the Galician interior.

Among the tribes the Celtiberians were singled out for special treatment, perhaps because of their long and bitter resistance to Roman domination. The name suggests a junction of cultures, hybrid communities between eastern Iberians from down the Ebro river and the Celtic background from the upper valley, Guadalajara and Soria; the Celtic people would have been attracted by the prosperity and richer lands of the Iberians. Ancient writers refer to a number of tribes, such as the Arevaci (Numantia and Thermantia) in the modern provinces of Soria,

Teruel and Cuenca, and Pelendones, famous for their short swords (*gladius hispanicus*), their solidarity in war and co-operative spirit in their working lives. They were the last to be reduced by the Roman legions, in 133 BC.

## Roman Hispania

The first experience the Spanish peninsula (including the Balearic archipelago) enjoyed as a unified territory under a single authority occurs with the Romans. These territories became imperial provinces and as such were eventually totally absorbed into the Roman economic, social and cultural world. Indigenous societies in remote areas of the Cantabrian fastnesses may have been left undisturbed and a resurgence of tribalism in periods of anarchy and after the fall of Roman power has often been suggested. Be that as it may, the fact remains that only the language of the people between the upper course of the River Iberus (Ebro) and the western Pyrenees has survived Latinisation, and even their language (Basque) is full of Latinisms, and the farmsteads of its users may well be an adaptation of the Roman villa. Roman writers described the two new provinces as Hispaniae, based on the Phoenician term for the Iberian peninsula as the land of the herbivorous mammal of the hare family peculiar to it.

The conquest of Hispaniae by the Romans began as a sequel to the contest between Rome and Carthage for political supremacy in the western Mediterranean. When Rome deprived Carthage of its spheres of commercial influence in Sicily, Sardinia and Corsica in the first Punic War of 241 BC, the Carthaginians sought to strengthen their hold over south-eastern Spain and expand their commercial activities as an alternative source of wealth. They had been in the area for some time as traders or involved in military expeditions to protect Phoenician colonies; they founded a colony in Ebusus (Ibiza) around the mid-seventh century BC. For their wars they had regularly recruited mercenaries among the Iberian tribes. The disaster of the first Punic War turned their attention to the rich silver mines on the east coast, where in 228–7 BC they established their capital at Carthago Nova to launch a determined bid from there against Roman hegemony.

At first the two powers agreed to share out the areas of influence, signing a treaty in 226 which set the River Ebro as the boundary line of Carthaginian expansion. But seven years later the great Carthaginian general Hannibal stormed and sacked the town of Saguntum (near Valencia). It was well to the south of the boundary line but it provoked an immediate response from Rome, who looked upon the town as an ally. Cnaeus Cornelius Scipio was sent to the Greek colony of Emporion (Ampurias) to stop Hannibal.

Scipio and his son were victorious, establishing Rome as the undisputed power in the western Mediterranean, which brought with it mastery over the unlimited mineral resources of the region. The loot obtained in the sack of Carthago Nova and the annexation of Gades, Carthage's last foothold, gave them a glimpse of the riches to come. Hannibal's challenge had been underwritten by the silver mines on the east coast. Rome probably had no long-term strategy for the Iberian peninsula when they took up Carthage's challenge. With their victory, however, the Romans showed every intention of wanting to settle there to exploit the enormous agricultural and mineral potential. They were not to be disappointed: according to the Greek historian Polybius, between 206 and 198 BC Rome received 6316 Roman pounds of gold bullion and 311,622 pounds of silver from Spain (three Roman pounds equal approximately one kilogram); and Livy records that Cato returned to Rome from his campaign of pacification in Spain (197–5 BC) with 25,000 pounds of silver, 1400 of gold bullion, 54,000 silver coins, and 123,000 other silver issues, and distributed 1610 bronze coins to each of his cavalrymen and 270 to each infantryman. To consolidate their victory at Ilipa in 206 they established a military stronghold of retired soldiers at Italica (Santiponce, near Sevilla) and divided their territories into two separate provinces, Hispania Citerior (east of the Iberus) and Hispania Ulterior. There followed 200 years of continuous battle until the provinces were firmly under Roman domination.

## ROMANISATION

The pacification of the northern territories presented Hispania Ulterior with a vast accumulation of lands and peoples to be supervised and incorporated into the same kind of administrative framework that existed in the eastern and southern areas. Peace was to be kept by small garrisons in the three provincial capitals (Córdoba, Mérida and Tarragona) and by three legions stationed in the north-western corner of the peninsula – the military strength in the north-west may be explained by the all too recent pacification of a troublesome area and Roman concern for the mineral resources there. By AD 69, when Vespasian quelled Galba's challenge to central authority from Tarraconensis Roman sway over the Spanish provinces was such that only one legion was thought to be needed, stationed at Legio (León) not far from the rich gold mines of Las Médulas. By this time the legions, originally composed of Roman citizens, were supported by auxiliary cavalry and infantry recruited to serve in other parts of the empire from among the native population, including the recently conquered people of the north. From the middle of the first century AD, one of the rewards for serving Rome was Roman citizenship upon completion of that service.

From the latter part of the first century BC to the end of the second century AD the Iberian peninsula played a key role in Roman expansion elsewhere, and in channelling the vast resources of the provinces to the imperial task, Rome transformed the landscape and moulded a new society with a new language and entirely different customs. The transformation worked upon both the physical and human landscapes of the Iberian peninsula is indelible everywhere in Spain to the present day, and especially so in the prosperous areas of the east, south and north-west. A comprehensive network of roads was built, in the first place to facilitate conquest, control and exploitation of natural resources, and Roman bridges are still in use today (Córdoba, Mérida, Salamanca, Zaragoza, and especially Alcántara, 194 metres long and 70 metres above the Tajo river). The main trunk roads carried milestones indicating distance and the name of the emperor under whose rule the road was built or repaired, and road stations provided food and shelter at regular intervals.

The thoroughness and durability of this *red viaria*, still basically the layout of Spain's present road system, was easily matched by the extent and effectiveness of the mining operation. The elder Pliny, who was mining administrator in Spain for a time, wrote that the gold mines of Lusitania, Gallaecia and Asturia yielded 20,000 Roman pounds of gold per month. In ancient times Río Tinto is estimated to have produced over 2 million tonnes of silver ore. The mines of Carthago Nova, already exploited by Phoenicians and Carthaginians, employed 40,000 people, mainly slaves and forced labour. The large mines were state-owned and run by procurators. The State gradually gained control of the smaller ones from private contractors and lessees. The profits made by mining contractors may be gleaned from the private donation of 20 million sexterces, the largest ever recorded in the western Roman Empire, made by someone who may have leased the cinnabar mine of Sisapo in Almadén.

The urbanisation of the Iberian peninsula was the crucial element in the assimilation of the local inhabitants to the Roman way of life. Apart from Bilbao and Madrid, there is hardly any town in Spain which has not been founded by the Romans or become an important centre under their rule. The process of Romanisation was long and thorough – a natural fusion of Roman and native. Rome did not seek, at least initially, to impose values and beliefs. By the mid-first century BC, according to Strabo, the Turdetanians, who lived along the River Baetis (Guadalquivir) had completely changed over to the Roman way of life, not even remembering their own language any more.

When Julius Caesar died in 44 BC there were only 30,000 Romans permanently resident in Spain. It was from then on that the process of colonisation gave way to Romanisation, with a dramatic increase of Roman citizens arriving in Hispania to stay. Twenty-one colonies were founded and existing semi-urban settlements were raised to the rank of municipium. Augustus re-formed the peninsula into three provinces: Baetica (in the south), Lusitania (south-west), and Tarraconensis. By AD 73–74 most communities had been granted Latin status and their inhabitants allowed full Roman citizenship. In the north and north-west native survival was stronger; apart from the exploitation of mineral resources and the maintenance of law and order, the Roman authorities seem to have allowed them to maintain their traditions, organised in family clans (*gentilitates*) and holding on to their Celtic names.

## PATTERNS OF LIFE UNDER ROMAN RULE

The administrative and economic centres of early imperial Rome were the provincial capitals like Emerita Augusta (Mérida) and Tarraco (Tarragona) under a governor, normally a Roman senator; colonies (*coloniae*) were founded to accommodate retired legionaries (like Itálica), to secure the mines and the northern borders like Gracchuris (Alfaro) and Pompaelo (Pamplona), or to relocate rebellious subjects such as the surviving Numantines who were translated to Valentia; *coloniae* and *municipia* were also judicial and fiscal centres like Urso (Osuna), Barcino (Barcelona), Caesar Augusta (Zaragoza). There were towns (like the Greek settlements at Emporion, Malaca and Gades) which retained their individuality and experienced little interference from Rome because of their early acceptance of its rule.

At the other end of the scale there were centres, such as Legio (León), which were under strict military rule since they were established exclusively to secure economic or strategic objectives. Fiscal obligations were also different, according to the origin and degree of assimilation of each centre; some were free from taxation, some were federated, and finally there were those which had to contribute full payment to the Fisc (such as *stipendium* and corn levy).

The size and abundance of public and private buildings in these centres signify the quality of life and civic pride of these urbanised communities. Water-supply systems (*aquaeducti*), public baths, sculpture and mosaics show the general level of commitment of the ruling élites. Power would be in the hands of a small urban oligarchy. They had to be rich since public office entailed private benefaction for the embellishment of towns and entertainment and adequate supply of basic commodities for the urban masses. Through this benefaction the enriched citizens gained public recognition and access to the executive orders (equestrian and senatorial), which made them eligible for public office in the provinces and Rome.

The countryside was part and parcel of this vast network of cities, colonies and municipalities. They had their own surrounding territories to provide basic commodities. Retired legionaries, for instance, were allotted plots of land in the vicinity, and other settlers cultivated small farms directly or through lessees. The basic products were the Mediterranean trilogy: grapes, olives and grain. The Iberians were already producing a grain surplus by the time the Romans arrived; from the second century BC they were exporting all three products to Rome and elsewhere. These agricultural exports enabled Iberians to purchase Roman luxuries like wines from central Italy, tableware, and so on. Wool and flax also appeared supporting a thriving textile industry. There were also building materials: tiles and bricks, and concrete which the Romans used in Spain to great advantage. In Roman times the fishing industry was also prospering; the main species were tunny, mackerel and sardine, supplying a flourishing internal market but also exported, as shown by the extent and variety of salt works along the main fishing areas, e.g. Torrevieja (Alicante). The main export by far in this particular field, however, and known throughout the Mediterranean, was garum (a spicy sauce from fish used for seasoning). In the first century AD Pliny the Elder concluded that next to Italy came Hispania: 'All its productive regions are rich in crops, oil, wine, horses and every kind of ore.'

The economic life of the country and exploitation of its resources were, then, not very different from the metropolis, but the main beneficiaries of that prosperity were Rome and Roman officials and settlers in the provinces of Spain. Intermarriage and a common purpose, especially in urban centres in the south and east, would have fused Roman and native into a Hispano–Roman society. Not much is known about a Hispano–Roman aristocracy: epitaphs and commemorative inscriptions mention names, but people of Iberian stock probably took Roman names, which makes it impossible to ascertain their background.

Hispania contributed a large share of prominent senators, illustrious writers and scholars, and even a few emperors. One Vibius Paciaecus appears to be the first Spaniard to be made a Roman senator, in the early part of the first century BC; later on there were very influential senators from Spain like Annaeus from Córdoba, and emperors like Trajan (AD 98–117) and his successor Hadrian (117–138), both from Itálica. Hadrian is believed to have been of indigenous stock but Trajan was from Italian colonial stock. There were writers like Quintilian, born *c.* AD 33 in Calagurris (Calahorra), who held the chair of rhetoric at Rome; Seneca the rhetorician from Córdoba, and his son the philosopher, forced to take his life by Nero after an alleged conspiracy in AD 65; the epigrammatist Martial from Bilbilis (Calatayud); and the geographer Mela. However they could in no way be said to be making a Spanish contribution to Rome's political life and culture. They were probably of Roman origin, second- or third-generation colonials whose economic power base was in the provinces in their large estates, but whose political or cultural aspirations were obviously fixed on the capital of the empire.

## Break-up of the Western Roman Empire

For nearly three centuries the provinces of Hispaniae enjoyed stability and prosperity. During the third century AD, however, this highly sophisticated, urbanised world came to a long, protracted crisis which led to the disintegration of Roman rule in the early fifth century and the split of the provincial components into separate and different political entities. They fell under semi-nomadic peoples from beyond the north-eastern boundary of the empire, themselves forced to overrun imperial borders by migrating hordes pushing westwards from central Asia. The collapse of imperial authority at the centre from 235 to 285 set the scene for the growing presence of Germanic tribes in Roman affairs. The peaceful transition of successive imperial dynasties in the first two centuries gave way to fifty years of internal strife, continuous civil warfare, military coups, usurpations and assassinations.

The western end of the Empire suffered a great deal of disruption, which began in AD 171–3 with the invasion of Baetica by tribesmen from northern Africa who swept through the Baetis valley on several occasions until 210. For a time between 258 and 270 the peninsula was left to fend for itself when Rome under the Emperor Gallienus could not prevent Frankish tribesmen from breaching the Rhine frontier and descending from Gaul in 262 to sack Tarraco. In 297 marauding Frankish tribesmen attacked and looted the eastern shores of Hispania again. Recent archaeological evidence shows a great deal of devastation and destruction of urban centres and country estates all along the coastal regions around 260. The scale of destruction, the loss of confidence in the imperial system and the fear and apprehension that seems to have gripped the country could not be simply the result of sporadic invasions.

What was at stake was obviously the ability of the imperial authority to maintain the *pax romana*. The weakening of Rome's sway over the provinces caused military expenditure to rise and silver coinage was debased to attract soldiers with higher salaries. The lack of confidence in the silver *denarius*, until then fixed to the gold coin (*aureus*), severely shattered the strong civic and community spirit of the urban élites. Diocletian, elected emperor by the legions in 284, restored the authority of the State for a while, introducing a system of co-emperors to strengthen the structure of command. He and Constantine I (306–37) also overhauled the fiscal and monetary system, and the provinces were more heavily garrisoned, with at least thirty major towns strengthened in their defences by a reconstruction of their walls: Barcino (Barcelona), Caesar Augusta (Zaragoza) and Lucus Augusti (Lugo) are still visible examples of these fortifications.

## CHRISTIANITY

The adoption of Christianity by Constantine in AD 312 is a further indication of the urgency of the situation. Diocletian had conducted major persecutions against the Christians obviously seeking to shore up the authority of the State through religious uniformity. But shortly afterwards Constantine, perhaps aware of the wide diffusion of Christianity – certainly in Spain where in 305 a church council at Illiberis (Granada) was attended by bishops from towns in all the Spanish provinces – decided to invest the new religion with pretensions of universality to help govern the empire.

Meanwhile, the pattern of life in Hispaniae continued to deteriorate. Urban oligarchies stopped lavishing their wealth on civic buildings and amenities; many buildings, basilicas and theatres were left to decay. This decline in public building was paralleled by the growing presence of churches and ecclesiastical buildings which came to represent the identification between the Christian religion and the State through the great church councils destined to play such a crucial political role under the Visigoths. The size and importance of private estates would suggest a ruralisation of the country and huge concentrations of land among Roman senators and the richest among the Hispano–Roman aristocracy, with the emperor as the largest landowner. One of those potentates was Count Theodosius, one of Valentian I's (364–75) most successful generals, who after restoring Roman control throughout the western empire retired to his estate in Hispaniae. His son, also called Theodosius, was born at Cauca (Coca; Segovia) to a mother called Thermantia, who took her name from one of the Celtiberian towns which so desperately resisted Roman rule in the second century BC. He was appointed emperor of the east in 379 and on two occasions appeared to have restored the power of Rome for a short period, successfully defending the western empire under Valentian II from usurpers and trying to impose a rigid Christian orthodoxy on all subjects. But there was no way of preventing the split between east and west and the disintegration of Roman authority in the west in the face of renewed pressure from several German tribes along the northern borders fleeing from the Huns, who made their first appearance in Europe *c.* 370. Roman aristocracy had deserted their military call for the sake of their political intrigues in the imperial capital or gracious living in their private estates. Constantine, Valentian and Theodosius I were still able commanders, asserting their personal rule in the field of battle, but less capable successors had to depend on the military support of others. It was Theodosius I's last descendants who had to watch helplessly the final stages of the dismemberment of the western half of the Roman Empire.

## Hispania Gothica

Rome's unified control was shattered by the invasion of some 200,000 Vandals, Suebi and Alans across the western Pyrenees in the early autumn of 409. Under their rule the Visigothic invaders never quite managed to restore the old Hispaniae to prosperity and stability, despite King Reccared's conversion in 587 to Catholicism, the religion of the Hispano–Roman establishment, and King Recceswinth's promulgation in 654 of a single unified code of law, *Forum iudiciorum*, very much based on Roman law. It is a period hardly known beyond the deeds and misdeeds of the rulers and the legal debates and enactments of the church councils – which does not explain the old school tradition in Spain, by now hopefully forgotten, of reciting the long list of Visigoth rulers starting with Alaric I (who would indeed be surprised by it since he died in 410 at the tip of Italy!).

After the first wave of Germanic invasions in western Europe, the

The votive gold crown of Recceswinth,
the seventh-century Visigothic King

Vandals settled in Baetica for twenty years and then moved on to
northern Africa via Julia Traducta (Tarifa), while the Suebi established
a firm hold over Gallaecia and from there campaigned year after year in
Lusitania and Baetica, and even pillaged Ilerda (Lérida) in the
Tarraconensis in 449. In trying to restore some form of control in the
Hispaniae Rome had to resort to the Visigoths for help as they had done
in 415 and 446. Suebic resistance was swiftly and brutally quelled and the
remaining Suebi were reduced to their original settlements in Gallaecia.
The Tarraconensis was still under some form of Roman control when, in
476, the last emperor Romulus Augustulus was deposed and the western
empire officially ceased to exist.

   The seat of Visigothic power was the old praetorian prefecture of the
Gauls at Arelate (Arles), and the Hispaniae, as provinces of the new

Visigothic kingdom, came under the authority of a count (*Comes Hispaniarum*) until 507, when Alaric II was defeated and killed by the Franks at Vouillé (near Poitiers). The Visigoths were displaced as the main force in the west and restrained to narrower and more defined boundaries in the Spanish peninsula where by 585 they managed to reduce the Suebic kingdom of Gallaecia to their control. There were still very fundamental geographical and political limitations to Visigothic domination.

In the north, the mountain people – Vascones, Cantabrians and Astures – had never been subjugated and remained a permanent nuisance, frequently raiding the lands of the Franks as well as those of the Visigoths on both sides of the Pyrenees. Their activities were particularly irritating to the Germanic authorities in that they tended to coincide with internal crises (normally ones of succession). In the south, between 552 and 621, Byzantium held southern Carthaginensis (Cartagena), eastern Baetica (Málaga) and the Balearic Islands as a province of the eastern Roman Empire known as Spania. Under Justinian (527–65) the Byzantine Empire, which was to survive another 1000 years, made a determined effort to restore Roman authority to the western provinces, first by overthrowing the Vandal kingdom of Africa in 533, annexing the Balearic Islands in 534 and invading Italy in 536, and then by setting a foothold in southern Spain and maintaining a presence there, partly assisted by the internal difficulties which the Byzantines could exploit so successfully.

The long century of Visigothic rule, or the little we know of it, is an uninterrupted litany of enthronements, depositions and usurpations. The sons of only two rulers (Leovigild and Chisdaswinth) ruled for more than two years after them. Such regular and frequent upheavals at the seat of the central government must have been replicated in the country at large. A divided monarchy could not remove the Byzantines' weak hold in the south, let alone withstand Islamic expansionism, before which the Visigothic kingdom of Toledo collapsed like a pack of cards.

It is thought that the Visigothic state was an elective monarchy. More accurate, perhaps, is to speak of an occupative throne, for rather than elected the holders of kingship came to it by prior association, designation and mostly usurpation. The rulers that survived long enough to attempt to leave some sort of imprint in the fabric of society were severely curtailed by the political necessity of having to reward their followers and keep them loyal through further grants of lands and money.

As a warlord, the Visigothic king would have need of regular campaigns to strengthen his base of support through participation of the warriors in military service to the Crown and share of the spoils; such royal dispensation of favour and property was also essential if the ruler wanted to provide some sort of protection for the surviving family. Royal patronage and munificence could not make up for the lack of continuity on the throne itself. Shifting allegiances among prominent members of the Visigothic establishment was bound to filter down the ladder to all levels of society, especially when an invading people, some 200,000 strong, were faced with the task of installing themselves and governing a large population of Hispano–Romans, perhaps four million strong, who had reached a higher level of material and political development.

The vast majority of newcomers settled between the upper reaches of the rivers Ebro and Tajo, in the northern meseta between Palencia, Calatayud and Toledo, the lands that had once belonged to the Celtiberian tribes. The Visigoths transferred the system of settlement which Constantine had surrendered to them in 418 as defenders and allies of Rome: Visigothic settlers received two-thirds of the large estates from the Hispano–Roman owners. Neither small farms nor church property were partitioned. The barbarians also took over the Roman system of management: life in the large estates and villas continued very much as before; the Hispano–Roman landowning aristocracy was not entirely displaced.

In the absence of any known rebellion on the part of the Hispano–Roman élites and any legislation deliberately intended to lower their social status or economic power beyond the initial redistribution of land, it can be argued that the Hispano–Roman population appears not to have been significantly disturbed or depressed by the new masters. No doubt the highest officials of the realm were of Gothic descent, but the fiscal and financial tasks of the State were in the hands of Hispano–Romans who alone had the experience and knowledge of such matters. There is very little evidence regarding urban living under the Visigoths. The signs are that town life continued to decline: the splendid civic monuments of the early Roman Empire continued to deteriorate or were ransacked for re-use in ecclesiastical buildings or defensive works. The Visigoths seem to have taken the repair and fortification of town walls quite seriously. No longer the open and thriving centres of trade and civic pride of the first and second centuries AD, cities and towns became small, fortified enclaves clustered around churches, convents and episcopal palaces.

The government of these towns was now in the hands of royal officials and the bishops. The importance of the Church authorities in civil administration was, if anything, strengthened with the arrival of an alien people. The practical collapse of the civil administration left the Catholic Hispano–Roman bishops as the senior authorities in the towns and cities. The new rulers were in no position to interfere and consequently allowed the Church considerable independence. The territorial division of the Roman Empire was retained. The towns would now be ranked according to the ecclesiastical dignitary in their midst. With the conversion of King Reccared to 'the Roman Religion' in 587, Church and State became more identified than ever before. The position of the king as head of the Church is clearly shown by the use of ex-communication as a penalty for breach of the law. The king ruled through the bishops in council. In exchange for services rendered to the State, the Church was sure to receive material rewards (donations, endowment, reversionary rights to property and exemption from taxes), which did not seem to satiate their rapacity. On no single subject did the bishops, Gothic and Hispano–Roman alike, spend more time than on the safeguarding of their churches' property.

A very significant example of their compliance with the civil authority was the lack of opposition, or even controversy, over the savage treatment meted out to the Jews, especially in the latter part of the seventh century when they had to choose between conversion or enslavement. Perhaps this excessively harsh attitude, not yet explained either in terms of the standards of the day or any popular feeling against them, is one more symptom of the very fundamental weaknesses that afflicted the neo-Roman realm of the Visigoths. Despite the religious and legal conversion of the invaders, the resulting entity was no more cohesive than it was at the beginning of the sixth century. The status of the monarchy, which Leovigild worked so hard to raise as the unitive element to break down the internal divisions, was at its lowest ebb on the eve of the Muslim landing. It is not improbable that the enslaved Jews may have been ready and willing to assist them or at least to rejoice in the downfall of their wilful oppressors.

There were also other indications that the situation was reaching crisis point. It is, in fact, rather ironic that the very body of the law, the Erwigian Code of 681, which stands out as the greatest legal achievement of western Europe at the time, in its preoccupation and detailed exploration of anti-Jewish legislation and of very strict measures required to return escaped slaves to their work, contributed to the feeling of crisis. It should be remembered that by the late seventh century the army was no longer composed of free Goths but landowners' and the Church's conscripted slaves. Existence of the law, however thorough, does not necessarily ensure its rule. All the same, able and resolute Visigothic rulers seemed to believe that adequate legislation could produce desired results; or they saw no hope of bringing on the change they wanted, but still expected to exorcise social evils through the sheer size and quality of their legislation.

No amount of legislation, though, was to extricate Hispania Gothica from her predicament. For nearly a thousand years Spain had been in close contact with the major commercial networks of the Mediterranean as a whole, and the provinces of the Spains were among the most productive and prosperous under the Romans. During the middle centuries of the first millennium AD Spain declined economically and demographically. In the last few years before its fall the Visigothic Kingdom of Toledo seemed to be plagued by famine, disease, a calamitous decline of law and order, monetary difficulties and restiveness along the northern frontier. Most importantly, there was a great deal of disaffection among the nobility and bishops about the way King Roderic had reached the throne a few months before by dispossessing his predecessor's sons. When the final moment came in 711 the Visigothic Kingdom collapsed before the Crescent without struggle.

The cultural imprint of the Visigoths was even less memorable than their military performance in the face of the invading Muslims. Administratively, legally and politically they were faithful heirs to the late Roman tradition. Their architectural and artistic attitudes were somewhat fashioned by the Byzantine east: only a handful of churches in Palencia, Zamora, Orense and Toledo bear witness to their slight contribution in this field. As for their linguistic legacy, only a few toponymic and patronymic relics and some lexical items referring to war and plunder have been recorded. Of the language they spoke when they arrived in the Iberian peninsula nothing is known. Their legal tradition was oral and any form of administrative or legal dealing with the population at large would be conducted in Latin by Hispano-Roman chancellors and secretaries who could attend to the business of drafting documents and interpreting the law of the land.

# CHAPTER TWO

# *Islamic Invaders*

In the early summer of 711 Tariq, with 7000 Berbers recently converted to Islam, landed at the Rock that still bears his name Gebel (Mount) Tariq (Gibraltar). They had been sent by Musa, the governor of Ifriqiya, the northern African province of the Arab Caliphate of Damascus, with the mission of helping King Witiza's sons recover their estates of which they had been dispossessed by King Roderic, their father's successor to the Visigothic throne of Toledo. The name by which they referred to the country north of the Straits of Gibraltar was al-Andalus, 'The Isle of the Vandals', which eventually became Andalucía.

Their arrival caught King Roderic engaged in one of the regular campaigns of pacification against the Vascones and Cantabrians. He turned back to face Tariq, who by now had been reinforced by an additional contingent of 5000 Berber troops. The two armies faced each other along the Barbate river (near modern Medina Sidonia). King Roderic, abandoned by prelates and magnates of the realm, was soundly defeated, losing his kingdom, and presumably his life (for no more was heard of him), in this one battle of 19 July 711.

Tariq proceeded to the capital, Toledo, meeting no further resistance. The governor of Ifriqiya himself joined him in Talavera in 713 with 18,000 Arabs from northern and central Arabia (Qaysites) and Yemen (Kalbites) and together they completed the occupation of the country by 714. They travelled to Damascus to render their accounts and to pay homage to their Caliph, leaving behind as governor (emir) of the new province Musa's son Abd al-Aziz, who had married Egilona, Roderic's widow. The first emir of al-Andalus established his capital at Sevilla but his tenure was cut short by a treacherous hand sent by the new Caliph of

Damascus, Sulayman, who had already put his father Musa in prison on arrival. The new governor sent from Ifriqiya in 716 was accompanied by 400 Arabs and moved the capital to Córdoba.

The first Berber contingent, some 12,000 men of military age under Tariq, appear to have settled in mountainous and peripheral areas of the Iberian peninsula, mainly in the north-west (not dissimilar to their original habitat as nomadic shepherds in the Atlas region of north Africa), and returned to their pastoral activities. They were the first to intermarry freely with the native population, many of whom would have converted to Islam and by the ninth century had ceased to speak their Vulgar Latin in favour of the local Romance dialect or Arabic, the language of the politically dominant groups.

The ethnic, tribal and religious differences among the invaders would have made their position in Spain quite untenable, had it not been for the apparent acquiescence of the indigenous population. Taking together the armies from Africa and small contingents of soldiers and officials of Arab origin, the population of the politically dominant groups was in the region of 40,000, with Qaysites (Arabs) pre-eminent in Sevilla and Valencia, and Kalbites also in Sevilla, as well as Córdoba, Badajoz, Elvira (Granada) and Murcia. Apart from the armies and escorts, and perhaps another 50,000 who were mainly north Africans, dependants and followers, no satisfactory estimate of the immigrant or invading population has as yet been advanced. The astonishing success of the invading armies against King Roderic perhaps exposes the weaknesses of the Visigothic State, but given the ethnic and tribal rivalries of the Muslim invaders, the equally successful establishment of a new regime and stable frontiers for centuries to come must have something to do with the equitable and fair nature of that regime, as against the divisive and arbitrary character of Visigothic rule. The teachings of Islam reinforced the basic egalitarianism of Arab and Berber tribal societies originally nomadic and pastoral in their way of life.

## Patterns of Social Integration

Abd al-Aziz, Musa's son and first emir of al-Andalus set the pattern of coexistence between the invaders and those who acknowledged their new masters in a treaty (713) with Theodomir, the Visigothic governor of a large region comprising Alicante and Murcia with Orihuela as the capital. By this treaty Theodomir, the former *dux* of Cartagena, retained a great deal of autonomy as military commander, subject to payment of one dinar, four bushels of wheat and four of barley, four measures of malt, four of vinegar, two of honey and two of oil per subject and half for slaves. This arrangement would be passed on to his son Athanagild and his successors, 'who would not be divested of their lordship for as long as they remained faithful and trusting servants of their master'. Within the jurisdiction of the secular lord, the 'people of the Book' – Christian and Jew – were not compelled to give up their religion and would be protected in exchange for land and poll taxes, and those freely converted to Islam were not liable to capitation, nor indeed were slaves who by their conversion could also win their freedom.

Such covenants, it has been suggested, may have applied to large areas of the country and so the land, to a large extent, would have remained in the hands of its previous owners now in a relationship of personal and territorial dependence on their political overlord no different from the bond of feudality which linked the Visigothic *seniores* to their king. People who had left the land, or had to be won over by force, lost their property. The confiscated estates were broken up into small and medium units which were cultivated directly by their owners through their servants and slaves, or more frequently handed over to local tenants as share-croppers. This form of exploitation of the land, still in operation in Spain, seems to have been adapted from Byzantium. The landlord provided capital equipment (land, implements and seeds) and the tenant his labour; the landlord's share of the crop varied from one-sixth to one-half.

The new ruling élites, therefore, appear to have shown some circumspection regarding land ownership and no taste for direct cultivation. The first wave of Arab soldiers were granted land as payment for military services, but Balj's 7000 Syrians could not be accommodated, as they expected since it was customary in Syria, because of the difficulty of finding available land without dispossessing anybody; instead, the various contingents were assigned to different military settlements in southern Spain and were paid a state stipend as professional soldiers. Like the Berbers, Arabs and Syrians were inclined to mix freely with the local population from the start: fair-haired ladies from the northern territories were highly regarded. By the tenth century miscegenation had mixed their bloods inextricably.

The indigenous population that chose to remain Christian, relatively few in comparison with the large majority of converts to Islam, was afforded the full protection of the law in exchange for a land capitation tax. They were judged by their own laws if they so desired, had their own churches, and selected their own secular and spiritual lords. They were known as *mozárabes* (*mustarib*: arabised, Arab-like) for their similarity with the invaders in manner and attire. They were to play a very significant role in the diffusion of Arab culture among the northerners when they migrated northwards as the Christian kingdoms progressed in their conquest. In this role they were ably supported by the Jews who were given the same degree of tolerance and freedom as the *mozárabes*; in fact, encouraged by this attitude, many Jews who fled the country under Visigothic rule returned to al-Andalus, the only country in Europe where they lived in large numbers. They settled mainly in Toledo, Córdoba, Málaga and Granada; they too contributed very prominently between the tenth and twelfth centuries to the culture and government of both Muslim and Christian Spain, helping to spread the superiority of Hispano–Arab civilisation throughout Europe.

Slaves (a generic term from Slav) from eastern and northern Europe and Sudanese negroes played a key role in this social mix. In their raids the Arab–Berber armies reduced those who resisted their rule to slavery, but many arrived as children, perhaps purchased from the Vikings – who from the end of the eighth century had a large share in the trade of those slaves they themselves had seized in their carefully co-ordinated expeditions in and around Europe – and then brought up in the Islamic religion. These men and women, emancipated when they converted to Islam, came to occupy important positions among the ruling élites and in the royal palace. By the tenth century there were some 8000 in Córdoba alone. As for male slaves, their favourable treatment by their masters, who allowed them to intervene in politics, contribute to the cultural and professional life, hold civil and military office, would have prevented them from leaving their former owners. Furthermore, armies and private guards came to rely very heavily on mercenaries and slaves for recruitment. By the second half of the ninth century, it seems, Slavic recruits had become a major component in these forces.

## TOWN

The social groups, resulting from the interaction between Arabs, Berbers, Hispani of Roman and Gothic descent, and Jews lived relatively at ease with one another. The new masters built and expanded on Roman foundations, re-creating old towns and founding twenty new ones. Like the Romans before them, strategic considerations were of paramount importance: the newly-founded or revived urban centres hosted frontier garrisons or connected the network of communications between sensitive areas. A new society emerged as a highly urbanised entity, surpassing even the Romans in the splendour of their cultural achievements. Palaces, public baths, schools, mosques, markets, fountains and gardens embellished them all and provided a surfeit of public amenities.

The Mosque of Córdoba which was begun in AD 785

Dominating this galaxy of industrious, prosperous and cultural centres, was Córdoba, until 1031 the capital of the independent Umayyad Emirate (756) and Caliphate (929). Rivalled in population (100,000) and splendour only by Baghdad and Constantinople, it is, with its Great Mosque (where it has not been spoiled by the Christian cathedral bursting through the middle), still the best example of the full flowering of Moorish culture in the Iberian peninsula. The foundations of the Great Mosque were laid by Abd al-Rahman I in 785, successive emirs and caliphs expanding and extending it. Abd al-Rahman III, the first independent caliph of Córdoba, built a new palace west of Córdoba, Medina Azahara, where 10,000 masons and labourers and 1800 camels and asses toiled for twenty-five years, at a cost to the caliph of 300,000 dinars. His son and successor al-Hakam II was a great poet and lover of books – he is believed to have owned a library with 400,000 volumes – and in his time Córdoba stood as the book centre of the world. His chief minister, al-Mansur, closed the Umayyad era with Medina Azahira to the east of Córdoba, which testified to his glorious military achievements.

## COUNTRY

The material prosperity and cultural allure of the large towns was matched by the variety and abundance of agricultural produce. New plants and fruit trees were successfully introduced; soils studied and enriched; and irrigation canals, cisterns, water-mills, draw-wells and ditches brought new land under cultivation. In addition to olives, corn and grapes, other produce normally identified with Spain began to appear in the eighth or ninth centuries such as rice, saffron, cotton, oranges, lemons, melons, figs, apples, pears, pomegranates, bananas, dates, chestnuts, quince, sugar cane from Almuñécar, honey from Alcarria (region of *alquerías*: from *al-qarya*, small farm) and pulses (beans, lentils and tares). The numbers of these fruits and crops testify to the dramatic advances in production, productivity and conservation, quite sufficient to feed a growing population and export some surpluses. Indeed, it is in these areas that the Castilian language is almost exclusively indebted to Arabic, e.g. *noria* (waterwheel), *acequia* (irrigation ditch), *aljibe* (cistern) and many others. Contemporary observers commented admiringly on the luxuriant landscape of farmhouses and small villages (*aldeas* from *al-daya*) dotted about the countryside, every bit of available land carefully cultivated, including the expertly terraced slopes which visitors can still admire in the Balearic Islands.

Along the coasts, fishing and fish-processing returned to pre-Visigothic levels of production; tunny, sardine and shad were the main varieties. The preparation of anchovies was the traditional industry of Málaga and the white salt of Zaragoza and Ibiza was used for the preservation of food which was exported far and wide. The pastoral and nomadic origins of Arabs and Berbers alike would have helped them to develop livestock farming, especially in the dry hilly areas of frontier territory. Sheep and cattle were found in abundance north of Toledo. Cuenca and Murcia became important wool-production centres. Like the Romans before them, Muslims practised transhumance, the system of pasturing on high land in summer and low land in winter. Andalusí horses were highly appreciated for hunting, war and tournaments: al-Mansur is said to have purchased 8000 horses a year for the State. Mules were available in very large numbers in Mallorca: with donkeys they were the backbone of transport, drawing carts and litters; they were also used in war, being adaptable to the mountainous terrain. Bullocks and oxen ploughed the fields.

## *The Umayyad Dynasty*

From 756 to 1031, under the strong and enlightened leadership of rulers peacefully succeeding one another, al-Andalus achieved a level of prosperity, learning and tolerance which contemporaries from all parts of the known world admired and envied, although the start of the golden age of Hispano–Arab civilization was not particularly auspicious.

### ABD AL-RAHMAN I

In one respect, at least, the unpropitious beginnings allowed the seeds of change to take root. In 756 Abd al-Rahman, the only remaining member of the Umayyad dynasty, managed to escape from the new ruling dynasty in Damascus, the Abbasids, and made his way to Almuñécar (east of Nerja). His ability and daring had already shown itself in the epic flight from one end of the Mediterranean to the other with the Abbasids' henchmen seeking to destroy anyone that might challenge their position. He was able to gather sufficient support to overthrow the emir of al-Andalus, and declared himself the independent emir of the province while still acknowledging the religious leadership of the caliph of Baghdad, the new capital of the Abbasids. Abd al-Rahman (756–88) restored order to the Emirate of Córdoba and brought a measure of consensus to the motley array of ethnic and social forces in the land. He allowed Muslimisation to proceed slowly, honouring the legal rights of tributaries and permitting religious freedom. When he felt he had stabilised his position, he embarked on a massive building programme to ratify his power and authority, thus laying the foundations of the greatness of Córdoba. In 785 he started the Great Mosque, much extended by his successors, and built the citadel adjoining it, as well as the summer residence modelled on the one his ancestor Caliph Hisham built amid the gardens irrigated by the Euphrates. He was succeeded by his second son and designated heir, Hisham I (788–96) who presided over seven years of uninterrupted peace at home, devoting himself to completing the work on the Great Mosque as well as his religious studies. Meantime, with the regularity of a harvesting expedition he dispatched his army every year to raid the northern territories outside his rule and exact payment from his tributaries, to plunder the land, rustle their cattle and collect slaves, or as a show of force in the marches and among the frontier towns of the emirate.

Hisham's successor, al-Hakem (796–822), had no time for razzias as he was obsessed with internal security and so determined to stamp out any sign of dissent. He would stop at nothing, and in his ruthless repression of protest or complaints managed to alienate large sections of the population in an ever-increasing circle of violence. In 797 he ordered the decapitation of the leading *muladíes* of Toledo (converts of some social standing) who had dared express discontent. In 806, on being informed of a conspiracy to replace him with a cousin, he executed the leading citizens of a Córdoba suburb. By 818 the whole suburb, representing a wide area of disaffection among artisans, labourers and intellectuals, rose against the atrocities of the despot and his fiscal demands. This time his personal guards and regular military units were needed to bring the insurrection under control. Retribution was implacable and the suburb was razed to the ground. Unlike his father, al-Hakam I did not seek to assert his authority and increase his revenue by regular expeditions against the infidel; besides, his high-handed methods and despotic attitude made him ever more dependent for his security on his own personal army. In addition to his personal Berber guard, he recruited an army of slave soldiers 6000 strong with regular pay, and employed secret agents. In turn this financial burden resulted in increased fiscal demands.

## ABD AL-RAHMAN II

He may have been aggrieved by his father's excesses, which on occasions he had been forced to witness, but at least Abd al-Rahman II (822–52) inherited a pacified kingdom. His thirty-year rule is one of the most fruitful and brilliant periods of al-Andalus. His patronage of the arts and the rich culture of the towns attracted men of taste and learning from all over the Islamic world and Christian Europe. But at the same time he resumed his grandfather's regular raids into northern territories. Under his son Muhammad I (852–86) al-Andalus continued to prosper. By the end of his reign, however, the fears of al-Hakam I seemed about to be realised.

Some Christian groups in Córdoba had grown restive and uneasy about growing acceptance of Muslim manners and culture among their brethren. Their provocative attitude and possible collusion with Ibn Hafsun, a convert to Islam, caused some harsh reaction from the State. The growing religious unrest was compounded by serious disruption along the northern frontier. The frontier territories had been left in the hands of local notables, with small garrisons, their own private armies and a great deal of autonomy. When the authority of the centre appeared to be fading, these frontier commanders failed to send tributes to their overlord and set themselves up as semi-independent states. From 886 to 912 revolt and dissension were rife; for a time only Córdoba appeared to accept the authority of the Emir. The brilliant political structure of the first Umayyads went through one of the most disastrous periods of its history. The power relationship between ruler and ruling élites was a personal one, the pre-eminence of the Umayyads resting on their military and economic power. Weak upholders of such power had to

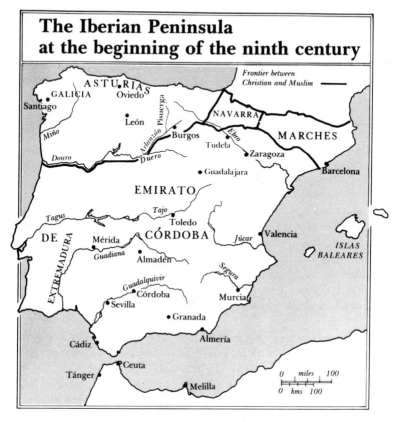

## The Iberian Peninsula at the beginning of the ninth century

witness the ethnic, tribal and religious rivalries surge to the surface and bring the country close to political disintegration. An efficient and authoritarian ruler could restore al-Andalus to its former glory and such a ruler could emerge in the midst of an apparently hopeless situation. Abd Allah (889–912) was alleged to have committed all manner of crimes against his own children because of his suspicious nature, but at least he picked the right man, his twenty-year-old grandson, to succeed him.

### ABD AL-RAHMAN III

Abd al-Rahman III (912–61) was a typical hybrid of al-Andalus – Arab father and Frank or Basque concubine mother. His grandmother was Princess Iniga, the daughter of King Fortún Garcés of Pamplona, who was sent to Córdoba as a pledge of her father's loyalty. Abd al-Rahman had red hair and blue eyes, and was excellently endowed both physically and intellectually, fluent in Arabic and in the Romance language according to Andalusí chroniclers. His first task on ascending the throne was to restore his authority and consolidate his power throughout the realm. He ended Sevilla's ten-year secession and dispatched regular expeditions to raid León, Navarra and Castilla, and assert his military pre-eminence on the frontier territories. To counter possible designs from the new Fatimid Caliphate in north Africa, he occupied Melilla (927), Ceuta (931) and Tangier (951). He also severed all religious connections with Baghdad and in 929 assumed the title of Caliph and Emir *al-muminin* (Commander of the Believers). He celebrated the splendour of his military and political achievements in the citadel which he had started to build outside Córdoba in 936. By the end of his life the Caliphate of Córdoba was the undisputed authority of the Iberian peninsula, with all the southern borders firmly secured against Fatimid interference. The three main territories of the north, León, Castilla and Navarra, had to pay annual tribute and were forced to recognise the sovereignty of the Caliph.

Al-Hakam II (961–76) presided over the zenith of learning and scholarship of al-Andalus under Umayyad rule. However, his son Hisham II (976–1013) had to rely on others to maintain his authority. His all-powerful minister, who came very close to asserting total Muslim control over the whole of the Iberian peninsula, was al-Mansur (938–1002) a Yemenite whose ascendancy over the Caliph went so far as to take the Caliph's mother, a Basque concubine, as his mistress. His military prowess inflicted terrible wounds on Christian territory. Barcelona was sacked in 985, and Santiago de Compostela in 997; its cathedral doors were carried off and the bells taken to Córdoba to hang in the Great Mosque. Al-Mansur died in Medinaceli in his last campaign against the Rioja in 1002. His son, Abd al-Malik, succeeded him as chief minister to Hisham II, and in 1003 forced Castilla and León to help him lay waste the county of Barcelona. Then another son, Abd al-Rahman (known as Sanjul or Sanchuelo), whose mother was the daughter of

Sancho II of Navarra, had the audacity to persuade the Caliph to designate him as his heir. While the Caliph was on a campaign in the north in 1009, members of the Umayyad family and the Arab aristocracy rose against Abd al-Rahman and in March 1009 executed him. A few months later Hisham II abdicated in favour of Muhammad II, who was himself deposed by Berber troops who proclaimed Sulayman, another grandson of Abd al-Rahman III, as Caliph. After twenty years of anarchy, Hisham III was deposed in 1031 and the Umayyad Caliphate ceased to exist as a unified structure of power.

## THE END OF THE UMAYYAD DYNASTY

The political collapse of the Umayyad Caliphate was not altogether unexpected. As indicated earlier, the original social and political ingredients lacked any kind of cohesion or established source of authority to make it durable. Umayyad ancestry helped Abd al-Rahman I to establish the first independent emirate in 756; however, his successful rule had been based on military victories against the infidel, substantial spoils of war for the armies and ruthless repression of protest and dissent. Perhaps aware of the precariousness of his situation Abd al-Rahman I did not fully break with the Caliphate of Baghdad and continued to recognise its religious leadership. While al-Hakam I had to increase taxes to pay for a permanent army, Abd al-Rahman III at the peak of his military power, and in possession of unimaginable riches according to contemporaries, is thought to have been the first to devalue the currency, presumably to keep up with escalating military costs. His chroniclers also commented on his isolation from his subjects and the growing division between the bureaucracy and a military élite pushing the Arab nobility from the centre of power. Al-Mansur was forced even further in that direction: his only power base was Hisham II's support, and only success in war and control of the army could keep him in power. He reorganised the army, finally breaking with its tribal structure and recruiting more Berbers from north Africa, and mercenaries and slaves, including Christians, from northern Europe. There must have been a limit to the spoils and tributes that could be exacted from the northern kingdoms and al-Mansur surely reached that limit in more than fifty raids in his lifetime. Furthermore, the establishment of a Fatimid

Caliphate in Kairouan in 909 added to the defensive costs across the Straits of Gibraltar and most probably siphoned off some of the African gold which had been flowing to Córdoba until then. In the twenty years after 969, on the strength of eastern trade with the Byzantines, Kairouan grew bigger than either Córdoba or Baghdad. Al-Mansur's son could not emulate his father's military victories and Sanchuelo's attempt to put himself forward as the successor to Hisham II was the final straw that broke the semblance of dynastic legitimacy under the Umayyads. In the absence of a strong and victorious ruler, the aristocracy of Córdoba removed the last of the Caliphs, Hisham III, and abolished the office. Al-Andalus split up into separate small states (*taifas*) centring round the main cities, usually under the strongest nobility and military commanders. Slave soldiers and servants of the Caliphate seem to have settled in Almería, Valencia and Denia (which included the Balearic Islands); Berbers dominated Málaga, Algeciras, Granada and Ronda; and the Muslim aristocracy of Arab and indigenous descent continued in central and southern cities.

The demise of the Umayyad Caliphate of Córdoba was not the end of Muslim Spain. Most of the *taifa* states managed to survive for two centuries and the kingdom of Granada (occupying approximately the modern provinces of Málaga, Granada and Almería) was not brought under Christian rule until 1492. Indeed, Hispano–Muslim civilisation reached a new peak in the eleventh and twelfth centuries. Córdoba's cultural and artistic monopoly gave way to several courts eager to emulate and surpass the achievements of the Umayyads. Al-Muktadir of Zaragoza built the most elaborate and intricate forms of decorative architecture in his new palace, Aljafería, in the second half of the eleventh century. Both the Giralda and the Torre de Oro in Sevilla belong to the following century. The Alhambra (*al-hamra*: 'the red one'), the best preserved symbol of Hispano–Muslim culture, dates from the thirteenth and fourteenth centuries.

But their split-up cost Muslim Spain dearly: unable or unwilling to act together against increasing pressure from the north they lost the military initiative to their Christian neighbours. Until 1031 the northern kingdoms had had to contribute a heavy toll to the Muslims for their precarious existence. It was now the Christians' turn to harass and raid the Muslim states regularly in search of tribute (*parias*). When the pressure proved unbearable Muslim Spain had to ask for help from northern Africa as in 1085 and again in 1146.

In 1085 Toledo fell to Alfonso VI of León and Castilla. The ruler of Sevilla requested military aid from the Berber Almoravids of North Africa, who defeated Alfonso at Zalaca (near Badajoz) in 1086 but also swept away the *taifa* rulers and restored a measure of political unity to al-Andalus until 1144 when the control crumbled once again and the petty rulers reappeared. They were soon brushed aside again; this time by the Almohads, products of another Berber religious revival, who entered al-Andalus in 1146 and restored order, until they were crushed by the combined Christian armies at Las Navas de Tolosa in 1212. After Las Navas the kingdoms of the north were able to proceed with the reduction of Muslim domination in Spain and by 1266 had nearly completed the task except for the Kingdom of Granada, which was re-established in 1238 by a Syrian of the Nasrid tribe, Muhammed I, who was allowed to retain his kingdom as a vassal of Fernando III.

## *Rise of Christian Spain*

When the Umayyad Caliphate ceased to exist, the territories lined along the Cantabrian coast and the Pyrenean foothills were just beginning to emerge from their mountain fastnesses in search of space for a growing population. Throughout the Roman and Visigothic periods, these mountainous peoples had remained outside the main course of events, locked in their tribal structures and narrow valleys, and engaged in pastoral and subsistence agriculture. They would descend occasionally to the lower and richer valleys of the Duero and Ebro to plunder the lowlands. The Romans had been happy simply to contain them; they saw no possible benefit in their total subjugation. The Visigoths, on the other hand, had settled in areas much closer and were consequently more involved in their supervision and control.

The arrival of the Muslims displaced the Visigothic élites to the shelter of the Cantabrian, Asturian and Galician valleys behind the mountain range which runs parallel to the coast and separates dry Spain from humid Spain. This additional pressure on the land must have prompted

The Mozarabic style: a view of the interior of San Miguel de Escalada,
incorporating the keyhole or horseshoe arch of the Visigoths

the surplus population to move out in the only direction possible:
southwards along the northern tributaries of the Duero river, the Esla
and Pisuerga. This was the first nucleus claiming a separate existence
from al-Andalus and seeking to expand. They were moving into
unpopulated territory and the very slow speed of their migration
southwards must be related to the paucity of their numbers.

## THE ASTUR–LEONESE KINGDOM

The mythical beginnings of the Astur–Leonese monarchy linked its first
incumbent, Pelayo, to King Roderic as his grandson and successor
elected by members of the royal family and ruling élites of the Visigothic
kingdom of Toledo seeking shelter in the north from the Islamic
invaders. Pelayo was the one to inflict the first symbolic defeat on the
Moors, at Covadonga in the inmost recesses of the mountains of Europe

in 722, through the spiritual mediation of St James, the Apostle, and to raise the banner of resistance against the infidel invader. It was also St James' intercession that helped them on the battlefield of Simancas against Caliph Abd al-Rahman himself in 939 and brought al-Mansur to his sudden death in 1002 as a punishment for the sacking of St James' cathedral and city (Santiago de Compostela) in 997. The hard-pressed Leonese were badly in need of the comfort of this faith to sustain them at the time. The version of events from the winning side was quite different: Ibn Hayyan (987–1076), the son of one of al-Mansur's secretaries, recognised the significance of the Apostle's shrine for all Christians as Ka'ba in Mecca was for Islam. As for their alleged right to repossession of land taken away from them, Ibn Hayyan was much less appreciative and referred to the northern rebels simply as 'thirty barbarians perched on a rock' who must inevitably die!

## FRANKISH COUNTIES

Charlemagne's disaster in Roncesvalles in 778 made him turn to the Mediterranean end of the Pyrenees as a more appropriate territory to set up a defensive buffer zone against the Muslims. He conquered Gerona (785) and Barcelona (801), aided by *hispani* who had been dispossessed by Abd al-Rahman in his punitive campaign against Zaragoza and had escaped to south and north of the eastern Pyrenees. He established the Marca Hispanica with five counties, limited to the west by the Llobregat and Cardoner rivers, under the counts of Barcelona who had become hereditary rulers free from Frankish interference by 800. Relatively free from Muslim raids, the Catalan counties grew demographically and developed along lines significantly different from the other nuclei of opposition to Muslim supremacy. Firstly, the early attempts to create a substantial social grouping of small farmers very soon gave way to a very rigid manorial system. The disappearance of a free peasantry, it has been suggested, went hand-in-hand with the rise of manorial castles; thus the name Catalunya as the land of *castláns* (castellans). It concentrated property in the hands of civil and ecclesiastical authorities and the main monasteries. Secondly, throughout these early times the Catalan counties remained very much in the cultural orbit of south-eastern France. Ripoll and Saint Pere de Rodes (San Pedro de Roda) monasteries were both built in the first half of the eleventh century, very probably with some of the money that Ramón Borrell I brought from his expedition to Córdoba in 1010. His spoils of war, no doubt, also gave him the means to mint coins with his own effigy – the first accoutrement of real kingship.

## ARAGÓN

Further west from the Catalan counties similar social groups lived along the upper courses of the tributaries descending from the Pyrenees to the Ebro valley, farming small plots of land and tending sheep and cattle. Their first recorded activities formed part of the Frankish defensive system. In the early ninth century an indigenous landowner by the name of Aznar Galindo was given the title of Count of Aragón, after the river which runs south along the Canfranc valley to its first capital, Jaca. He ruled the county as a military outpost dependent on Toulouse. His successors extended their wings slowly, providing basic administration and occupying the territories between the Aragón and the Gállego, with the monastery of San Juan de la Peña as the spiritual focus of the region in the same way that the commemorative centre built in Covadonga was to the first Asturian kingdom. By the beginning of the ninth century the county of Aragón became linked through marriage to the neighbouring kingdom of Navarra, which under Sancho III (*el mayor*, the Great, 1005–35) played the leading role amongst the incipient Christian states.

## NAVARRA

First mentioned in an early ninth-century Frankish text, the name taken from the Basque 'Nafarroa' referred to two nuclei of Vascones centring round Pamplona ('Baskunis' according to Arab texts) and Sangüesa and Leyre ('Glaskiyun'), who evolved a separate identity in the wake of the break-up of the frontier governorships which had defended Charlemagne's empire until 814. At the centre of the region stood Pamplona as a fortified enclave at the crossroads between Jaca, Tudela and Logroño, and the main mountain pass through the Pyrenees, Roncesvalles. Its strategic situation made it not only the natural centre of influence in the area, but also the pole of attraction of powerful neighbours. Early Arab historians commented on this nucleus of resistance as inhabited by poor people forced from their mountain abodes by sheer necessity. A *modus vivendi* with the Banu Qasi, who controlled the upper frontier of al-Andalus (Tudela, Zaragoza and Huesca), ensured its survival. In 778 the Banu Qasi together with the Vascones of Pamplona are reported to have routed Charlemagne along the Roncesvalles valley after his failure to take Zaragoza, co-operation which was later reinforced by marriage.

South-east of Pamplona, the second centre of resistance round Sangüesa and Leyre remained closer to monastic colonisation. A family called Jimena, made a successful bid to establish their hegemony in Pamplona. In the first decades of the tenth century they extended their sphere of influence to Estella and down to the Ebro valley west of Tudela into Rioja and Alava (923) and in 922 incorporated the county of Aragón through marriage. Settlement of the territory across the Ebro river was entrusted to monasteries like San Millán de la Cogolla or San Martín de Albelda. The strength of this political and cultural formation brought Navarra to a prominent position in the Christian part of the Iberian peninsula under Sancho III. The rulers of Barcelona, León and Zaragoza rendered homage to him and recognised his supremacy. Pamplona was also the main route of entry for the pilgrims from Europe on their way to Santiago, which the king facilitated by rerouting it on the site of the old Roman way.

Sancho III's pre-eminence over Christian lords or his protection of Muslim rulers, from whom he was the first to receive tribute, were typical of the personal character of kingship. The idea of sovereignty was not yet mooted; nor was there any indication that Sancho was aiming to establish any permanent claim to hegemony under the aegis of Navarra. By the time of his death in 1035 his intervention in León was already spent and he had been forced to retreat from further interference behind the Pisuerga river. Furthermore, his will clearly differentiated between the Navarrese territories (including La Rioja, Alava, Guipúzcoa and Vizcaya) which he bequeathed to his first-born García (as the family patrimony), and the counties of Castilla, Sobrarbe and Ribagorza (between Aragón and the Catalan counties), and Aragón (the latter with the title of kingdom) which went to his other sons, Fernando, Gonzalo and Ramiro respectively; they had to recognise and render homage to their elder brother as their sovereign lord. This practice was carried out by his successors also, thus creating a semi-permanent state of civil war among the beneficiaries of royal wills, with the strongest heir eventually attaining some form of authority over all others.

Amid this uncertainty and aided by the emergence of strong warlords, Castilla and Aragón forced their way to the centre of the struggle for territorial growth, first at the expense of the other Christian principalities and then of the Muslims. In 1076 Navarra was shared out between Fernando II of Castilla and Sancho I of Aragón. However, in 1134 Navarra managed to find a new independent ruler in the person of García Ramírez, under the suzerainty of Alfonso VII of Castilla. Effectively barred from expansion to the south by Castilla and Aragón, Navarra continued its separate existence more and more within the orbit of France, especially from 1234, but still a key point of entry for European ideas and pilgrims on their way to Santiago.

## *The Birth of Castilla*

Between Navarra and Asturias, from the ninth century onwards Cantabrians and Vascones were on the move to settle the territories around the head-waters of the Ebro river and the upper Duero valley. From the start, their chance of success depended on their ability to hold their position against the Muslims whose customary route for their regular raids against the northern territories was along the road from Toledo to Zaragoza, along the Henares and Jalón rivers, and from Zaragoza to Briviesca. From the eleventh to the thirteenth centuries the long frontier stretching from the Atlantic to the Mediterranean along the Duero and moving southwards was dotted with defensive settlements, castles, fortified towns and bridges. But it was the early line of defence along the right bank of the Ebro above the gorges of Pancorbo that came to typify the structure and spirit of this line of fortifications, most of which had been built initially by the Muslims who referred to this area as al-Qila (the castles). This was the region at the receiving end of Muslim onslaughts and the people of this buffer zone were the first to turn the tables on the Muslim frontier states after the break-up of the Caliphate. The Castilian people brought with them an individualistic and adventurous spirit well suited to their rugged existence along the dangerous border. They governed themselves through open councils or assemblies and settled newly-occupied lands through the squatters' principle. The new territories were assigned to military commanders with a defensive mission. In 1035 Sancho III of Navarra bequeathed Castilla as a county to his second son, Fernando.

## FERNANDO I

Like his father before him, Fernando I made no attempt to increase his territorial holding at the expense of the Muslims, other than extracting tribute (*parias*) from Zaragoza, Toledo, Sevilla and Badajoz in return for protection against Muslim and Christian alike. His aspirations pointed in a more personal direction: the establishment of his authority over Castilla vis-à-vis León and the reassertion of his father's pre-eminence among other rulers. He proceeded to raise his county to political hegemony by first incorporating the old kingdom of León, after defeating and killing Vermudo III at the Battle of Tamarón in 1037. In 1054 he meted out the same treatment to his elder brother, García III of Navarra, at Atapuerca. Shorn of the territories west and east of the upper Ebro (La Rioja, Alava, Vizcaya and Guipúzcoa) which Sancho III had taken from Castilla not long before, Sancho IV (1054–76) was allowed to succeed his brother García to the throne of Navarra as Fernando I's vassal. The loss of these lands effectively barred Navarra from further expansion into Muslim territory.

## ALFONSO VI

Castilian supremacy was only a phase. Alfonso VI had to build it up all over again. At Fernando I's death in 1065 his dominions and the *parias* he was getting from Muslim rulers were divided among his children. As the second-born, Alfonso inherited León, Asturias and the *parias* the Muslim ruler of Toledo was paying, i.e. the dominions Fernando had acquired in his lifetime. Those he had inherited, the dynastic heirloom, together with the *parias* from the Muslim Kingdom of Zaragoza, went to the first-born, Sancho. The third son, García, received Galicia, northern Portugal and the *parias* from Sevilla and Badajoz.

It was Sancho who first attempted to reassemble Fernando's territorial holding under his own rule; Alfonso and García were dispossessed. But in 1072 Sancho was assassinated and Alfonso, who in the meantime had fled to Toledo, returned to appropriate all dominions, including those of his brother García, and set himself up as Alfonso VI of Castilla (1072–1109) and León (1065–1109).

## *The fall of Toledo in 1085*

The capitulation of the capital city of the Muslim middle frontier on the Tajo was the final act of five years of internal plots and counterplots involving both Christian and Muslim rulers, with Alfonso VI pressurising al-Mutamid of Toledo for higher and higher contributions, for protection or support against all others. By 1080 Toledo was sinking under severe inflation and crippling taxation, and deeply divided as to whether to buy Alfonso VI off at all costs or resist his demands for more protection money. After years of skirmishes, sallies and devastation to the countryside, the usual form of warfare at the time, the city surrendered to Alfonso VI, despite the protection money, and the King of Castilla and León made his formal entry in 1085. The surrender terms were still in keeping with the tolerant and conciliatory attitude that the Muslims had shown when they were ahead: immediate surrender meant that the local inhabitants could continue practising their own religion in the great mosque of Toledo and keep their lives and property in return for the same taxes they had been paying their previous masters; they could freely leave the city and return without forfeiting their possessions; only if a city had to be stormed, would the citizens be killed or enslaved.

Alfonso VI may not have aimed beyond the political prestige and financial rewards to be reaped from the occupation of the capital city of the old Visigothic Kingdom and one of al-Andalus' greatest centres, famous for its magnificent court and cultural excellence. He may even have felt gratitude for Toledo's erstwhile ruler, al-Mamun, who so lavishly entertained him when he had to flee for his life from his brother Sancho. His own claim to royal authority was considerably strengthened by its possession. He adopted the title of Emperor of Toledo, Emperor of the Two Religions. The appointment of Count Sisnando Davídiz as governor indicated his desire to ensure a conciliatory interpretation of the capitulation terms. Davídiz was a typical product of the majority section of the new community, straddling two or even three cultures, and making a stand for religious and political toleration between Muslim, Christian and Jew. He himself was a *mozárabe* (Arabised Christian) who had served the Emir of Sevilla and entered the service of Alfonso VI as a royal councillor; a man well experienced in frontiers and communications, commented a contemporary Arab scholar.

Whatever Alfonso VI's intentions, the loss of Toledo could not fail to be seen by Muslims other than as part and parcel of a wider design on the part of the Christian ruler to pursue his march southwards, or at best to make them all his vassals and tributaries. No sooner had he settled the question of Toledo than he turned on Sevilla for higher tribute, against Davídiz's counsel of prudence and moderation as to the amount lest Muslim rulers should decide to appeal for help to their fellow Muslims in Africa. It was, in fact, al-Mutamid of Sevilla, with the *taifa* rulers of Badajoz and Granada, who after much hesitation decided to throw al-Andalus to the mercy of the Almoravids for deliverance from Castilla. In the last instance, he is reported to have said, he would rather be a camel-driver in Africa among people of his own religion and culture and keep al-Andalus from the infidels, than a swineherd in Castilla.

## *Almoravids and Almohads*

The first wave of support from Africa was a new Muslim revivalism from the Atlas region of the north-west brandishing a stricter interpretation of the Koran and a rekindled crusading spirit. Their name Almoravids derives from the Arabic, meaning the inhabitants of the 'ribat' (place of retreat or frontier–convent combining prayer and military service in pursuance of the holy war against the non-believers). Spanish place-names bear witness to the dispersion of these establishments, e.g. Rábida-Huelva, Rápita-Tortosa. Under Yusuf Ibn Tashunin, already in control of an African empire four times the size of al-Andalus, the Almoravids came across the Straits and by October 1086, just over a year after the capitulation of Toledo, were facing Alfonso VI at Sagrajas, north-east of Badajoz. The conqueror of Toledo, seriously wounded and bleeding profusely, barely escaped with his life to the safety of Coria, while his army lay in tatters. Christian heads were dispatched to the main cities of al-Andalus for their rejoicing and edification; and the *taifa* rulers no longer had to pay tribute to their Christian overlords.

Yusuf then returned to Africa and had to be summoned again. In 1089 he returned to seize al-Andalus for his own people, on the grounds that the *taifa* princes were no better than the infidels, indifferent to religion, imposing illegal taxes on the population and paying tribute to non-believers. The Castilians were dealt severe blows again at Consuegra and Uclés but Toledo held out. The Almoravids, for their part, lost their zest for war and fell into the same habits and libertinism from which they had come to rescue the *taifa* rulers.

Within half a century a new star was rising from the Atlas mountains. Ibn Tumart (1082–1130) was preaching a new creed of unity in God for the Almohads, the true believers, and war against the Almoravids who were no better than pagans. His followers displaced the Almoravids from power, entering their capital Marrakesh in 1147, and when Almoravid control in al-Andalus crumbled in the late 1140s, they moved in to restore their own brand of unity to their brethren across the sea. Almohad supremacy was even more precarious than that of their predecessors, who were still holding the Balearic Islands and the region around Cuenca and Murcia and drawing Almohad fire until 1172, thus enabling some Christian advances from the north-east along the Ebro valley and from the west along the silver road of the Romans. In addition, the Almohads were being challenged in Tunisia by constant rebellions. Their spectacular victory over Alfonso VIII of Castilla in 1195 at Alarcos, north of the Despeñaperros pass, was their last great action: a Pyrrhic victory since the Almohads could not follow it up and the terrified Christians from all over Europe came to the rescue, compounding their differences at least long enough to save Christian Spain from the clutches of the Almohads.

## *Christian advances in the twelfth century*

Toledo, and indeed Castilla, just about held out in this century of constant and uncertain struggle between north and south, fought mainly in the area south of Toledo along the main routes to Andalucía. Castilla la Nueva, the new land of castles and fortified towns, had to contend with Muslim revivalism as well as territorial designs on her on the part of Aragón and the newly-created county of Portugal. Alfonso VI had ruled over both Castilla and León but when he died in 1109 his dominions were divided among his children and there followed a long civil war which threatened the territorial integrity of both dominions. Castilla was not yet firmly established as a separate kingdom; its start, as an offshoot of the territories disputed by León and Navarra, ruled by the same dynasty, explain the succession crises which became an endemic feature of Castilla. If the first half of the century was dominated by the civil war that followed Alfonso VI's death, the second half of the century was a replay of all the problems of the first, this time occasioned by the death of Alfonso VII in 1157 and Alfonso VIII's minority crisis.

Alfonso VI's daughter Urraca (1109–26), successor to the twin crowns of Castilla and León, had first married Raymond of Burgundy, who was given an extensive appanage in Galicia while his brother Henry, married to Urraca's sister, Teresa, was granted the county of Portugal. It was the offspring of this latter marriage, Alfonso Enríquez, who in 1143 declared himself King Alfonso I of Portugal, still under the suzerainty of León. Availing himself of the instability in Castilla–León, and the struggle between the Almoravids and the Almohads in the east, he consolidated his rule over Portugal by expanding along the west, competing with Fernando II of León (1157–88), who had married his daughter, for the territories of the Muslim ruler of Cáceres, Badajoz and Trujillo, which fell to Portuguese and Leonese armies between 1165 and 1170. Portugal was the first to reach the southern seabord in 1249, and in 1267 Alfonso III agreed with Alfonso X of Castilla–León to set the Guadiana river as the boundary between the two countries.

In the east it was left to Alfonso I of Aragón (1104–34) to challenge Muslim domination along the middle and lower course of the River Ebro. His crusading zeal has been portrayed ever since as the new conquering spirit of Christian Spain in response to the Almoravids. To start with, though, his first sphere of interest was Castilla–León. His marriage to Urraca of Castilla–León was childless; the Castilian nobility successfully opposed an alliance which might weaken their position in relation to the Crown. Alfonso I, *el batallador* (the redoubtable champion of the faith), turned to the middle Ebro to pursue the inroads made to the Kingdom of Zaragoza by his father Sancho (1063–94), the first King of Aragón, who had conquered Barbastro in 1064 with the help of an army of knights from Aquitaine, Burgundy and Normandy. Alfonso I conquered Zaragoza in 1118, Tudela, Tarazona and Calatayud in 1120, and conducted a raid on Andalucía in 1125–6 which brought back several thousand *mozárabes* to repopulate the occupied territories. Following the action against Barbastro, probably the first one on the Iberian peninsula to enjoy the juridical status of a crusade, i.e. with total spiritual and material support from Rome, Alfonso I's campaign drew a great deal of support from abroad. The plunder taken from Barbastro, which was not an important city, had caused excitement throughout Europe. Alfonso I also introduced the military order of the Templars and willed his kingdom to them, indirectly causing the amalgamation of Aragón and Catalunya through the marriage of Petronila, the daughter of Alfonso I's brother Ramiro III (1134–7), and Ramón Berenguer of Barcelona (1137–62).

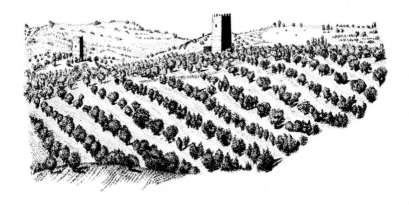

# CHAPTER THREE

# The Making of Castilla

## Las Navas de Tolosa

The northern principalities' final act in their struggle to shake off Muslim military hegemony took place in 1212 at Las Navas de Tolosa. The rulers of Castilla (Alfonso VIII), Aragón (Pedro II) and Navarra (Sancho VII), with large contingents of French knights, friars of all military orders and town militiamen from Castilla, crushed Almohad military power. Victory for the Christian forces had been very much in the balance and Alfonso VIII felt that Castilla was gambling on a decisive battle. However, he was no more able to capitalise on this military victory than the Almohads after Alarcos. Co-operation among Christian rulers and their ruling élites against the Muslims was the exception rather than the rule. During these centuries Christian princes and their warlords could be seen fighting one another for land and status as frequently as raiding Muslim territories, or in the service of Muslim lords, like Rodrigo Díaz de Vivar, 'el Cid Campeador' of the epic 'El Cantar del mío Cid' (from the Arab 'sid' meaning lord) who carved himself a separate dominion out of Muslim Valencia (1094–9), or the Christian mercenaries who helped the Almoravids in their fight against the Almohads until 1172. The Almohads, from 1213 under a new caliph Yusuf II (a young boy who hardly ever left Marrakesh), never recovered from the defeat at Las Navas. At Yusuf's death in 1224 Andalusí provinces split and supported three different claimants to the caliphate As for the victors, they could do nothing but lick their wounds. Famine and sickness ravaged the forces still encamped after Las Navas; furthermore, there was no proper harvest until 1220. Pedro II of Aragón died in 1213, bequeathing five years of civil wars for his five-year-old son Jaime I (1217–52). In Castilla, Fernando III (1217–52) had to fight for his throne against the powerful Laras and his own father Alfonso IX of León before he could turn his hand to further expansion south of Despeñaperros in 1225.

## *A World at War*

The long century between the conquest of Toledo and Las Navas de Tolosa set the seal on Castilla as a society dedicated to war but badly

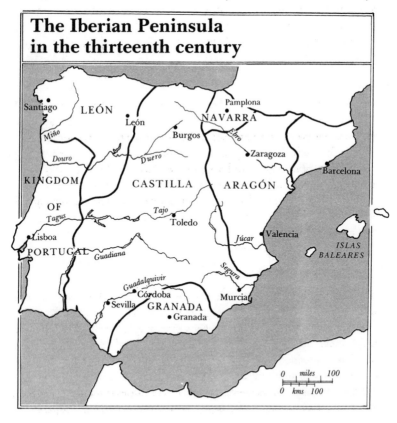

# The Iberian Peninsula in the thirteenth century

equipped and organised. Royal authority was very slowly emerging as a unifying force but the limitations to such claims as may have been made at the time were all too evident. Monarchs had to struggle during the first years of their reign to establish their authority within the dynasty or against the nobility. Financial muscle or territorial holdings were the essence of the authority of a prince, or indeed the standing of his/her vassal, and the only source of patronage to reward loyal service and attract faithful servants. In the absence of any legitimising principle, successful war was the only means of acquiring the trappings of authority. The basic dilemma of war as a self-financing mechanism bringing the additional bonus of acknowledged kingship was that it had limited prospects even if successful. Warfare in the twelfth century was expensive, e.g. long sieges of increasingly better-fortified towns and castles, and the spoils of war ever less gratifying on account of the methodical and systematic devastation wrought upon the countryside surrounding the military targets. Warlords who had to reward their warriors adequately diminished their own standing by the same amount. The Crown's share of spoils was substantial but never large enough to overawe a powerful formation of ecclesiastical and territorial lords. The monopoly of war leadership on the part of the monarchy was the only way of strengthening the authority of the Crown and encouraging the growth of new social forces closer to the leadership of the war; royal authority was seeking to balance out the military and territorial weight of the peers of the realm, who lorded it over large estates and vast numbers of vassals. These new forces came from the towns, the ecclesiastical authorities and the military orders.

## URBAN DEVELOPMENT

The first towns to experience a revival in the eleventh century were those along the Road to Santiago (Pilgrims' Way). Merchants and artisans, travellers and town-dwellers, profiting from improved communications, trade opportunities and circulation of money, began to show a communal spirit and struggled to free themselves from ecclesiastical or nobiliary lordships. Thereafter, the towns grew along the frontier line of the eleventh and twelfth centuries from the Duero to the Tajo; they could profit from their extensive *alfoces* (adjoining countryside) and enjoy the administrative autonomy enshrined in their royal charters (*fueros*), electing their own magistrates and officials from among the urban notables. A contemporary legal text described a town as a 'walled population centre'. Their military function enabled them to assemble powerful militias which played a very prominent part in the last stages of the war against Islam, bringing to their municipal councils territorial and personal rewards to enhance their power. Those among the *villani* (town-dwellers) who could afford to maintain a horse and equip themselves for war competed in the battlefield and entered the ranks of the lower nobility – *hidalgos:hijos de algo* 'men of some substance', as the Arabs say to refer to people of some standing in society. The *caballeros villani* were the element of social mobility in a war situation which no doubt bound these people to the Crown.

## The Church Militant

From the very beginning priests and monks had been very heavily involved in the work of repopulating and colonising the lands taken from the Muslims. Some of these territories contained important sections of the communities which had been able to retain the Visigothic tradition of the Toledan Church; this mozarabic rite was the traditional view, trying to transmit a vision of coexistence and peaceable transition from Muslim to Christian, which we saw in conflict in Toledo in 1085 with a more intransigent attitude towards the Muslims coming from Rome and France. The pioneers of this Christian revivalism were the reformed Benedictine monks of Cluny (Burgundy). They had been established in the Catalan and Aragonese counties from the tenth century and were very closely integrated with the first independent rulers of these Pyrenean valleys, who endowed them handsomely with subsidies and lands. The Cathedral of Jaca, built from 1053 to 1063, exemplifies the Romanesque style of French architecture in the wake of Cluniac monasticism, as do San Martín de Frómista, San Isidoro de León, started in 1075, and Santa María la Real de Nájera, founded by King García of Navarra with the proceeds of the investment of Calahorra in 1052.

In his attempt to raise Castilla to political pre-eminence after Sancho III of Navarra, Fernando I must have seen Cluniac monasticism as a

Santa María de Naranco, the chapel of Ramiro I (842–50). One of the earliest
Asturian Christian churches after the Muslim invasion

powerful instrument for he was the one to establish in favour of Cluny
an annual subsidy, worth more than the total income of the abbey's
important landed possessions, out of the tributes he was exacting from
his Muslim neighbours in the mid-eleventh century. By the end of the
century the Roman rite had been imposed throughout León and Castilla,
the mozarabic liturgy surviving only in Toledo. By the mid-twelfth
century, though, the environment had changed quite dramatically: the
successive waves of Almoravids and Almohads required a determined
effort on the part of the Church militant to come to the rescue of the
Crown, which was incapable of providing adequate defences.

## MILITARY ORDERS

The Cistercians provided the new impetus needed to hold out against the

Almohads. The first Cistercian foundation in Christian Spain was Fitero (Navarra) in 1140. In the early stages of the war against Islam the Cistercian monks did not have as great an impact as Cluny; however, they played an important part in the creation of the Castilian military orders who were to bear the brunt of the Almohad attacks in the second half of the twelfth century. When the Templars, whom Alfonso I of Aragón had introduced at the beginning of the century, proved unable to hold the town of Calatrava against the Almohads, a group of Cistercian monks from Fitero came to the rescue and in 1157 set up the Order of Calatrava. There followed the Order of Santiago, to whom Fernando II of León entrusted the custody of the town of Cáceres taken from the Almohads in 1170, and the Order of Alcántara.

The military orders are the most explicit manifestation of the war ethos of the twelfth and early thirteenth centuries. Half soldiers, half monks, the friars of the military orders held firm for Christendom in the hard years of Almohad attacks, their convent-fortresses, like the 'ribats' of the Almoravids, dotting the strategic lines of access and defence along the great expanses between the Tajo river and Sierra Morena, from Peñíscola in the east to Tomar in the west. Their contribution to the great action of Las Navas de Tolosa was invaluable, not only in human endeavour and commitment in the fight against the enemies of the Faith, but most importantly as part of the Church establishment in the financial contribution they made directly to the Crown. The clergy of Castilla and León surrendered half their annual rent to Fernando III; the papacy allowed him to use the third of ecclesiastical tithes normally used for the upkeep of the churches and gave its full spiritual backing by preaching the campaign as a crusade, which attracted large numbers of men from all over Europe.

## CHURCH AND MONARCHY

The Crown, therefore, was able to call on years of generous foundations and endowments to the Church, and the Church profited enormously from their contribution to the final stages of the conquest of the south. Episcopal sees like Toledo grew into one of the most extensive territorial holdings in the land. The military orders were granted whole provinces between the Tajo river, Teruel and Sierra Morena. Alfonso X founded

Ciudad Real in 1262 to counterbalance the excessive power of the Order of Calatrava in the area. The Church reached a peak of power and prestige, as witnessed by the extensive building: the Gothic cathedrals of Burgos and Toledo were started in 1222 and 1226 respectively, and Léon was started in 1254 and actually completed in the fourteenth century. However, after the large territorial rewards that followed the conquest of Andalucía, the Castilian–Leonese secular church, especially Toledo, was in a parlous state. In the second quarter of the thirteenth century they had invested a massive amount of money in the expectation of sweet returns from the conquest of large cities, such as Sevilla and Córdoba, which never materialised. They had also surrendered future income, like the *tercias*, which successive monarchs retained and used freely from then on for purely political purposes. Church income also suffered from the drift of population southwards; there were no tenants to pay the rents and jurisdictional dues. The Crown offered no financial comfort but capitalised on the situation by strengthening its own control. Fernando III in 1236 and Jaime I in 1238 officially started to exercise the right of presentation of candidates to church office, and Alfonso X enshrined in *Las Partidas* the formalisation of this form of patronage and authority over the Church.

## Fernando III and Jaime I

Fernando III of Castilla–León and Jaime I of Aragón-Catalunya were the protagonists of the most important phase of the conquest of al-Andalus. The former, after a long struggle to assert his authority in Castilla and León, marched south to take Córdoba in 1236 (triumphantly bringing back to Santiago the bells that al-Mansur had taken to the Great Mosque of Córdoba in 997), Jaén (after four sieges) in 1245, and Sevilla, still the greatest city in western Europe, in 1246. His death in 1252 left his son and heir, Alfonso X, with the task of completing the conquest of the south by taking Cádiz, Murcia and Cartagena in 1264. As for Jaime I, also impeded by succession crises, and by aristocratic unrest at home early in his reign, he first directed his armies to the Balearic Islands, which he occupied between 1229 and 1235, and then proceeded along the Mediterranean coast to take hold of Valencia and Játiva and expand as far south as the Briar Castle (1253), near Calpe promontory. The Treaty of Almizra of 1244 identified that area as the boundary line between Castilla–León and Aragón–Catalunya.

## AFTERMATH OF THE CONQUEST AND OCCUPATION OF AL-ANDALUS

Five political entities emerged from the long centuries of Muslim domination; Navarra, Portugal, Granada, the Crown of Aragón and Castilla-León. Navarra, still locked out by her neighbours from southern expansion, managed to maintain her independence in the orbit of France until the early sixteenth century. Portugal settled down to digest its large territorial acquisitions and by the early fifteenth century was ready to launch into a period of unprecedented maritime discovery and overseas expansion, leading the way for Castilla. The other three made up what we now call Spain, their territorial definition no more precise than the political outlines of the authority of their rulers.

Granada was totally woven into the political life of Castilla as a tributary of the Crown. The full implementation of the terms of the treaty of foundation of the Nasrid Kingdom of Granada, i.e. payment of tribute and obligation to support Castilla militarily against other rulers, was very much related to the ability of Castilla's military machine to enforce it. Through cunning, diplomacy and a defensive system pretty well impregnable, Granada managed to survive and prosper, finding comfort and security in the internecine struggles of Castilla–León and the territorial designs of the Christian kingdoms on one another, offering a safe refuge to exiles and deportees from their civil and succession wars, and contributing to their conflicts through famous companies of mercenaries contracted out to the highest bidders, like the Catalan mercenaries and the free companies from Europe which played such an important part in the peninsular phase of the Hundred Years' War.

The fact is that the Iberian peninsula, from the middle of the thirteenth century to the Black Death of 1348, continued to exist as a cosmopolitan, open society, mediating between Islam and Christendom, where Jewish financiers, Moorish minstrels and artisans, warriors, friars and canonists mixed together fairly freely, not least on account of the uncertainty of the political boundaries of crowns and countries. The art and literature of the period underline the conjunction of Islamic, Hebraic and Christian elements.

## The Crown of Aragón

This was like a federation of autonomous principalities. The Crown of Aragón and the county of Barcelona, the latter exercising an overall feudal authority over all other counties, including Roussillon and Cerdenya on the northern side of the Pyrenees, came together as the result of the marriage of Petronila and Ramón Berenguer in 1137. Jaime I incorporated the kingdoms of Valencia and the Balearic Islands. The titular head of the Aragonese federation ruled the various member-states separately and in each case there was an individual contractual relationship between monarch and vassals, institutionalised through a representative chamber, *cortes*, which the Catalans first assembled in 1218, the Aragonese in 1247, and the Valencians in 1283. The contractual relationship between the ruling élites was embodied in the oath of allegiance and mutual recognition of rights and duties. In the early part of the twelfth century the Aragonese put it to their king, Alfonso I, in no uncertain terms: 'We who are as good as you and together are more powerful than you, make you our king and lord, provided that you observe our charter and liberties, and if not, not.'

### POPULATION AND PATTERNS OF LAND OCCUPATION

The population of these territories had undergone some fundamental changes in the early years. Alfonso I of Aragón brought a few thousand mozarabic families from Andalucía in 1126 to repopulate the newly occupied territories along the middle Ebro valley, and colonists from Aragón, Catalonia and southern France moved into towns like Valencia, which was almost exclusively Christian. By and large the population of Aragón, Tarragona, Tortosa and the central and southern parts of the kingdom of Valencia and the Balearic Islands, about 30–35 per cent of the population, were Muslim (*mudéjares*). So were the popular form of architecture and the artisans of these areas. Throughout Aragón we find the small parish churches of the thirteenth century which represent this *mudéjar* style. The ornate wooden ceilings and elaborate doors from jointed pieces (*artesonado*) and the pottery and tile-making techniques of the *azulejos* of Manises and Paterna (where Moorish kilns are still in use) are also part of the same cultural tradition. The Jewish element was not as large as in Castilla but still constituted 5–7 per cent of the total population of three-quarters of a million.

The initial pattern of occupation by Christian immigrants in the coastal areas between Tortosa and Murcia showed a desire to come to terms with the natives. Jaime I, fully aware of the human and military limitations of his expansionist campaign, allowed Muslims to carry on with their religion, civil institutions and farms, under the jurisdiction of civil and ecclesiastical lords. The fertile Levantine *huertas* that he so much admired, with their orderly *alquerías* and elaborate system of irrigation, surely contributed to his desire to retain such a productive system. In Mallorca, however, he showed much less concern for the former owners of the land; he divided up the islands in halves, between himself and the nobility and the Church, reducing the native Moorish population to working the fields as tenants tied to the land. The region of Murcia, which had been acquired by Castilla in 1243, was granted special status as a semi-autonomous Muslim kingdom. From 1257 King Alfonso of Castilla appeared to put pressure on the Muslim king and the local chiefs to give up their land to Christian colonists, which helps to explain the wave of protest and rebellion spreading through Valencia, Alicante, Murcia and Andalucía in the 1260s. When Jaime I restored order, resettlement of the territory by a strong Catalan contingent followed the pattern set by the occupation of Andalucía: large tracts of land were granted to municipal councils, military orders and the nobility. Retaken from the Muslims by Jaime II, Murcia was surrendered to Castilla in 1304.

Catalunya's substantial contribution to the repopulation of Murcia may indicate that the expansionist urge of the north-eastern counties under Jaime I had not been exhausted. When the expansion southwards reached the boundaries agreed with Castilla, Catalunya turned her attention to the Mediterranean. She established a permanent presence in north Africa and intervened in Italian internal affairs, acquiring rights over Sardinia. In addition, consulates were opened up from the Levant to Flanders, and the two Greek duchies of Athens and Neopatras, which the *almogávares* (Catalan light infantry units) had wrested from Byzan-

The Generalitat Palace in Barcelona

tium, were incorporated into the Aragonese federation. With this maritime expansion went growth in Catalan industrial exports in return for slaves and spices from the east, which made their language the lingua franca of Mediterranean exchanges and their trading customs the first set of rules of maritime law, codified as *Llibre del Consolat de mar*. This golden age of mercantile and maritime expansion reached its apogee by the mid-fourteenth century. Spectacular evidence of this power and prosperity is abundantly visible in Barcelona, the epicentre of this expansion, with its Cathedral, the Church of Santa María del Mar, Consell de Cent, Llotja (chamber of commerce), the palace of the Generalitat (the permanent committee of the Catalan parliament), and Reales Atarazanas (shipyards), now the Maritime Museum.

Urban development in the Iberian Levant came later than in Castilla but by the thirteenth century places like Barcelona and Valencia, and their institutions of direct government, were growing very rapidly. The urban oligarchies, 'honourable citizens' of the community, were connected with the landed aristocracy but these eastern cities developed a greater degree of political participation on the part of successful burgesses and merchants. The civic virtues of these urban patriciates were not so closely identified with the feudal aristocracy of the countryside, and over the centuries provided a more open and enterprising atmosphere.

## ECONOMIC AND DEMOGRAPHIC DECLINE

If the splendid expressions of Catalan prowess are still quite obvious, the factors contributing to this magnificent era show no such clear projection. Attention has been drawn to the good fortune of some remarkable rulers succeeding one another from 1213 to 1410 and enjoying a considerable degree of stability. Stable authority, monetary stability, capital growth and slave and spice trading were obviously highly conducive to adventure and enterprise. The Crown's contribution may have been rather limited, to judge from royal moans about resources. As for the view that an early form of constitutionalism (pactism) encouraged the Catalan expansionist spirit in the second half of the fourteenth century, the alleged freedoms and liberties of the Aragonese federation were obtained only after a long struggle with the monarchy between 1265 and 1348, and redounded to the exclusive advantage of the nobility and urban oligarchies.

Whatever the explanation for this burst of energy and expansionist endeavour, it was very short-lived and began to slow down even before the Black Death of 1348, which made its appearance through the Balearic Islands and then hit the Iberian peninsula, and especially the Catalan counties, in successive waves for the next forty years. Between 1340 and the end of the fifteenth century Catalunya lost half its population. Aragón, the Balearic Islands and Valencia were probably as hard hit but showed earlier signs of recuperation, with Valencia actually growing quite steadily from the end of the fourteenth century.

As usual pestilence came in the wake of famine and war – the last straw in a series of crises which affected the whole of the Iberian peninsula. Throughout the fourteenth century there was a general deterioration in weather conditions, coupled with nobiliary wars and wholesale devastation of the countryside. Landowners responded to rising inflation and general decline in profits from the land with an equally brutal determination to recoup their dwindling income by raising their exactions or increasing their holdings at the expense of the Crown or municipal land. These social and economic disasters were compounded by the ten-year war (1356–66) the Crown of Aragón had to wage against Castilla's territorial ambitions. In the process Aragón was forced to make further concessions to the nobility and their representative assemblies, while wrestling in vain to prevent political domination from Castilla. By 1412 Castilian hegemony was beyond dispute and the very dynasty that some believe provided the stability and continuity underwriting Catalan expansionism became extinguished. Castilla was called upon to provide the Crown of Aragón with a new dynasty from a junior branch (Trastámara) of the reigning Castilian family.

## THE FIFTEENTH-CENTURY CRISIS

The sorry tale of economic and political conflicts afflicting the social fabric of the eastern kingdoms came to a head in the civil war of 1462–72. From 1435 the festering conflict of the countryside was aggravated by growing unrest among the urban lower classes. Artisans and craftsmen, producers and exporters confronted the town oligarchies of rentiers and importers for a restoration of the productive capacity of the economy and a broadening of the basis of municipal government. The final confrontation came on the occasion of the family quarrel between Juan II (1458–79) and his son Carlos. The Catalan élites rallied to Carlos as the champion of Catalan privileges and liberties. By the early 1460s, the prince already dead, the Principality of Catalunya offered itself to Enrique IV of Castilla, also a Transtámara. The Catalan élites were in open revolt against Juan II who was supported by Aragón, Valencia and Mallorca. Waiting on the sidelines was also Louis XI of France, offering help in the hope of obtaining the two Catalan provinces, Cerdenya and Roussillon, north of the Pyrenees.

A new agrarian revolt was needed to make King Fernando II, Juan II's son and heir, move towards the resolution of the conflict by satisfying at least the aspirations of the better-off among the peasants, who before these events were freeholders in the northern region of Catalunya where property was less concentrated and seigniorial encumbrances more endurable. The Sentence of Guadalupe of 1486 allowed those peasants for a relatively small sum of money to buy themselves free from servile status. This settlement helped create a strong rural peasantry in Old Catalunya that would play an important part in the development of the region. These events underlined the extent of the demographic and commercial decline of the Principality and its political dependence on Castilla at a crucial time in its history. In the meantime Aragón and Valencia continued their slow but steady recovery.

## The Kingdom of Castilla

Unlike the Crown of Aragón, with its succession of enduring rulers from the dynasty founded by Petronila of Aragón and Ramón Berenguer IV of Barcelona in 1137, the seat of monarchical power in the Iberian interior was not peacefully occupied by a lawful successor until the middle of the sixteenth century. In a very real sense monarchical authority in Castilla had been and continued to be based on personal success, *de facto* primacy; like Visigothic princes, Castilian rulers had to win their crown in the field of battle. With victory and gains came ratification of their right to rule and the means to recompense their loyal and trusted vassals who alone could give substance through their allegiance to that rule.

### POPULATION AND RESETTLEMENT

The absorption of half as much territory again into the polity of Castilla in the first half of the thirteenth century presented as many problems as the actual conquest of Castilla la Nueva and Andalucía. Its demographic landscape was altered far more substantially than the landscape of the Levantine provinces and the Ebro valley. In the first place, from the tenth century and especially from 1125 when the Almoravids decreed their general expulsion from Muslim territories, there was a more sizeable migration of *mozárabes* from al-Andalus to León, Zamora, Tierra de Campos and Toledo. Secondly, some 200,000 Jews seem to have migrated northwards in response to the same intolerant attitude on the part of both Almoravids and Almohads; many of them must have returned to Andalucía with the conquering armies of Fernando III. There were many more than in the Crown of Aragón but they still represented the same proportion, 5–7 per cent of the total population of Castilla, estimated by 1340 at about 3.7 million. Thirdly, in the 1260s the pressure on the land from the newcomers from the north caused large sections of the Muslim population to rise against the invaders. The rebellion was put down by the two crowns of Castilla and Aragón acting together, and there followed an exodus of *mudéjares* to North Africa or the Kingdom of Granada, which is said to have doubled its population as a result. Finally, the new opportunities which might have come with the acquisition of vast tracts of land, some of it extremely fertile, failed to attract Christian migrants from the north or to retain them if they hopefully moved southwards in the early days of the post-conquest period. The few who stayed in the new territories tended to settle in the fortified towns. Even before the Muslim rebellions of the 1260s Sevilla was depopulating and lands along the Guadalquivir were being abandoned. Shortage of manpower conditioned the distribution of the land in large grants to the few who, in turn, could not exploit it in any way which would require a significant supply of labour. The new configuration of the occupied territories south of Toledo was therefore a surfeit of land and not enough men able or willing to work it: *tierras sin hombres, hombres sin tierra* ('deserted fields and landless peasants').

The Islamic Kingdom of Jaén was distributed between the Orders of Calatrava and Santiago and the See of Toledo. In Córdoba and Sevilla, like Carmona, Niebla, Arcos and Cádiz, large municipal councils under a royal charter were established, extending their authority in some cases beyond the boundaries of the modern provincial areas; again the Orders of Calatrava, Alcántara and Santiago received huge land concessions in these regions. In Lower Extremadura, for instance, the three military orders were granted 700,000 acres of land each and, failing or unwilling to offer such terms as would attract Christian colonists from the north, predictably opted for sheep-, horse- and cattle-raising, which required only the help of small numbers of subject Muslims. This vast surrender of land ownership and jurisdictional authority to the nobility, the Church and the military orders is the overwhelming legacy of the conquest, which would shape the history of Castilla for centuries to come.

## Monarchical Power

Land distribution in Castilla created a powerful nobility which was able to hold the authority of the Crown in check. As in the eastern kingdoms, they were each of them as good as the king and together more powerful than the king. The greatest hurdle, and in a sense the greatest stimulus to action in the promotion of their aspirations, was for both nobility and Crown the general depression of the thirteenth and fourteenth centuries and universal lack of money. From the 'great conqueror' Fernando III on, successive monarchs had to resort to all sorts of expedients to make ends meet; devaluations, export of bullion, sale of royal property. In the context of the continuing fight against the Kingdom of Granada and their allies from North Africa, Castilian rulers sought to strengthen their position vis-à-vis the nobility. In the middle of the thirteenth century Alfonso XI of Castilla (1312–50) building on the legal foundations of his great-grandfather, Alfonso X, made a very significant contribution to a theory of kingship which aimed to depart from the contractual relationship between a lord and his vassal towards a more universal relationship of the king and his 'natural' subject, i.e. all that lived within the territorial boundaries of his realm, without the mediation of prelates or lords. In the *Ordenamiento General de Alcalá* (1348) he placed castles under the protection of the Crown in the hope of putting a break on nobiliary wars. His advances in the direction of a powerful Crown were cut short by the Black Death in 1350. In any case, his ability to bring the nobility under control was not there: the same 1348 Act firmed up the economic and legal foundations of their landholdings by allowing manorial lords prescriptive rights over jurisdiction in their domains.

His son and heir, Pedro I (1350–69), *el cruel*, was much more resolute in his determination to assert the authority of the Crown. The nobility, equally determined to withstand his intention to curtail their power, conspired to have him removed, and to that end invited French and English intervention in peninsular affairs, which very nearly caused the partition of Castilla or its subjection to foreign domination. In their struggle against royal authority the nobility found a leader in Pedro's bastard half-brother, Enrique de Trastámara, the eldest son of Alfonso XI's mistress, Leonor de Guzmán.

His victory over Pedro I and the latter's assassination in the Battle of

Montiel in 1369 could not have contributed a great deal to the emerging principle of strong, hereditary rule. His only claim to the Crown was based on the notion that Pedro I was a tyrant, who abused his authority and trampled on the rights of his vassals. And his apologists observed the considerable skill with which Enrique II managed to reconcile an absolutist view of royal authority with an elective process of selection of the ruler best suited to counter the impious monster; the support of the Church for the usurper turned the struggle into a crusade. However, in the final analysis Enrique II owed his successful bid to his ability to capitalise on the support of the many interests and individuals that Pedro I had antagonised in his desire to keep the nobility in check and to establish Castilian hegemony in the peninsula. The price he had to pay for this support further weakened the patrimonial strength of the monarchy, which resulted in heavier taxes on the people to make up for the loss of revenue.

The French and Aragonese allies who came to Enrique's aid, his relatives, lesser nobility and ecclesiastical magnates who assisted him in his long struggle with Pedro I, all had to be amply rewarded with the manorial estates of Pedro I's erstwhile followers, towns and Crown lands, offices and benefices. His recognition of the debt of gratitude for his supporters brought a new breed of men to the forefront of Castilian politics and territorial power. Only one-fifth of the old families (seven out of thirty-four) survived the civil wars of the period. Enrique III's troubled minority (1390–6) and the confused reigns of Juan II (1406–54) and Enrique IV (1454–74) added new noble families, drawn mainly from the northern periphery of Castilla (Alava and Navarra). These sought to endow substance to their new position and status with those inalienable blocks of land (*señoríos*) which were to be transmitted intact to the first-born (*mayorazgos*). The grant of these entailed manors multiplied from the mid-fourteenth century onwards, conferring upon the lord full authority over land and villeins, that is to say both jurisdictional and property rights. This concentration of lordship over land and men meant that some twenty-four leading families, including bishops, abbots, masters of the military orders and other officials who came from among their members, owned or controlled half the land of Castilla.

Dynastic wars and nobiliary feuds continued to plague Castilian progress through the fifteenth century. Nevertheless, royal authority made significant strides forward. Juan II and his favourite Don Alvaro de Luna managed to wage a successful war against a large section of the nobility and bring them to heel at the Battle of Olmedo in 1445, whereupon there followed a very strong assertion of 'absolute power' based on God, whose deputy in temporal matters the monarch was. The strength of a general interest in a stronger monarchy was shown during the disastrous reign of Juan II's successor, Enrique IV. Despite repeated plots against his rule and personal abuse of power, the authority of the Crown was further strengthened. Thus, the foundations of monarchical royal power had been formally laid in a long struggle with the nobility, old and new. But the claim to that authority was not yet clearly stated; indeed, those among the nobility that conspired against Enrique IV had tried to justify their opposition on the following grounds: first, the abuse of authority on the part of the king; secondly, the favour he showed towards Moors and Jews; and finally, the elective nature of the monarchy of Castilla. In the previous century those who had helped Enrique II defeat and murder the rightful king, Pedro I, used the same arguments; but then they were victorious and their leader managed to found a dynasty which endured. The descendant of that Transtámara family, Enrique IV, was now upholding the hereditary principle vested in that family, and by and large succession difficulties in the fifteenth and sixteenth centuries were kept within the family, brothers and half-brothers, sisters and half-sisters. As for the practical extent of that authority and the accretion of benefits from such powers, they were still determined by the strength of purpose and political ability of individual rulers. Juan II's daughter, Isabel I de Castilla, would aim to bring this constitutional legacy of royal absolutism into full play in the favourable circumstances of the latter part of the fifteenth century.

## THE CASTILIAN FISC

The growth of monarchical authority was sustained by a real increase in the revenue-raising power of the Crown. Against a general background of deterioration of seigniorial finances, the Crown of Castilla introduced new taxes to replenish its coffers. With increased resources there followed a more elaborate system of financial management and a greater involvement in regional and territorial administration. The Crown was also able to introduce military reforms which made it more capable of dealing with the problems of war and civil unrest, and to promote naval expansion which made Castilla by the mid-fifteenth century the leading power and merchant in the Bay of Biscay and the northern seas. The Iberian phase of the Hundred Years War was partly brought about by French and English efforts going back to the end of the thirteenth century to secure the services of Castilian naval power. Basque, Cantabrian and Andalusian mariners and traders were also active in the Mediterranean and west Africa, where they clashed with the Portuguese who embarked upon voyages of exploration across the globe attracted by the prospect of gold, slaves and spices. The Treaty of Tordesillas of 1494 shared out Castilla's and Portugal's areas of influence overseas.

By mid-fifteenth century, therefore, the power of the Crown was fairly well-founded financially and could command a large number of offices and sinecures as the most important source of patronage in the land. Through a judicious balance of rewards and confiscations Castilian rulers were better able to keep a rein on the nobility, who in fact became more dependent on the favours and good disposition of their liege lord as a consequence of their financial difficulties.

## FINANCIAL STRAITS OF THE NOBILITY

The uncertainty of the times, the precariousness of life, the changing moods of political fortune and, indeed, opportunities for social and economic advancement, all were part of the mood of the period between the assassination of Pedro I in 1369 and the end of the succession war between Isabel and Juana in 1480. The large number of castles and fortified manor houses built or restored at the time seems to suggest a desire to seek shelter from the political confusion of the age: Fuensaldaña, Peñafiel, Torrelobatón, Mota and Coca. The nostalgic return to chivalric ideals and the polite rituals of love and courtship, which experienced a very powerful revival in the fifteenth century, first in the court of Aragón and then of Castilla, also express the feeling of anxiety and insecurity of the first estate of the realm, the nobility who had watched great changes in their ranks and witnessed Don Alvaro de Luna by 1445 build up a semi-monarchical position of power and influence

The castle of El Real de Manzanares on the Guadarrama hills near Madrid.

second to none in the Iberian peninsula, only to be ruined by court intrigues and executed in 1453. There was a crisis of confidence among the nobility, most of them dating no further back than 1369, as to their role in society in the context of their secular struggle against the Muslims. Enrique IV's Islamic court and the war games against Granada enraged and irritated the nobility, who vilified him for dressing and eating like a Muslim, keeping a large Moorish guard, and abdicating his responsibility as a Christian soldier for not pursuing the holy war against Granada seriously. He was also accused of all sorts of heretical and unnatural vices for his penchant for young beautiful males of any denomination or race. The frustration and resentment of the nobility showed up in the shifting allegiances from 1464 to 1480 towards Enrique IV, his daughter Juana, his half-sister Isabel and half-brother Alfonso.

Perhaps the underlying explanation for this aristocratic rebelliousness and nostalgia for a bygone and heroic past ('cualquiera tiempo pasado fue mejor', wrote Jorge Manrique at the time) is to be found in the financial misfortunes of noble and ecclesiastical lords through the continuing fall in disposable income from land and jurisdiction. The diminution of their income coincided with a long period of increasing costs in their military equipment and defensive works in a situation of almost endemic warfare. The Black Death, the long, successive waves of bubonic plague, caused a sharp rise in prices and labour wages and a long period of monetary instability, which reached dramatic proportions in the middle decades of the fifteenth century. The land and jurisdictional resources of the nobility were dwindling both in nominal and real terms, and this at a time when Crown revenues were increasing by a third.

Over the years the nobility had recourse to a variety of expedients to make up for the shortfall: greater exactions from their subjects, usurpation of wealth and land from towns, monasteries and the Crown, depredations from one another, pastoral farming, perquisites and profits from commercial and distribution networks and from protection rackets. The noble lords offered the Church protection in return for a share of ecclesiastical income. But most of all the nobility were compelled by their financial difficulties to resort to the Crown for a share of the royal revenue, in the form of outright grants and concessions or office in the administration, the Church or the royal forces. It is estimated that 60–70 per cent of royal income went to pacify the nobility or strengthen their loyalty to the service of the Crown. In the last resort, the importance of co-operation between the two parties for the effective maintenance of the status quo vis-à-vis the majority of the people was never missed for very long on either side.

## SOCIAL AND RACIAL CONFLICTS

The abuses and depredations of the noble lords placed an intolerable burden on the peasants of Galicia, who in 1467 rose to the cry of 'Long live the King and death to the caballeros'. Some hundred lords were forced to flee for their lives, but soon returned in 1469 with the support of the monarchy to put down the rebellion. No other similar movement in the Castilian countryside has been recorded but the urban anti-Jewish pogroms of 1348–51, 1391, 1449 and 1473 were indicative of the general malaise in the country among the lower orders.

No doubt complex religious factors as well as resentment against the wealth and social success of the Jews who settled normally in urban centres contributed to their persecution. At first there were some legal impediments that kept them from certain offices and occupations. After 1391, however, mass conversions led to the removal of these impediments, which enabled some of them to advance socially, marrying into the leading families of the country, amassing riches (and purchasing entailed estates) as financiers and traders, doctors and officials, administrators of the nobility as well as money-lenders and tax-farmers, and exercising great influence as distinguished members of the Church and royal councils. They were particularly strong in Andalucía. For example, the tax administration of Sevilla, the city which set the spark to the 1391 massacres, was handled by *conversos* and so was that of Toledo, the epicentre of the 1449 riots and massacres. Burgos and Segovia were also controlled by *converso* families, and successive monarchs, especially Pedro I, Juan II and Enrique IV, seem to have sought their company and services, allowing them their special protection. No doubt, too, as individuals and perhaps even as a group they involved themselves and were involved in the social and political struggles of this uncertain and conflictive age.

The background to these social conflicts was always bad harvests, acute food shortages and heavy taxation, which could easily be made attributable to the presence of 'abnormal people' in the body politic. The anti-Jewish nature of this antagonism became progressively clearer. In 1449 Toledo banned civil and ecclesiastical office to *conversos* and the notorious statute of its Cathedral Chapter spread like wildfire to other parts of Castilla: it introduced the notion of purity of blood as a qualification for public life. It may be suggested that to a large extent the established forces of the country allowed these outbursts of resentment and frustration to be directed against groups who could be marginalised without upsetting the status quo. The large Moorish population was left largely undisturbed, at least for the time being, perhaps because they lived mainly in the small villages tied to the land on the margin of a monetary economy and posing no threat to the established order. The peasant unrest in Galicia, on the other hand, was put down swiftly and effectively by the nobility with the support of the monarchy.

The Jewish question was used and abused in the struggle between the monarchy and the nobility and in the private wars among the civil and ecclesiastical lords. The nobility, the Church and the town oligarchies must have welcomed a target that left them off the hook; furthermore, there is no indication that the ruling élites with Jewish blood in their blue veins which included the Trastámara family, were seriously affected by the popular witch-hunt. As for the attitude of the Crown towards the end of the period under consideration, its hand may have been stilled by the increasing use made from the mid-fifteenth century of popular protest and unrest as a weapon against the monarchy. The Catholic Monarchs, Isabel of Castilla and Fernando of Aragón, regained the initiative by setting up the Inquisition in 1478 and in 1492 expelling all Jews who refused conversion. These eminently popular measures, together with the long war of attrition against the remaining Muslim enclave of Granada, were part of the long process of assertion of monarchical authority and the rise of the modern state, in which the joint rulers of Castilla and Aragón attempted to consolidate a consensus of support for an orderly society and bring to a conclusion the chaos and disruption of the preceding century and a half. To this end, the relatively peaceful coexistence of earlier times between creeds and races (*convivencia*) was sacrificed on the altar of a formalised social structure and a unified system of beliefs which would hamper the spirit of enterprise and the thirst of adventure. Still, within the main framework of its immediate past Castilla was yet to show sufficient ability and resilience to guide and harness a world revolution for the best of two centuries.

## The Union of Castilla and Aragón

Isabel I of Castilla and Fernando II of Aragón succeeded to their respective crowns in 1474 and 1479. Their marriage in 1469 had taken place not without some difficulties since, in addition to other suitors to formidable Castilla and internal opposition to such a powerful combination of monarchical power, the two members of the senior and junior branches of the Trastámara family were second cousins and therefore required special dispensation from Rome for their wedding. They both ascended to their respective thrones after long civil wars which they had survived with each other's support. The reunion of the

Trastámaras had been foreshadowed from the moment of the election of Fernando I of Antequera as titular head of the Aragonese federation in 1412. In the third quarter of the century Juan II of Aragón was forced to realise the crucial importance of Castilian support in the face of the challenge of the Catalan oligarchies and French territorial aspirations both across the Pyrenees and in Italy. Furthermore, there were very strong ties with powerful economic interests in Castilla. As for Isabel, her own succession to her half-brother Enrique IV had to be wrested from the king's daughter and heiress, Juana, and her Portuguese supporters at the Battle of Toro in 1476. As in the past, supporters had to be rewarded with titles of nobility, grants of land and royal offices. The power of the monarchy was still based on the collective support of the leading families of the country.

## THE CONQUEST OF GRANADA (1492)

To bind them in a joint enterprise and heal the wounds of the internecine struggle of the 1470s, the rulers of Castilla and Aragón relaunched in 1482 a determined campaign to bring the Muslim Kingdom of Granada to the fold of Christendom. It took ten years to reduce Granada, which was not only 'one of the greatest and most beautiful cities', according to an Egyptian traveller, but also a redoubtable natural fortress which, despite internal strife and economic recession, could still hold the might of the Castilian armies in check. Warfare was not very different from earlier times – long and expensive town sieges and devastation of the surrounding countryside, rather than raids; nor indeed the composition of the armies, which consisted of infantry mainly from town councils and brotherhoods, cavalry from the nobility, the military orders and the Church, and royal troops which were a very small proportion of the total. The private armies of the nobility were still the most important component. What was new in this final act on the peninsular stage of the struggle of the Cross against the Crescent was the more extensive use made of infantry and artillery, including a primitive version of the arquebus. As before, the largest financial contribution towards the war came from the revenues of the Church.

The surrender came at the beginning of 1492 and the terms granted to the vanquished were as generous and conciliatory as they had been in the twelfth and thirteenth centuries. Perhaps as a token of their conciliatory disposition, the joint rulers were dressed as Muslims when they officially entered the city. However, despite the generous terms granted to leading Muslims, by 1494 most of them had left for northern Africa. As for the large majority of the population of the kingdom, believed to number some 300,000, after a period of peaceful coexistence the new rulers decided to speed up the process of conversion. New exactions from the Crown and a more intolerant attitude provoked them into a series of revolts, to which the Crown responded by offering them in 1502 the choice between conversion and exile. Since they had to pay to leave the country and leave without their children, most of them chose to stay, that is convert to Christianity, and were moved to reservations in the Alpujarras (the mountainous region south-east of Granada). They were to be known by the rather derogatory name of *moriscos*. As in earlier times Christian immigration into the south-east settled mainly in fortified towns and castles under the Crown, and the countryside was granted to the nobility, the military orders and the town councils.

The conquest of Granada was the best possible start for the joint monarchs. For ten years they had the best troops of southern Castilla under the royal banner engaged in a royal enterprise. Their final victory brought them the means to shower their royal favour upon the most faithful and valiant among their loyal vassals. The emotional impact for contemporaries was beyond description: 'infinitely greater than the discovery of America', 'the end of the calamities of Spain'. In this atmosphere of self-congratulation over the successful conclusion of the centuries-old conflict the ruling couple, still encamped with the armies six miles from Granada in the newly-established Christian city of Santa Fé, may have pondered that this was the opportune moment to strengthen their standing in their respective countries with further triumphs.

## THE EXPULSION OF THE JEWS

Perhaps they saw the military victory over the Moors as the best chance to pursue popular policies which would bring recognition from the urban centres. The monarchy needed to widen its support base in order to reduce the power of the nobility. The establishment of the Inquisition in 1478 was their first step in that direction; apart from the popularity of the measure among the people and the Church, it introduced a centralised institution of monarchical power – the only one covering all the territories of the joint monarchy. The expulsion of the Jews was obviously seen as a way to further their monarchical power in the country. It came only three months after the surrender of Granada. Jews were to convert to Christianity or leave the Crowns of Castilla and Aragón within four months. The number of those who chose to leave has been the subject of heated debates; the latest estimate is between 60,000 and 70,000, and it has been suggested that many of them went back since the edict of expulsion allowed them to return and recover their property if they could prove that they had been baptised. According to this view the impact of the expulsion on the economic and demographic future of the country has also been greatly exaggerated.

## COLÓN AND THE INDIES

1492 was also the year that Isabel and Fernando finally decided to listen to the Genoese adventurer Cristóbal Colón (Christopher Columbus) who, for years, had been peddling his dream of a western passage to the Indies to the leading Crowns of Europe. It was, in fact, two weeks after the edict of expulsion of the Jews, and not surprisingly the support for the Genoese came from Andalucía. The only competing nation for the new enterprise beyond the Atlantic was Portugal, who had pioneered the way and by 1492 was believed to have gained control over the gold and spice routes. The great lords of western Andalucía controlled the ports, like San Lúcar de Barrameda, Gibraltar and Cádiz, and had grown rich and greedy on their raids on North Africa and the exploitation of their vast estates through colonial labour. It was the monarchs' determination to retain the initiative in as wide an area of government and enterprise as possible that finally swayed the royal minds in favour of such a risky venture; as happened in 1482, when they rushed against Granada for fear that the large territorial magnates of the south should occupy and share out the Muslim kingdom among themselves.

From the number of references in his writings, Colón himself had a very clear notion of what he wanted: gold. But he also insisted that he wished to bring heathen nations to the Church of Rome. It was after

Colón's first voyages in 1494 that the Pope conferred the title of 'Catholic Monarchs' upon the joint rulers in recognition of their mission. The acquisitive urge went hand in hand with this civilising mission, which raised Castilla to be the champion of Christian Europe against the Infidels; all who contributed their efforts or provided finance for the enterprise expected a good return on their investment. Gold was then 'the most lucrative as well as the most symbolic of all commodities', according to the eminent French historian Pierre Vilar. The Church militant and the crusading army, which had just proved their valour and resolve in the final contest against Islam on peninsular soil, were now to extend their sway beyond the seas. Furthermore, the Cross and the Sword also had a new weapon to help them establish their moral authority: the Castilian language. In 1492 Elio Antonio de Nebrija (1444–1522) dedicated his *Arte de la lengua castellana*, the first vernacular grammar of Europe, to Isabel I as the 'instrument of empire', the yoke by which to bind together the old and the new subjects of the Queen of Castilla.

## *Fernando II of Aragón and Regent of Castilla*

Having completed the first and most significant stage of their rule, i.e. the affirmation of their authority on the peninsula, the Catholic Monarchs turned their attention to securing their boundaries with France and furthering Aragonese aspirations in Italy. By the Treaty of Barcelona of 1493 Charles VIII of France agreed to return Roussillon and Cerdagne, the two Catalan provinces north of the Pyrenees, which France had held since 1462. Hispano–French rivalry shifted to Italy. After some years of diplomatic skirmishes, a large fleet with a small army under the command of Don Gonzalo Fernández de Córdoba, the *Gran Capitán*, was sent to southern Italy against Charles VIII and a series of brilliant military victories (the Battles of Cerignola and Garigliano in 1503) brought Naples permanently under the full domination of the Hispanic monarchy.

The grandeur and splendour of the dual monarchy as a formidable coalition of forces both at home and abroad were not to be taken for granted. The history of Spain, and indeed of western Europe, might easily have been quite different from 1504 when Isabel I of Castilla died, leaving behind a succession problem no less complex and fraught with difficulties than the one she had faced herself in 1474. Fernando was only the King Consort of Castilla and, apart from his considerable economic and political power in Castilla as a Trastámara, the territories he brought to the dynastic alliance in 1479 were in no position to challenge the leadership of their western neighbours. Castilla was three times larger than the combined kingdoms of Aragón, Valencia and Mallorca and the Principality of Catalunya; more heavily populated with five million inhabitants as against well under a million; and much richer in taxable wealth and disposable income, more dynamic and expansionist.

On Isabel I's death her consort returned to his own dominions. The dynastic plans for their progeny (which Fernando had laid so brilliantly in a skilful diplomatic game that gained him Machiavelli's admiration) did not materialise. Their first son, Juan, died in 1497; their grandson, Miguel, born to Infanta Isabel and King Manuel I of Portugal in 1498, also died two years later; while in Ghent (Flanders) their daughter Doña Juana, next in line to the throne, was delivered of a son, Carlos, by Philip, son and heir to Mary of Burgundy and the Holy Roman Emperor, Maximilian I. In her testament Isabel I expressed her great regret at the prospect of an heir 'of another nation and other tongue'. Some misgivings regarding Doña Juana's ability to govern had already led Isabel I to dispose in her will that, should her daughter not be able or willing to take up the burden of government, her husband Fernando would rule in Castilla as Regent until such time as Don Carlos would become of age. It was then left to Don Fernando to have to endure the interfering opposition to his rule on the part of Juana's husband, Don Felipe, until the latter's early death in 1506, and the prospect of a foreign successor to both Castilla and Aragón.

Fernando returned to Castilla in July 1507, bringing a small army from Naples which proved sufficient to crush open opposition, but concessions had to be made to those who had been hostile to Fernando's recall. He governed Castilla until his death in January 1516. Eastern dominions were left to viceroys; Castilla's resources were the sinews of his international aspirations and he turned his attention to Navarra, which an army under the Duke of Alba conquered, and North Africa, where a number of ports were taken as further security against attack from that region.

On Fernando's death, the unruly and autocratic nobility reverted to their private feuds and personal loyalties and allegiances, disregarding or challenging the authority of the Crown. Anticipating such developments Fernando had appointed Cardinal Cisneros to maintain some semblance of law and order in the midst of a crisis which revealed the full extent of the precarious balance achieved by the Catholic Monarchs. Between 1515, when Don Carlos was declared of age in Brussels, and June 1517 when he was making ready to go to Spain, there were two centres of power: Cisneros in Castilla and Don Carlos himself and his advisers in Brussels. Cisneros had to wrestle with an impossible situation: when he attempted to create a permanent police force to maintain law and order in the realm and to eradicate certain administrative abuses resulting from the power vacuum, he met determined opposition from the nobility, from Brussels, and from cities like Burgos who were conspiring in the Castilian parliament to strengthen their power vis-à-vis the monarchy.

The dynastic uncertainty of these years was punctuated by a series of poor harvests from 1502, famine in 1506, and a bout of plague in 1507; the Andalusian countryside was devastated by locusts in 1508. For the first time the population of Castilla had to be fed from large-scale cereal imports from Flanders, France, North Africa, Sicily and even Turkey. A bumper cereal crop in 1509 sent prices down, ruining merchants and small farmers and causing a general exodus from the countryside. Unrest on the land was mirrored by discontent among the manufacturing towns of Castilla which resented the Burgos monopoly on sales and exports of first-quality wool to northern markets, condemning them to dependency and unemployment. This, then, was the scene upon which a ruler of 'another nation and other tongue' was to enter in the autumn of 1517.

# CHAPTER FOUR

# Imperial Spain

## Carlos I

'Don Carlos, by the grace of God King of Castilla, León, Aragón, Two Sicilies, Jerusalem, Navarra, Granada, Jaén, Valencia, Galicia, Mallorca, ... West and East Indies, ... Lord of Biscay ...' was already Count of Flanders and titular ruler of the Netherlands and Franche-Comté on his father Philip's death in 1507; a total of seventeen titles with their respective domains. His coronation in 1515 took place in the Parliament Hall of the Ducal Palace at Brussels, his first capital, where he returned forty years later to give his farewell speech and abdicate his vast empire 'where the sun never set'.

Born and bred in the Burgundian Court of Mary and Maximilian, the spiritual and political centre of the Holy Roman Empire, he knew no Castilian or any other peninsular language and spoke only French. Surrounded by Flemish advisers he arrived in Laredo (Santander), one of the northern ports of Castilla which were experiencing growth and prosperity from increasing trade with Flanders and northern Europe. From the start he was aloof and dismissive of those, like Cardinal Cisneros, who had served the Crown of Castilla in the difficult period following his grandmother's death. As for his mother, Doña Juana, still *Reina y Señora de Castilla*, he visited her in Tordesillas but only to ensure her enforced seclusion from political intrigues in a tower overlooking the River Duero. Ignored and forgotten by the world, as much as she had been neglected by her father, husband and son, she lived to be seventy-six and died in 1555, six months before her son's abdication in Brussels. The Infante Fernando, the King's brother and his junior, born and bred in Castilla, familiar with its habits, customs and language, was also spirited away, and put on a ship in Santander bound for Flanders, lest support might gather round him to threaten the King's own position.

The rapacity and arrogance of the King's Flemish and Burgundian entourage fanned the flames of disappointment and discontent among Castilians who gave vent to their feelings in no uncertain terms when the King first met the *cortes* in Valladolid in February 1518. There was no challenge to his right of succession to the Crown of Castilla but he was firmly reminded that he must recognise the laws and liberties of the realm and govern in accordance with the guiding principles laid down by Isabel I in her will, which contained an explicit prohibition against appointing foreigners to Castilian offices; that he was their 'paid master and for that reason his subjects share with him part of their profits and benefits and serve him with their persons whenever called upon to do so'. He was urged to learn Castilian and take cognisance of the fact that Juana was still Queen and Mistress of Castilla and allow his younger brother Fernando, first in the line of succession to the throne, to return to Castilla until the King should marry and father an heir. After some conciliatory gestures, Carlos I was granted a subsidy of 600,000 ducats for the next three year.

Don Carlos then proceeded to Zaragoza to meet the Aragonese *cortes* where he encountered similar opposition. It took him eight months to obtain recognition and a subsidy of 200,000 ducats. In February 1519, on his way to the Catalan *cortes*, he was apprised that his grandfather, the Emperor Maximilian, had died. His main concern now was the election to the Holy Roman Empire; he made haste to the capital of the Principality of Catalunya to be sworn by the Catalan parliament and obtain additional financial support for his imperial campaign to succeed to the Holy Roman Empire.

## Holy Roman Emperor

Don Carlos' candidature to the imperial crown was probably the strongest. The seven German electors had already made promises to his grandfather, the deceased emperor, and the Habsburg and Burgundian hereditary holdings in central Europe gave him a significant advantage over his main rival Francis I, the King of France. But in the last analysis the decisive factor was money; the electors' and their councillors' palms had to be greased extensively and Carlos I of Castilla had the credit worthiness with the financial houses of Genoa and Augsburg to provide the cash payments needed to purchase their votes. And so Carlos I of Castilla succeeded his grandfather to the Holy Roman Empire as Charles V on 28 June 1519.

The news reached him in Barcelona. A visit to Germany was now imperative. From France came warnings of Francis I's machinations for a political alliance with Henry VIII of England against him. Parliamentary business kept him in Barcelona for the rest of the year and at the beginning of 1520 he hurried through Aragón on his way to Castilla for more funds to finance his trip to Germany. After paying his respects to his mother in Tordesillas, he proceeded to Santiago de Compostela in the Kingdom of Galicia where against all precedent he summoned the Castilian *cortes* for the end of March, in the hope of setting sail from La Coruña as soon as he managed to obtain further subsidies for his imperial progress. The assembled deputies, however, insisted on satisfaction for their grievances before considering the question of a grant. Bribes and threats brought no change to the proceedings and Carlos I had to reassemble the *cortes* at La Coruña, with the members from Salamanca and Toledo refusing to attend. After twenty-two days of debates he was voted a *servicio* of 400,000 ducats by a majority of one. Throwing caution to the wind, or confident of his authority as an hereditary ruler of these territories, Don Carlos set sail from La Coruña for Dover, leaving behind as his personal representative in Castilla his old tutor Adrian of Utrecht. From England, where he signed an alliance with Henry VIII aimed at keeping Francis I from any aggressive action, he travelled to Aachen, the city of Charlemagne, to be crowned Emperor on 23 October 1520.

## THE REVOLT OF THE CASTILIAN COMUNEROS

Meanwhile Castilla was seething with discontent. The *cortes* deputies still assembled at La Coruña saw the Emperor's decision to leave Adrian of Utrecht as Regent as contravention of his promise not to appoint foreigners to the government of the realm. Toledo, whose archbishopric (the richest and most powerful of all the Castilian dioceses) had been bestowed upon a Flemish youth, was in open revolt, having thrown out the *corregidor*, the chief royal executive in the administration of the city, and taken the *Alcázar*, the symbol of royal authority. All other towns in central Castilla followed suit and their representatives assembled in Avila at the behest of Toledo. A solidarity pact was signed and as the Holy Junta (*Junta Santa de las Comunidades*) the signatory towns reminded the King that Castilla was not to defer to the Empire nor contribute to its expenses; furthermore, in the absence of its ruler the towns as represented in the *cortes* had a right to intervene in the government of the realm. Failing to obtain a response, in September urban militias from Toledo, Madrid and Salamanca under Juan de Padilla, commander-in-chief of the Junta, proceeded to seize Tordesillas and the Junta from Avila followed suit. Thirteen out of the eighteen towns with a right to vote in the *cortes* were represented. In reaching Tordesillas they expected to gain Queen Juana to their side and place themselves under her authority; but the wretched Queen refused to sign any document or give any indication of support.

This confrontation brought to the surface all the social conflicts, private feuds, economic anxieties and political rifts of the previous decades between Crown and the nobility. Doña Juana's refusal or inability to provide the insurrectionists with a legitimate banner to further their conflicting aims added to the extreme fluidity and confusion of the early months of the revolt. To start with, the town notables appeared to be leading the rebellion: as part of the nobility they were incensed by the way the main offices and perquisites of the Crown were now going to foreign advisers. For a short while they seemed to be hedging their bets, perhaps gloating over what appeared to be a serious conflict between municipalities and the overbearing Crown, and expecting to gain by it sooner or later.

The spread of the conflict beyond the urban movement helped to define the contending elements. Independent of the towns' rising but occasioned by it, a wide anti-seigniorial revolt broke out in the countryside. In a significant number of cases the rebellious villeins were reacting against nobiliary abuse and asking for protection from the Crown; they saw their escape from the misery and exploitation in being placed under the jurisdiction of the King. In the circumstances the nobility were quite happy to make peace with the Crown, and Carlos I, equally mindful of the fact that their support was vital to his own position in Castilla, met them half-way by inviting them to the royalist cause and promising financial compensation for any losses suffered in the ensuing conflict. He also invited the two leading members of the Castilian nobility, the Constable and Admiral of Castilla, to join in government with Adrian of Utrecht as co-regents, and while waiting for the Imperial Coronation at Aachen he further strengthened their economic position and social status by presenting the apex of the social fabric of the realm with the formal trappings of Burgundian titles and honours. The *ricos hombres y ricas hembras* of the past were given twenty-five titles of *grandeza* (dukedoms) concentrated in twenty ancestral lines – twenty in Castilla, four in Aragón and one in Navarra. Below these, thirty-five titles of nobility (marquises, counts and viscounts) were created. In the meantime the urban movement was losing momentum and showing signs of serious disagreement between the leading centres. The drift of the nobility towards the royalist camp was paralleled by a similar slide of some of the cities towards a more subversive stand in support of the anti-seigniorial rising. The *comunero* Junta redefined their aspirations to strengthen the *cortes* as a representative, legislative assembly to counterbalance the alliance of nobility and Crown. Valladolid and especially Burgos expressed their opposition to these revolutionary initiatives. Burgos was the main base of a powerful financial and commercial community centring round a prosperous wool trade with northern Europe. Carlos I had given them some assurances in writing (18 January 1520) regarding trade with the Low Countries. They were able to obtain further concessions for their monopolistic control over such trade from the Constable of Castilla, who not only shared in the profitable business of wool production and exports but also, like the notables of Burgos, was fearful of the subversive ideas gaining ground among the lower orders. Burgos joined the royalist camp, carrying with it Soria and Guadalajara. In Valladolid the more subversive elements of the rising gained the ascendancy over the authorities of the city, and when Tordesillas fell to the royalist armies on 5 December it became the bulwark of the movement and its third capital.

Internal rivalries both in the *comunero* and royalist camps, shifting allegiances, and financial difficulties explain the long months between the royalist seizure of Tordesillas and the final defeat of the *comunero* army on 23 April 1521 at Villalar, a small village to the east of Tordesillas. That was the end of the revolt except for Toledo, which held out until February 1522 because the royalist armies had to rush to Navarra to repulse the French invaders. The uprising had been from the beginning a very confused affair, expressing an overall hostile reaction to a foreign ruler bringing a reluctant country into the centre of world affairs, with what that meant, in the short term, in extra cost, exertion and sacrifice of Castilla's own interests.

## THE REVOLT OF THE AGERMANATS IN VALENCIA

In Valencia and Mallorca the so-called *agermanats* (brotherhood) showed a more distinctive social outlook when they rose in the spring of 1520 against the appointment of a Castilian, Don Diego Hurtado de Mendoza, Count of Mélito, as viceroy. The region was suffering from a serious decline in seigniorial income and a resulting increase in the level of rent and taxation on the lower orders with which the nobility tried to restore their financial position. There was also the danger of attacks by pirates from northern Africa and the especial composition of the population of Valencia: 35–40 per cent of the local inhabitants were of Moorish origin (*moriscos*), who in periods of social and economic stress were resented for their hard work and frugal living as well as their servile and docile attitude towards the nobility in the countryside. At the time there were also serious deficiencies in cereal production and corruption in quality and supply from abroad. When Carlos I left Barcelona for Castilla on 23 January 1520 in search of funds to secure the Imperial election he had shown no sympathy or understanding for any of the grievances put to him by the *agermanats*, nor had he been sworn in by their *cortes*. The *agermanats* mustered an 8000-strong militia which in July 1521 defeated a royalist army with a very strong *morisco* contingent. Soon afterwards Viceroy Hurtado de Mendoza, with reinforcements from Murcia under Vélez destroyed the *agermanat* army at Orihuela and made his triumphal re-entry into the capital of the kingdom. The pacification of Mallorca by March 1523 was entrusted to a separate force sent by Carlos I himself.

The *agermanat* and *comunero* risings could be said to have originated from a similar unease among the middle and lower sections of the urban communities regarding the changing economic climate of the period and the arrival of a new ruler who offered no hope of redress in the face of deteriorating circumstances. The social dimension was emphasised in the case of Valencia by the anti-*morisco* movement, while the Castilian rebellion appeared to contain a stronger political element – a political aspiration to strengthen the contractual nature of sovereignty and the power of the *cortes*. In one respect, at least, the similarity between developments in central Castilla and Valencia was almost perfect, and that is in the way the Crown and the nobility joined forces to bring order and restore the status quo – in Valencia from the start of the protest, and in central Castilla after some hesitation and ambiguity intended mainly to exact better rewards from the Crown in full recognition of their services. Equally similar was the fierce repression which followed and the high level of compensation for damages levied on the rebellious towns for years to come. The alliance of Crown and nobility was unassailable. At Villalar the bulk of the nobility were present, ostensibly to save the Crown for Emperor Charles V, but first 'por temor que temían a las Comunidades, ca tenían propósito de tomarles sus tierras y reducirlas a la corona'(for the sake of their land), wrote Cardinal Adrian of Utrecht. Their self-seeking attitude was prominently displayed in the fat bills for compensation they submitted to the Crown.

## War against Francis I of France

Two weeks after Villalar, on 10 May 1521, the nobility's royal fervour was rekindled by the French invasion of Navarra. The western Pyrenean country was one of the three areas of territorial rivalry between France and Spain prior to the Imperial election. Taking advantage of Castilla's internal conflict and claiming to be acting on behalf of the Albret family, dispossessed by Fernando in 1512, a French army under Lesparre occupied Pamplona and Estella and laid siege to Logroño, across the Ebro river, the south-eastern border of the kingdom. The flower of the aristocracy with an army three times the size of the French, led by the Admiral and Constable of Castilla, rushed from Villalar to drive them back, gleefully anticipating further shows of royal favour for the additional services. The formidable gathering of the aristocracy included those nobles, like the Vélez of Murcia or Don Pedro Girón, who had foolishly flirted with the *comuneros*, in the early stages when they appeared to be posing no threat to their status or wealth. It also included active participants who had not been singled out for summary retribution, anxious to make amends for their insubordination. The towns which only a few weeks before were fighting the co-regents' armies had also sent important contingents of foot-soldiers. On 30 June the invading army was totally destroyed at the Battle of Quirós (Noaín, near Pamplona). A second invasion in September was immediately pushed back, except for Fuenterrabía which had to be invested until September 1524 when the French were forced to surrender the town to the Duke of Alba, in the presence of Emperor Carlos V. Navarra was then placed under the viceroyalty of the Duke of Nájera.

## RESTORATION OF ORDER IN CASTILLA

The Emperor was back among his Castilian subjects from 16 July 1522, at the head of an army of German mercenaries several thousand strong and an artillery train of seventy-four cannons, the like of which had never before been seen south of the Pyrenees. From Palencia, where he stayed for two months, he proceeded to Valladolid, with no desire to show clemency to the defeated *comuneros*. In fact, the repressive tone and punitive compensatory settlements inflicted upon them were only mitigated after representations from the Valladolid *cortes* of 14 July 1523; an occasion used by Carlos I to state firmly that from then on he expected subsidies to the Crown to be voted before he would listen to their petitions. It was unopposed.

As for the nobility, at first Carlos I seemed to ignore their high expectations of compensation and rewards for services rendered to the Crown, but in the next few years, like Isabel and Fernando, and countless predecessors before them, he was forced to recognise that the strength of his position was based on the power and loyalty of the upper reaches of society. A measured blend of punishments and rewards was the only way to assert his authority among his peers; they still liked to perceive the position of the monarch as *primus inter pares*, and the leading families of the country could rally round to protect one of their own as easily as they could band together to keep any one of their members from rising too high. To satisfy their social and economic aspirations the Crown required an inexhaustible supply of offices, grants and sinecures to oil the wheels of monarchical power.

In 1486 the Catholic Monarchs had obtained from Pope Innocent VIII the right of patronage and presentation to all the major ecclesiastical benefices in Granada. In 1508 Fernando managed to extend the royal prerogative to the New World and in 1523 Pope Adrian VI, Carlos' former tutor and viceroy of Castilla, expanded the Crown's right of presentation to all episcopal sees in the Hispanic kingdoms. Adrian's bull also ratified the royal incorporation of the three military orders of Castilla, Santiago, Calatrava and Alcántara, in perpetuity. Through the *Patronato Real* and the grand mastership of the military orders the Crown was able to prop up the royal purse and to imprint substance and status on the social order.

## VICTORY OVER FRANCIS I AND A ROYAL WEDDING

In 1525 all the signs pointed to a long and glorious imperial and colonial career for the first Trastámara–Habsburg emperor and his peninsular subjects. On his twenty-fifth birthday (24 February) his powerful neighbour and erstwhile contender for the imperial crown, Francis I of France, was soundly defeated on the outskirts of Pavia, in northern Italy, and taken prisoner to Madrid, where he was obliged to sign a treaty surrendering all claims to Milan and Naples, the Duchy of Burgundy and several towns along the northern French frontier. He also promised to participate in a crusade of all Christians against the Ottoman Empire threatening Christendom from east and south.

It was also in 1525 that Carlos I sealed a strong dynastic alliance with his western neighbour, the King of Portugal, master of the routes to Guinea and the East Indies and reckoned to be the wealthiest monarch on earth. He married the Portuguese princess, Isabel, who brought a dazzling dowry of 900,000 ducats. Their first encounter took place against the beautiful backdrop of the *mudéjar* Alcázar of Sevilla and the royal couple spent their honeymoon amid the splendours of the Alhambra Palace in Granada. To commemorate these events the

Emperor ordered the construction of a palace in the best Italianate tradition. Two years later Empress Isabel bore him a son and heir, Felipe, in Valladolid. She also proved to be an able ruler, governing Castilla during the Carlos' long absences, until her early death in 1539.

## American Treasure

Meanwhile, between 1519 and 1525 Hernán Cortés and his handful of followers had taken possession of half a million square kilometres in central México for the Crown of Castilla. The conquest of Perú by Francisco Pizarro followed ten years later. By 1540 the contours of the American continents had been mapped out. The 250,000 sq. kms which constituted the first colonial holding of the Catholic Monarchs, centring round Santo Domingo and Cuba, were to expand by the end of Felipe II's reign to a permanent control over one and a half million sq. kms. No more than 100,000 Spaniards crossed the Atlantic in the sixteenth century to explore overall some 4–5 million sq. kms. The vast territorial expansion by such small numbers allowed only an extensive exploitation of the land. It conditioned an itinerant form of conquest and occupation, with ever-increasing distances dictating a very expensive system of production. Only the most profitable commodities could offer adequate returns for such huge investment in human endeavour and material costs. The American continents offered a large supply of expendable labour for the seemingly inexhaustible extraction of precious metals, gold at first and then, from the mid-sixteenth century, silver. Other produce, such as spices, pearls, sugar and dyestuffs, contributed bountifully to the rich pickings from the Indies. It was the heavy premium on risk and distance which fixed a colonial pattern of exploitation as a monoculture of the Americas geared to the production of luxury items.

Between 1540 and 1560 some churchmen and administrators struggled for justice, for a more equitable system of domination. But against the harsh realities of distance, the heavy hand of the powers at work and Castilla's ever-increasing reliance on the American treasure, their efforts came to nothing. From 1555 onwards a more intensive exploitation of mining resources had to follow, less dependent on human labour, which had been decimated in the early stages of the occupation

# The Spanish Empire

EUROPE

AFRICA

INDIA

CHINA

*Macao*

PHILIPPINES

*Ceylon*

EAST
INDIES

*INDIAN OCEAN*

AUSTRALIA

Territories of the Crowns of
Castilla and Aragon

Portuguese territories

Habsburg and Imperial territories
under Carlos V

and exploitation of the mineral resources. It was based on the introduction of amalgam techniques to isolate the silver by means of mercury, which was imported mainly from Almadén. It brought silver production to record levels towards the 1580s. The high level of dependence on human suffering continued to devastate the demographic landscape of the New World.

Whatever the long-term consequences of this pattern of conquest and colonisation, America unleashed the embarrassment of riches which underwrote Castilian preponderance in Europe and overseas for a hundred years. In the first half of the sixteenth century taxes on the wool trade provided the main source of income for the Royal Treasury, and the cost of Empire was shouldered by Castilla, the Netherlands and Italy. By the late 1540s, however, Castilla took over as the financial and administrative hub of the Caroline Empire. Precisely at the time when the resources from sheep-farming ceased to keep pace with the growing requirements of the Imperial enterprise, America came to the rescue; without its timely arrival Spanish ascendancy in Europe would not have survived the financial straits of the mid-sixteenth century.

The gold consignments rose from 5000 kgs in 1503–10 to record receipts of 42,620 kgs in the 1550s; and silver remittances climbed from 86 tons in the 1530s to a peak of 2707 tons by the closing decade of the sixteenth century. The most precious of all metals remained top of the table of imports until the 1550s because of a value ratio of gold to silver of 12 to 1, and it was still 10 per cent of the total bullion consignment in the 1590s. It is estimated that between 1503 and 1660 some 25,000 tons of silver-equivalent reached Sevilla, increasing Europe's holding of precious metals threefold.

## SEVILLA AND THE ATLANTIC TRADE

Sevilla was indeed the first port of call of these riches and the gate to the transatlantic trade until 1680 when it had to share this trade with Cádiz. In 1503 the *Casa de Contratación* ('Chamber of Commerce') was set up to oversee and regulate all shipping from and to the Americas, from 1543 exercising a monopolistic control over imports and exports in combination with the Indian Merchants' Association of Sevilla, organised into a chamber of commerce on the Burgos model. All goods were congregated there ready for shipment to the Indies and the American *galeones* laden with expensive commodities sailed up the Guadalquivir river to make Sevilla by the end of the century into one of the largest cities of Europe, behind only Paris and Naples. A regular system of fleets (*Carrera de Indias*) was established from the 1560s to ensure safe passage of the Atlantic crossing; it consisted of two convoys (*flotas*), sailing from Andalucía in the spring and late summer, and returning together in March of the following year. The mid-Atlantic trade route was extended to the Philippines (which had been discovered for Spain in 1521 by the Portuguese Fernando Magalhães ) by means of an annual *galeón* which carried out a triangular trade between metropolitan manufactured goods and agricultural produce (wine and oil), American bullion and eastern spices. In terms of security the convoy system proved its worth; only on one occasion did the treasure galleons fall into enemy hands: on 8 September 1628 in the Bay of Matanzas off the Cuban coast almost the entire Mexican silver-fleet was captured by the Dutchman Pier Heyn.

## THE ROYAL FIFTH

Following the old Muslim Custom this was the proportion of American bullion for the Crown of Castilla in return for renting or disposing of the mines which, according to Castilian legislation dating back to the thirteenth century, belonged to the royal patrimony. In addition to the *quinto real* there was payment of taxes levied on goods exported to America. Protection costs fell on the Royal Treasury as regards Castilian territorial waters but naval security of the convoys in the open seas was financed by direct contributions from trade profits. The Royal Fifth increased tenfold in the course of the second half of the sixteenth century, from 250,000 to two million ducats a year, while in the same period ordinary and extraordinary revenue for the Castilian Crown only doubled, and ordinary revenue, that is income from taxation, which is normally the backbone of a country's contribution to the enterprise of the State, could not even keep up with inflation and was in any case usually mortgaged well in advance. The American bullion was 'the only fresh money in the land', the only disposable income to pacify creditors and to finance escalating imperial defence costs.

## The Cost of Empire

The growth of public expenditure was a general phenomenon in sixteenth-century Europe, and most western states were, in fact, spending a large part of their income in defence, e.g. 70 per cent of the Castilian budget in 1574. All the same, the cost of maintaining Castilian hegemony throughout Europe was really staggering. On acceding to the throne in July 1556, Felipe II discovered that his Spanish revenues were spoken for in full up to and including 1561; and between 1572 and 1576, when he was fighting on two fronts (the Ottoman Empire and the rebellious Dutch), he was spending double his yearly income, which brought him to bankruptcy in 1575. By the 1660s the Crown debt amounted to between ten and fifteen years' revenue and the annual servicing charge represented well over half the total income, i.e. 70 per cent.

From the early sixteenth century the Castilian Treasury entered into a permanent and ever more expensive system of deficit financing, with liquidity crises as a regular feature (eight bankruptcy decrees between 1557 to 1662). By converting unpaid short-term loans into redeemable annuities these decrees were intended to reduce the rate of interest payable on the debt and free revenue which normally would have been previously mortgaged to financiers and speculators. It was a prohibitively expensive, spiralling process which left very little room for manoeuvre. However, as long as the inflow of American ingots continued to arrive safely and regularly to Sevilla there were always bankers, south German, Genoese and Portuguese, ready to bail out the Hispanic Crown and advance the cash required to pay the soldiers and functionaries of the Empire in Flanders, Germany and Italy. The large intakes of gold and silver were the collateral security underpinning the vast borrowing requirement of the Imperial enterprise. Furthermore, monetary stability was a constant, from the currency reform of the Catholic Monarchs in the late fifteenth century to the 1620s. For a long time the Crown enjoyed a near monopoly of the best currency in Europe, easily and frequently minted, with high purchasing power and highly versatile. Such a vast accumulation of capital has not been seen in Europe again until Victorian England. Sixteenth-century Spaniards may well have believed that El Dorado was indeed inexhaustible, that they were in the midst of a Golden or at least Silver Age.

## LANDS OF OPPORTUNITY AND PLENTY

In his *Historia de las Indias*, Francisco López de Gomara gives a vivid account of Pizarro's share-out among his 200 men of the treasure requisitioned by Atahualpa, the Inca chief, in the vain hope of purchasing his freedom. The Crown of Castilla was allotted its fifth, each soldier was apportioned 18.6 kgs of gold and 41.4 kgs of silver, and the captain ten times that amount. It was an exceptional situation, but not unique. Service in the king's army in Europe could also bring unexpected and no less spectacular windfalls. Soldiers' pay may not have kept up with inflation but the army still exerted a very strong attraction on many Europeans from the depressed areas of the Empire. The high purchasing power of Castilian currency throughout Europe, where prices were increasing less rapidly than in the centre of the Hispanic monarchy, continued to offer a chance of riches and social advancement. Soldiers' pay and welfare were top priority in paymasters' calculations, in that success in battle was closely linked to regular and satisfactory delivery of wages. And then there were the spoils of war, the loot taken from the enemy and the authorised plunder of conquered cities. The sacking of a town was regulated by law and limited to three days, as in Malouines in 1568 or Harleem in 1573: Castilians on the first day, and then Walloons and Germans. Sacking and looting could be avoided by a substantial ransom, and when privations and delayed payments tested their endurance to the limit, the *tercios* sacked and pillaged entire cities in the most brutal manner. The sack of Antwerp in 1576 according to a Fugger agent netted twenty million ducats, including two million in gold and silver coins – not an improbable sum considering the importance of Antwerp at the time as the distribution centre of American treasure.

## AGRICULTURAL AND COMMERCIAL GROWTH

Sustained demographic and economic growth in Castilla from the latter part of the fifteenth century was apparent in all areas of production: textiles, agriculture and intermediary activity, finance and trade. The increasing demand of a growing population at home and settlers abroad requiring almost everything from the home market – food, wine and clothing, arms, horses, corn and mercury – stimulated production at home. The 'political money' which had to be shipped across continents to Flanders, Germany, Italy, to finance Imperial defence was lost to potential Spanish development but it was only a quarter of the bullion imported from the Indies. In theory at least three-quarters of the American treasure arrived in Sevilla as private consignments to repay investment in the American enterprise and cargoes shipped to the New World. This huge influx of new capital, added to the revenue arising from the export of traditional primary produce such as wool, moved more slowly through the interstices of the peninsular economy, fostering textile industries in Castilla, Levant and Catalunya, leathers from Ocaña, Toledo steel, Talavera ceramics, Biscay and Navarrese foundries, northern and Andalusian shipbuilding, and financial and administrative services. Agriculture was particularly responsive to the increasing demand. The main produce by far was cereals, with areas such as Tierra de Campos, between Burgos, León and Palencia, or La Sagra in Toledo almost exclusively under cereals, i.e. 90–95 per cent of arable land. As the century wore on this preponderance gave way in part to olive groves, mainly along the Guadalquivir river, and vines in Galicia and Old Castilla, attracted by increasing prices. The Mediterranean provinces had always enjoyed a more diversified form of agricultural production: Granada and Murcia, for instance, were important silk producers, and Valencia was profitably engaged in the silk trade. There was also sugar cane between Málaga and Almería.

Trade and commerce, industry and agriculture offered opportunities aplenty to all the King's subjects. The second-born of the upper nobility, the offspring of the lesser aristocracy, the impoverished hidalgo, merchants and prosperous farmers could also make their way up the social ladder through the Church, colonial service and royal administration.

## A New Service Class

The requirements of a world-wide enterprise gave rise to a large service class trained in the new centres of learning which sprung up throughout the empire. In so far as the advance of royal authority always meant possible diminution of aristocratic power, the monarch needed to rely on new men whose power and status originated from royal patronage. The

Catholic Monarchs promoted the rise of a new breed to fill the ranks of the state councils, local government, management of the royal patrimony and administration of justice. From 1493 servants of the Crown had to be jurists qualified in common or civil law after a minimum of ten years' study at a university. Sixteenth- and seventeenth-century rulers had to respond on a much grander scale to new requirements.

Castilla inherited only two centres of higher education from the Middle Ages (Salamanca and Valladolid) but by the end of the sixteenth century seventeen had been founded, and they reached a total of thirty-four including those in Aragón and the five founded in the New World. At their peak in the 1580s Castilian universities had an annual intake of 20,000 students. There were several other centres providing higher education, and a strong educational revival among the religious orders, led by the Jesuits, probably added some 10,000 students, to give a total participation rate of more than three per cent of the 15–24 age group, probably the highest in Europe. The rise of the Castilian language and literature and the high regard for the profession of letters contributed to this university expansion. The humanist content of some of the new universities, like Alcalá de Henares, provided an excellent measure of the range of interest in philosophical, literary and linguistic pursuits. The information and statistical evidence gathered by these highly-trained servants of the Crown may be seen in the archives of the period (Archivo General de Simancas and Archivo de Indias), among the best repositories anywhere in Europe for the quantity and quality of documentation. In the long term, however, the increasing emphasis on legal subjects and the career orientation of the type of studies pursued at the universities was detrimental to the quality of education.

## SPREAD OF LITERACY AND GEOGRAPHICAL MOBILITY

Without a large reading public it is difficult to imagine the quantity and variety of literary endeavour in sixteenth- and seventeenth-century Spain. Recent research points to a great leap forward towards widespread literacy, as shown by the number of publications, easy access to books through lending libraries or purchase at auctions, and the spread of teachers in practically all towns teaching reading and writing to children from very modest backgrounds. The richness and complexity of

Castilian literature is also evidence of the spread of education and range of literary creation: from the chronicles and surveys of the new discoveries to the legal tracts relating to all spheres of government, social justice and treatment of the Indians; from the popular staging of plays that showed the abuse of royal power and the irritants of the billeting of soldiers in private homes to the theological disputations of the morality plays; from the mystical to the pornographic. The chequered lives and careers in all corners of the globe of the most accomplished exponents of the art of writing bear witness to the variety of experience and richness of their message.

The range of writing includes the *Arte de la lengua castellana* of 1492 (already mentioned), *La Celestina* of Fernando de Rojas published in 1499 and the Italianate poetry of Garcilaso de la Vega, the soldier-poet who died in battle in France in 1536. Especially noteworthy was the protector of the Indians, Bartolomé de las Casas, internationalist Francisco de Vitoria, the mystical experiences of Santa Teresa de Avila, San Juan de la Cruz and Fray Luis de León, and the erotic poetry of Luis de Góngora (1561-1627). The satirical invectives of writer and diplomat Francisco de Quevedo, and the subtle irony and narrative skills of Miguel de Cervantes (1547-1616), culminated in the flood of theatrical works in the best populist tradition from the three great masters of the stage Lope de Vega (1562-1635), Tirso de Molina (1580-1648) and Pedro Calderón de la Barca (1600-81) in the 1620s, 1630s and 1640s. Calderón's morality plays (*autos sacramentales*) and Baltasar Gracián's linguistic sophistication in the third quarter of the century signalled the end of Castilla's literary and intellectual 'golden age'.

Geographical mobility was, indeed, one of the perquisites of empire. From the northern regions of Spain a constant flow of migrants moved southwards and beyond to the Americas. The southern provinces were the main contributors to migration overseas. In the second half of the sixteenth century it was estimated that one-fifth of the Catalan population had been born north of the Pyrenees, and in 1626 a French diplomat estimated that there were some 200,000 French immigrants in Spain, attracted by the high level of salaries paid in good and solid currency. Military and administrative requirements in Europe also attracted large numbers to the main theatres of war. The armies were mainly recruited among Germans, Walloons and Italians, and no more than 20,000 Spanish soldiers are believed to have fought at any one time outside the peninsula during the reign of Felipe II. Nine thousand men a year were levied by the Council of War between 1580 and 1640, and mortality was especially high among the Spanish infantry because the fame of their invincibility brought them to the first line of combat in any serious situation. Even in peacetime 4000 Spaniards had to be recruited yearly to maintain army numbers in Italy in full strength. Writers and scholars, soldiers and administrators may have thrived on the geographical mobility afforded by the imperial and colonial enterprise, but the adverse effect on the long-term prospects of the centre of the empire soon began to show.

## Conspicuous Wealth

The financial muscle of the Hispanic monarchy at the zenith of its hegemony was not exhausted in the military struggle to retain that preeminence. Despite centuries of war destruction and the wholesale spoliation of village churches over the years, there is not a town or even a village in Spain which cannot boast of some work of art from this period. With very few exceptions, such as Córdoba and Santiago, the urban landscape of the Iberian peninsula was transformed. Modern visitors cannot fail to notice that art in all its manifestations – architecture, sculpture, painting, gold, silver and metalwork – must have been the first and most lasting industry of imperial Spain, drawing 5–7 per cent of the nation's income. From 1480 to the mid-seventeenth century the whole country must have appeared to contemporaries as a gigantic workshop anxious to accommodate the requirements of Crown, Church and wealthy patrons – all seeking to signify their position in the social order and to reinforce its cohesion and the enduring qualities of their world. Most of the cathedrals so much admired by travellers today were erected or completed in the first half of the sixteenth century: Jaén, Granada, Málaga, Calahorra, Astorga, Plasencia, Coria, Barbastro, Salamanca, Segovia and Sevilla. When Felipe II wanted to accelerate the completion of El Escorial, he was employing 1500 artisans and labourers, investing 2–3 per cent of the Crown's income from 1562 to 1598. And Felipe IV spent 250,000 ducats a year, one-tenth of the cost of the war in Flanders, to build El Buen Retiro (1631–40) in Madrid.

The nobility, the newly rich and the municipal authorities were also lavish investors in the trappings of excellence and amenities of life. The Plaza Mayor in Valladolid, with its fourteen streets converging onto it, built after the fire of 1561, was designed according to plans personally supervised by Felipe II. The architect Lorenzo Vázquez was responsible for the construction of the university college of the Holy Cross also in Valladolid based on a Gothic design with a Florentine facade. He was the architect of the powerful Mendoza family, Duque del Infantado, for whom he built a new palace at Guadalajara (which is now the Museo de Bellas Artes) to serve as a fitting venue for the marriage of Felipe II to

The Palace of Monterrey in Salamanca also known as the *Palacio de las Conchas* (House of Shells) because of the pilgrim's scallop shells worked in relief in the façade

his third wife, Elisabeth de Valois, the daughter of Henry II of France and Catherine of Medici; he also built the castle of Calahorra in the province of Granada for the Marquis of Zenete. Gil de Hontañón completed the Gothic Cathedral of Salamanca and the Renaissance palace for the Counts of Monterrey (*Palacio de las Conchas*). Juan Bautista de Toledo and his pupil Juan de Herrera were the masterbuilders responsible for El Escorial, which typified Spain's imperial grandeur under Felipe II.

Sevilla, the gateway to the Indies, was the centre of architectural and artistic endeavour throughout the sixteenth and seventeenth centuries. Its Cathedral was completed at the beginning of the sixteenth century. There were also the Royal Chapel, the Court of Justice, the Chamber of Commerce and the Town Hall, as well as *Casa de Pilatos* built for the Duke of Medinaceli and *Casa de las Dueñas* for the Duke of Alba, various hospitals and convents, and the Irish College. The artistic, intellectual and literary circles of the city were among the most highly regarded in the whole of the Empire. In Extremadura and Old Castilla (Plasencia, Trujillo, Cáceres, Burgos and Medina del Campo) the spoils from the conquest and exploitation of the Americas as well as the profits of wool production and trade went to embellish those towns with houses and palaces that bear witness to the success of merchants and conquistadores.

Apart from 'the Greek' (El Greco), Domenico Theotocopoulos, born in Crete in 1540, whose life and work has come to be identified with Toledo, it was Sevilla which played host to the main school of painters in the land, such as Francisco Pacheco, Francisco Zurbarán, Bartolomé Esteban Murillo, Juan de Valdés Leal and Diego de Velázquez, Felipe IV's court painter. A recent book on the building of the Buen Retiro, the ill-fated royal palace in Madrid, refers to the 'Sevillian connection' as the main artistic input in Felipe IV's grand artistic enterprise. Francisco Ribalta, born in Solsona (Catalunya), settled in Valencia, and José Ribera 'el españoleto', was born in Játiva (Valencia). Sculptors like Alonso Berrugete, Juan de Juni, Alonso Cano, the Arfe family, Juan Martínez Montañés, Juan de Mesa and Gregorio Fernández represented a much wider geographical spread and their main works may now be admired in the National Museum of Religious Sculpture in Valladolid.

By the seventeenth century the nobility and the wealthy seemed to be

The monastery of San Lorenzo de El Escorial

turning to less financially demanding pursuits. Unable to compete with the Church or the Crown, who were still building the most impressive churches and convents in a more ornate and theatrical style than the rather austere and sober classicism of the builder of El Escorial, Herrera, they turned to the patronage of authors and painters. Emulating the collecting spirit of their royal masters, they gathered books, paintings and tapestry. Gondómar and Olivares were famous, among other things, for their impressive libraries; the Count of Monterrey, who served as ambassador in Rome from 1628 to 1631 and viceroy of Naples to 1637, through purchases abroad built up an invaluable gallery of pictures, and so did the Marquis of Leganés who was said to own 1333 paintings when he died in 1655. Felipe IV commissioned his brother, Cardinal Infante Fernando, the victor over the Swedes at Nördlingen in 1634, and Rubens to buy works of art for him in Flanders, and by the end of his days he is believed to have added 2000 paintings to the royal collections.

## The end of Hispanic Supremacy in Europe

The achievements of the *Monarchia Hispanica* and its contribution to the common stock of European civilisation were remarkable. It opened the confines of the globe and retained cultural and political supremacy over western Europe for well over a century. No other country was faced with the logistic problems of a worldwide enterprise when administrative techniques 'had scarcely advanced beyond the stage of household administration'. From 1492, the year of the conquest of Granada and the discovery of America, to 1636, when the Spaniards reached Corbie, very close to Paris, their military and naval power seemed unstoppable. But the end of the apparent invincibility of the Hispanic armies was near. At sea the failure of Felipe II's Armada to bring about the invasion of England in 1588 exposed the limits of Spain's maritime and financial power. On the occasion of the recent anniversary of the momentous event, a spate of detailed and scholary lectures and publications have come to the conclusion that the *Armada Invencible* was not defeated but, all the same, failed to achieve its main objective and had to return home severely battered. Such a vast and costly enterprise could not be put together again. In 1643 the French inflicted the first serious military defeat on the Spaniards, and the victory of the Dutch under Tromp at the Battle of the Downs in 1639, together with the defeat of a combined Hispano–Portuguese fleet off the coast of Brazil, were the first irreparable naval disasters. The spell of Spanish supremacy was breaking and the agony of the forced withdrawal from Europe was as long and traumatic as the brilliant beginnings had been unexpected and spectacular. The dismantling of Hispanic hegemony lasted from 1640 to 1714 and very nearly brought in its wake the disintegration of the Spanish realms themselves.

1640 was also the year of rebellions in Catalunya and Portugal. In Andalucía the Marquis of Ayamonte and his cousin the Duke of Medina Sidonia conspired to set up an independent state. In 1647–8 Neapolitans and Sicilians staged a separatist revolt and the leading grandee of the Crown of Aragón, the Duke of Híjar, was plotting separation from Castilla under French protection. After eighty years of war Spain was finally forced to recognise the independence of the United Provinces (the Low Countries). The end of the Dutch war gave Spain some room to manoeuvre and for a while in 1652 it looked as though she was regaining ground from the French by recapturing Barcelona, Casale (Milan) and Dunkirk. But in 1655, after fifty-one years of peace with

England, Cromwell joined France in the fight against Spain. Blake's navy destroyed the Indies treasure fleet in 1656 and 1657, and in 1658 Anglo-French troops defeated the Army of Flanders at the Battle of the Dunes and recaptured Dunkirk for the French. The Portuguese, fighting for their independence from their eastern neighbours, inflicted a humiliating defeat on them at the frontier town of Elvas in January 1659. By the Peace Treaty of the Pyrenees in November of the same year Louis XIV acquired Cerdagne, Roussillon, Artois and several fortresses in the Spanish Netherlands and agreed to marry María Teresa, Felipe IV's daughter, in return for a dowry of half a million ducats and her renunciation for herself and her descendants of any right to succeed to the Spanish Crown. Attempts now to bring Portugal under control

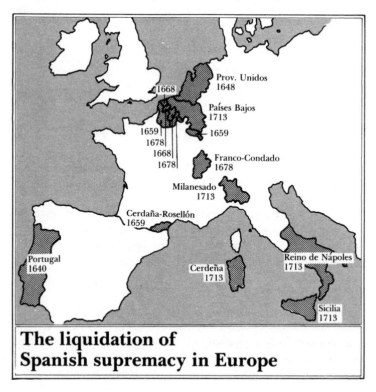

**The liquidation of Spanish supremacy in Europe**

resulted in ten years of attrition along the Extremaduran border and final recognition of Portuguese independence in 1668.

## THE FRENCH CHALLENGE

Meanwhile, Louis XIV continued to gnaw away at Spain's European possessions on all fronts until the end of the century, when he had no further desire to weaken the Spanish empire since through diplomacy he was planning to install a French Bourbon, his grandson Philip of Anjou, on the Spanish throne. The incumbent from 1665, Carlos II, a rather miserable epilogue on the Trastámara–Habsburg dynasty, suffered from chronic ill-health and was unable to father any children. When he died on 1 November 1700, he left his vast dominions enmeshed in a civil war to resolve the succession crisis between the French claimant, Philip of Anjou, and Archduke Charles of Habsburg, supported by his brother Emperor Joseph, England and the United Provinces. A month before his death Carlos II with almost unanimous support from his Council of State named Philip as his successor, in the belief that the protection of Louis XIV would secure the territorial integrity of the Spanish inheritance. Philip actually made his formal entry in April 1701 as Felipe V of Spain, but the United Provinces and England, unwilling to countenance a Franco-Spanish alliance even more formidable than the old Trastámara--Habsburg block, declared war on France in May 1702.

## THE WAR OF THE SPANISH SUCCESSION (1702–1714)

Spain was no longer the master of her own destiny. She now became the theatre of war for other countries' ambitions. If in the long war that ensued Spain lost only her European dominions it was due to the rivalry and mutual suspicions of the contending parties rather than to her own part in the struggle. The end of the War of the Spanish Succession came when Archduke Charles left Barcelona at the end of 1711 to succeed Joseph to the Imperial Crown as Charles VI. His former supporters were no more likely to countenance a repetition of the old Hispano-Imperial connection than a Franco-Spanish dynastic merger. As long as Felipe V abandoned any pretension to the French throne, they were prepared to recognise him as King of Spain and her overseas colonies. Any adjustment to be made to the map of Europe would be at Spain's expense. Spain was not even a party to the second peace settlement at Rastatt in March 1714 (the first was signed at Utrecht in April 1713). The Spanish Netherlands and the Italian possessions (Naples, Sardinia, Milan, Tuscany and Mantua) went to Emperor Charles VI, Sicily to Savoy, and England kept Gibraltar and Minorca (seized during the war) and gained very substantial advantages in the New World, which would prove to be the death-knell of Castilian control over the Atlantic trade.

From the spring of 1618, when Spain entered the Thirty Years War to help Ferdinand II put down the Bohemian rebellion, to the General Pacification of 1714, she had been involved in a semi-permanent state of war on all fronts. From the very beginning the main antagonist to Spain's imperial career in Europe was France, whose own potential growth and security as a nation-state seeking also to strengthen her territorial base were threatened by the Trastámara-Habsburg connection surrounding her on all sides. The permanent confrontation with France exposed the limitations of Castilian imperialism. British historians sympathetic to the enduring qualities of the Hispanic enterprise constantly refer to their almost miraculous resilience and ability to bring hidden reserves of strength to so many occasions in the seventeenth century when everything seemed utterly lost. It may be so; nevertheless, where France was concerned the *Monarchia Hispanica* was from the start on the defensive. In 1545 the future Felipe II wrote to his father how difficult it was to gather financial resources in Spain and how it took years to recover from a bad harvest; France, on the other hand, was a fertile and united country which time and time again could afford to supply its rulers with the sinews of war. In the 1630s, for instance, the development Spain most feared was France's entry in the Thirty Years War. Only when France was being torn apart by religious differences and civil wars, as in 1652, did Spain recover some sort of military initiative over events. In 1665 Felipe IV expressed in his will and testament the limits of his power and the painful necessity of having to fight on in defence of the royal patrimony.

## *A Case of Financial Exhaustion*

The taming of Spanish power in the European battlefields was the result, in the first instance, of the inability to sustain a level of expenditure which not even the seemingly inexhaustible riches of the Indies were equipped to keep up with. In our own times we are witnessing a similar situation: a powerful nation becoming the world's leading debtor in the process of maintaining military hegemony on a global scale, with 40 per cent of the annual tax revenues to service the interest payments of the devouring national debt. Similarly, rather than changes in international competitiveness or the growing strength of opposing or rivalling nations reflecting internal changes, as has been suggested, the case of Imperial Spain suggests unwillingness to change, inability to depart from the attitudes and beliefs that brought her to pre-eminence in the first place. The seizing-up process was, then, the consequence of excessive friction or failure to improve the oiling elements of the imperial apparatus. The long years of ascendancy locked the leading forces of the country in the firm belief in the profitability and rightness of their cause. For a long time they could argue that their short-term advantage and gratification were vindicated by the durability of their eminent position in the world.

Power and wealth were then as they are now ultimate ends of national policy. Their congruence was clearly understood by the rulers and the ruling classes. It was felt that war was the only way to ensure Spain's economic survival. In a world where wealth was believed to be finite, the acquisition of it could only be at the expense of others. Spain was therefore pinned to an endless struggle which she was for ever hoping to resolve by a final, decisive battle. For a hundred years of supremacy in Europe she had to maintain a permanent army, the first ever, of up to 85,000 men fighting a costly war of long sieges and stalemates. Castilla's formative years in the struggle against Islam had shaped her into a society made for war; the prolongation of this conflictive situation well into the modern period defined its material base as an economy under siege, closing in on itself to protect its territorial and spiritual integrity against all enemies, and further reducing the ability to opt for a different course of action.

The growth in defence expenditure and in the number of challengers of Hispanic supremacy eventually caught up with the human and financial resources of the monarchy. The success of the sixteenth century carried with it the seeds of failure in the seventeenth. By dragging into the maintenance of the imperial enterprise an ever-larger proportion of the available capital, investment in wealth creation was crowded out. The riches of America went to finance defence and to purchase foreign products. Spain was the most expensive country in Europe; the more that was spent in defence and foreign imports, the higher the price to be paid. Money as a non-renewable resource was thus spent for good and the country found itself in a situation with no way out from the vicious circle of dependency and underdevelopment.

To make ends meet the Crown resorted to new forms of taxation and sale of all manner of disposable assets: royal offices, titles of nobility, estates, villages and towns, and ecclesiastical offices and benefices. The sale of knighthoods of the military orders, certificates and titles of nobility went unchecked from the time of the Catholic Monarchs, who granted about a thousand new *hidalguías*, through to Carlos II, who created 328 new titles, bringing the total from sixty titles in 1525 to 745 in 1700. In trying to cope with the short-term liquidity problems monarchical power was constantly being reduced; for, in the first place, the massive alienation of royal patrimony placed the jurisdiction over lands and vassals beyond the authority of the Crown. Sixty to seventy per cent of the Spanish territory and its inhabitants were under ecclesiastical or civil lords. Secondly, by auctioning its patrimony the Crown was also selling up future revenue sources, becoming more dependent on the support of the peers of the realm.

## POPULATION DECLINE: THE EXPULSION OF THE MORISCOS

From 1480 Castilla and Valencia experienced a steady growth in population, while Catalunya trailed slightly behind. A hundred years later this growth was over; the *Relaciones topográficas*, the census which Felipe II commissioned in 1575, responded to the general impression of a slow-down in the population of the country. The great epidemic of 1598–1602, preceded by the 1594 famine and the bankruptcy of 1597, depleted the population of central Spain which was already failing to keep up the birthrates of the middle decades of the century. Famine and bubonic pestilence, with attendant diseases such as croup, smallpox and diphtheria, raged throughout, with special virulence in the heartland, Avila and Segovia, taking half a million lives mainly from among the poor and destitute. Mediterranean Spain and the whole of Andalucía, which were spared in the first great epidemic of the turn of the century, suffered the same, if not worse, mutilation fifty years later (1647–52). This time the bubonic plague made its first appearance in Valencia in June 1647, coinciding with the worst harvest of the century, and by October 1648 it had claimed 34 per cent of the population. The hellish cycle of dearth, malnutrition, famine and pestilence struck again between 1676 and 1689, scourging the breadth of the country in a cortège of harvest failures, floods, drought and even locusts.

In the midst of these disasters, endemic in Europe at the time, the population of Castilla continued to bleed in the direction of the Indies and the European battlefields. And Felipe III, despite early warnings about the loss of population, decided in 1609 to amputate the *morisco* communities (280,000 mainly farmers) from the fertile plains of Játiva, Gandía and Valencia, where they constituted 26 per cent of the inhabitants, and from the Ebro valley where they were 15 per cent. The social fabric of the country was incapable of assimilating and unwilling to tolerate them. Forty years before, Felipe II had already made it clear that the population of Muslim origin would have to abandon their religion, customs, attire and objects of personal ornament and 'above all that most un-Christian, most peculiar oddity of taking a daily bath'. The total population loss to the peninsular kingdoms between 1580 and 1680 is estimated as one and a half million; not until 1750 did Spain return to the population level of 1575.

## SOCIO-ECONOMIC STAGNATION

The patterns of financial exhaustion and demographic recession were paralleled by blockages to change in the social and economic structures of the country. From the early sixteenth century there were those who saw quite clearly how the country was irrevocably heading for a point of no return. The *comunero* revolt in 1521 may be seen partly as an early protest against the heavy demands imperial costs made on Castilla. By the late 1550s there was a chorus of voices commenting on price inflation, loss of competitiveness abroad, the drift of non-productive investment and scarcity of capital as the first signs of a check to economic expansion. By 1600 the most famous of all *arbitristas* (projectors, ρ.anners), Don Martín González de Cellorigo, lawyer of the Valladolid Court of Justice and himself enjoying the substantial rents of a most profitable marriage, wrote a brilliant memorial on the ills of the Castilian economy. After Cellorigo, many others joined the throng of critical and, at times, very perceptive analysts of the Spanish condition. The arguments centred round the perceived correlation between military and economic power, population and productivity. The symptoms of friction and imbalance were clearly diagnosed: excesses in the money supply, lack of productive investment, excessive government expenditure and fiscality, price inflation, loss of manufacturing competitiveness, agricultural stagnation, depopulation, foreign imports and bankers, loss of markets in Europe and America, and so on. They were all examined in great detail and on occasions with great venom against the non-productive classes of society. But in their critical projects not many went beyond the framework of the restoration of the past, normally identified with the reign of the Catholic Monarchs. Rather than innovation, reputation and restoration defined the boundaries of the debate. Quevedo, one of the most savage critics of his age, saw the return to the past as the only way out of the moral decline of the nation: 'Let us do as we have always done.' Very few dared tackle the basic premises of societal organisation: the relationship between high prices and profits, rentier mentality and leisure: nor follow through the implications of Cellorigo's contrite or cynical comment that foreign bankers and traders treated Castilians as if they were Indians ('Spain devoured the New World but it was the Low Countries that grew fat on it').

## Values and Attitudes of the Aristocracy

But even the most constructive and genuine criticism had little chance of success against the main stream of aristocratic values and imperialist conviction. Those firmly in control of the social and economic power of the land would argue that these were the attitudes that had made Castilla great. It is no surprise that they should view the situation as requiring no departure from ways and means that had brought them such a large share of the riches of the world. The Crown endeavoured to build on the promising fits and starts of the late fifteenth and early sixteenth centuries to promote change, but the ever-pressing requirements of a large military and naval undertaking left very little room for manoeuvre; there was never any time for planning the future and whenever pressure reached breaking point the monarchy had to fall back on the support of the established forces.

The powerful confederation of caste and privilege solidly founded on landed wealth and jurisdiction over people reinforced their imprint on society, unchallenged and unchallengeable, since new social groupings who might have intended to bring diversity and movement to the social and economic processes were easily attracted to or driven towards the twin accomplishments of the nobility: status and rents (*honra y provecho*). Birth and wealth were the distinguishing features of social pre-eminence – the possession of a family coat of arms (*ejecutoria de nobleza*) and inherited wealth – for in no way were rank and position to be conferred on those who toiled and laboured for their material gains. 'Hidalguía', wrote Fernán Mexía, 'is nobility of man by birth'; the Duke of Nájera stated that the commoner was different from the nobleman in his subjection to personal and pecuniary servitude; that is to say, the nobleman, even if he were a 'mere hidalgo' (*hidalgo a secas*), was so by virtue of the all-important exemption from personal taxation. Thus the determined opposition of the rich and powerful to several attempts on the part of the Crown to levy a tax on land and other rental properties and to gain control of the taxes which the nobility was farming for the Crown.

## THE LIMITS OF SOCIAL MOBILITY

The growth of civil and royal administration, ecclesiastical and military careers, and the vast range of opportunities in finance and trade in the Old World and the New, brought forth new service classes which might have populated that wide harmonious centre of consensus that some *arbitristas* wrote about. Bankers, traders, metropolitan and colonial officials made fortunes which went towards the purchase of social recognition. The new social groups were never numerous or distinctive enough to challenge the structure of society. Landownership, jurisdiction over vassals and rents were the hallmarks of true nobility. 'Riches, for the most part, may lead to nobility,' Fray Benito de Peñalosa wrote in 1629, for how was a gentleman going to enjoy the privileges of the nobility if he had not the means by which to live in the manner of an aristocrat. Don Toribio in Quevedo's *El buscón* states quite categorically that 'no puede ser hijo de algo el que no tiene nada' (a man of substance must have means); and Sancho Panza in *Don Quijote* concluded that there were 'but two families in the world, the haves and the have-nots'.

Social mobility took place within the very narrow bounds of the ten per cent of the population, mainly from the northern provinces, among whom practically everybody claimed noble status and the possession of wealth, inherited or at any rate unearned. Very rarely did commoners, engaged in mechanical trades, manage to climb socially. The great court painter, Diego Silva de Velázquez (1599–1660), could draw the attention of his liege and patron to obtain special dispensation from the Pope for a knighthood, but only after a lengthy and humiliating genealogical investigation. Juan Cristóbal de Guardiola, a jurist on the royal council, purchased the large estate of La Guardia (Toledo) from Felipe II, but it took the family a hundred years to obtain a marquisate. The Church offered an easier avenue of social advancement; high-ranking ecclesiastics usually combined a career in the Church with service to the Crown. One such cleric was Juan Martínez de Guijarro ('Siliceo'), Archbishop of Toledo, who climbed to that exalted position from peasant stock. It was he who in 1547 introduced the *Estatuto de pureza de sangre* into the metropolitan see of Castilla. Freedom from semitic blood was made a prerequisite for dignities and prebends. An old Christian of peasant stock thus claimed a compensating social code of his own (based on service to the Church and, allegedly, honourable endeavour) to challenge the exclusive claim of lineage and inheritance from the established nobility.

## THE SURVIVAL OF THE NOBILITY

The titled lineages of the country continued to monopolise positions of power and prestige, such as Crown representation, viceroyalties, governorships, embassies, high ecclesiastical dignities and military and naval high command. The second layer of the administration, civil and legal officials, town and municipal administration, army and naval officers, came from the middle and lesser nobility (with the second sons of the titled nobility in very prominent position), and recruited mainly from the six major colleges of Castilla's three main universities, four at

Salamanca and one each at Valladolid and Alcalá de Henares and from the Spanish College in Bologna. Originally these colleges were founded to provide access for students of humble origins, but from the start they were barred to all save the powerful and well-connected on account of the length of the course of study, six to eight years, requiring a high level of financial and intellectual commitment.

The financial muscle of the nobility and the purchasing power of traders, speculators and financiers came in the first place from landownership and jurisdiction over people – 'the greatest single source of revenue in the Mediterranean,' wrote Ferdinand Braudel. Secondly, America and the Atlantic trade were also spectacular providers of riches. Last but certainly not least were *juros y censos*, most profitable form of investment and socially acceptable source of income. *Juros* (IOU's) were negotiable Crown bonds, that is loans to the Crown in return for perpetual or life annuities yielding 10 per cent interest a year; *censos* were short-term agricultural improvement loans, repayable in annuities until the extinction of the debt at a similar rate of interest, and guaranteed by a mortgage on the borrower's land, with a right from 1535 to repurchase at any time. Failure to keep up payments meant repossession. While agricultural production was expanding and capital was relatively scarce, there was a considerable demand for these credits; but in the seventeenth century the agricultural situation worsened and these *censos* became a liability. Lands and houses which had been offered as security were repossessed by the lender, thus contributing to further extension of large estates and continuing diminution of peasant propriety.

In the circumstances no amount of moral exhortation or economic argument could have diverted the holders of capital from investment in *juros y censos*, which offered a safe return and could be converted to land. How could it be otherwise, wrote the economist Caxa de Leruela: 'As every man could see that a capital of 2000 ducats brought in 200 a year in return, and that the capital was repaid at the end of six years, it seemed to them a good investment.' And Cellorigo admonished that 'for the sweetness of the sure profit from *censos* the merchant leaves his trading, the artisan his employment, the peasant his farming, the shepherd his flock; and the noble sells his lands so as to exchange the one hundred they bring him for the five hundred the *juro* brings'. Eventually, though, the general depression which began in the latter part of the sixteenth century and spiralling inflation started to erode their income, at a time when both production and rent returns were falling. No longer could they turn the screw on the starving tenants and landless peasants, as happened in Valencia where the secular and religious lords sought to compensate for the loss of revenue because of the expulsion of the *moriscos* in 1609 by increasing rentals by fifty per cent between 1582 and 1648, even though the population had been halved. Tenant farmers either vacated entire villages to join the urban dispossessed or resisted violently or turned to banditry, which became endemic throughout the whole of the seventeenth century.

Growing unrest and the continuing deterioration of law and order brought the Crown and traditional élites closer together. Disgruntled and factionalist grandees did, on occasion, engage in dissident behaviour and rebellious acts against overbearing royal officials and persistent calls from the Crown for financial and military support, but they were only isolated incidents. The landed aristocracy, struggling under an increasing burden of debt, found their monarchs always ready to bail them out with awards and grants, extension of their seigniorial powers and dispensations to quash their debt obligations at the expense of their creditors. For their part, secured in their entailed estates and dominating the higher reaches of the administration, they were well placed to appropriate common land, purchase on favourable terms, and sell local offices and state revenues. The massive Crown expenditure of the Thirty Years War brought the situation to a halt. When confronted with urgent requests for troops and money, the nobility complained of their indebtedness and inability to live in a manner befitting their social rank: they were strong on fixed assets but very short on liquidity. Of course it was a short-term financial crisis caused by the decline in value of *juros y censos*. They were sheltered from the worst of the storm with the aid and support of the Crown, as they were able to flee from the epidemics of the century to the safety of their estates, or stay away from the wars by paying for a substitute or purchasing an office which carried exemption from military services.

When the situation started to improve from the 1660s, when rents and production levels began to rise, land became once again the major 'refuge of value'. The Duke of Infantado, whose debt in 1637 amounted to 897,731 ducats, could die in the comforting knowledge that he had fully paid this debt by 1693. The aristocratic revival of the seventeenth century, assuming that there was a crisis of the aristocracy in the first place, amounted to a process of refeudalisation of the peninsular kingdoms which continued unabated until the early part of the nineteenth century, with sixty per cent of productive land firmly held in entail (*señoríos*) or mortmain (church estates), that is inalienable so as to secure the foundations of the first and second estates of the realms against their own improvidence or economic fluctuations. A very explicit corpus of Castilian law dating back to 1348 perpetuated the privileged condition of the ruling estates. It was expanded to Biscay in 1754, Asturias in 1756 and Catalunya in 1760, and restated in the *Novísima Recopilación* of 15 July 1805.

# CHAPTER FIVE

# The End of the Spanish Colonial Empire

## The establishment of a new dynasty: Felipe V de Borbón

The close identification of means and purpose between the monarchy, the lords of the land and the notables of towns and cities was strengthened during the twelve-year War of the Spanish Succession. The established forces of the country were prepared to accept Carlos II's testament in favour of the French pretender. They believed that the integrity of the Hispanic realms and colonies would be better served by a Bourbon monarch who could count on Louis XIV's support against the colonial and commercial ambitions of the main trading nations of Europe. In the Catalan *cortes* of 1701–2, Felipe V introduced himself as the zealous protector of their liberties, promising to grant them rights to trade with the Indies directly. When the war ended he helped to win over those who had supported the Austrian pretender by giving them a free pardon and permission to return to Catalunya and have their property restored. As for the war itself it caused very little disruption to the social and economic fabric of the country. The trials of those years derived from natural disasters rather than the passage of troops: from 1708 to 1711 there were poor harvests, heavy rains and great famine, which perhaps explains the political and military failures of 1709–10 and the general relief when in 1711 the war seemed to be coming to an end. The enlightened politicians of the eighteenth century believed that the war had been positively beneficial in bringing the country together.

Seventeen years old when he entered Madrid in 1701, like his Trastámara–Habsburg predecessor Carlos in 1517, Felipe V had no knowledge of Spain or Spanish and was surrounded by a retinue of foreign advisers, first French and then Italian. He was to become the first 'Spanish' monarch, the first ruler of a politically united Spain. In June 1707 he abolished the regional charters of Aragón and Valencia, and of Mallorca (1715). The new constitution of 16 January 1716 (*Decretos de nueva planta*) did the same for the Principality of Catalunya. The first casualty of this 'political revolution' was the regional parliaments and executive institutions of the various kingdoms, except for Navarra and the Basque Provinces which continued to enjoy their fiscal and political autonomy (*Provincias Exentas*) because of their loyalty to the Bourbon pretender from the beginning.

The authority of the Crown was made more pervasive through the creation of departmental secretaries of state to replace the old regional councils; the Consejo de Castilla remained as the chief legislative organ of the nation. The supreme authority over the provinces was vested upon a royal appointee as a military governor and lord justice in conjunction with the newly-created provincial law courts under a professional judge. The internal legal system was largely left untouched.

In addition, a new royal official (*intendente*) was sent to Valencia and Aragón in 1714 and then in 1718 to all other provinces, to supervise army payments and supplies, billeting of soldiers and war finance; from 1718 his job included a vast range of administrative, judicial, fiscal, financial, information-gathering and promotional tasks. In 1749 Fernando VI completed the installation of the intendant system in peninsular Spain and his half-brother and successor, Carlos III, extended it to colonial Spain.

The main purpose of these reforms was to bring all the various kingdoms and principalities under the same laws, i.e. the laws of Castilla 'universally acknowledged for their equity and practicality', and to provide equal access to all state posts. If the real objective of the political unification was to bring the eastern provinces to share the financial burden of the State, they were a great success for the former Crown of Aragón which contributed almost nothing to the Castilian Fisc prior to 1707, by 1734 was supplying nearly 14 per cent of State revenue. The new dynasty brought about some of the changes the central government of Castilla had tried to introduce in the 1630s and 1640s. On taking his leave of the House of Austria a Spanish grandee expressed the satisfaction of the realm at the return to the prosperity under the Catholic monarchy, before the interests of Spain had been sacrificed to the imperial grandeur of the Habsburg enterprise. The Spanish Treasury grew richer with the revenue from the eastern provinces and the increasing remittances of bullion from the Americas. From the low ebb of a five year total of three million pesos in 1656–60 (the treasure from America was now reckoned in pesos which was equivalent to forty-two grams of pure silver), the returns from the New World climbed back to a new record of 40 million pesos in 1691 and average five-year totals of 50 million pesos from 1671 through to the end of the eighteenth century, representing by 1791 over 12 per cent of state revenues.

## ECONOMIC RECOVERY

Much more significant as a break with the predominantly Castilian past, and pregnant with consequences for the future of a unified Spain, was the commercial and agricultural recovery from the 1680s of the northern and eastern maritime regions, heralding a slow but steady growth. These were the regions that had been allowed to plod along on the margins of the Empire, denied a large share of its profits and glamour but also spared the worst of the human and financial burden of endless wars. Population began to expand generally from the 1660s. In 1680–6 inflation was brought to a brutal halt, which must have caused severe dislocation, but restored monetary stability and initiated a steady rise in prices and investment in productive activities. Chambers of commerce and trading companies were set up to promote exports and encourage trade with the Indies. The Sevilla–Cádiz–Puerto de Santa María–SanLúcar de Barrameda complex continued to be the main centre of commercial activity, geared mainly to the American trade, but smaller ports, such as Valencia, Alicante, Bilbao and Barcelona–Mataró, started a long period of growth.

The increased activity and growing prosperity of these coastal towns depended on internal and foreign trade, but most importantly on agricultural growth and development, i.e. extension of the land under the plough, increased productivity and diversification. The introduction of maize from the Indies to the northern soils in the early seventeenth century, for instance, raised yields quite considerably: by the beginning of the ninteenth century it exceeded the land surface under wheat. Beans and turnips (and potatoes in the nineteenth century) also became familiar features along the northern valleys, while less fertile soils were turned over to grass in support of livestock. Catalunya was also laying the foundations for a long period of sustained growth, with agriculture and especially viniculture as the key. The vine and its main product, brandies, which found very receptive markets both in Europe and overseas, provided large capital gains which were used to further agricultural improvements, new cultures and manufacturing investment (wool, cotton and silk). A distinctive feature of this part of the country which undoubtedly contributed in a very significant way to the general feeling of growth and prosperity throughout the century, was the existence of a strong contractual tradition in the land-tenure system, which gave a great deal of security to the small farmer. Unlike Catalunya, the region of Valencia was not able to capitalise on the very hopeful beginnings of the turn of the century because of a very rigid and oppressive manorial structure, which obstructed change.

The central and southern regions of the peninsula showed also some signs of an upturn in agrarian production and population by the end of the seventeenth century, which marked the way for a modest expansion throughout the next 100 years. However, unlike the eastern provinces which saw considerable improvements in productivity, the Castilian mesetas achieved their modest expansion through a shift from wheat to higher-yielding and lower-quality cereals, and by bringing marginal land under cultivation. By and large, the pattern of culture, range of produce and land-tenure system continued undisturbed until the 1830s. The eighteenth century, therefore, may be recorded as the time when the weight of human and economic resources shifted from the centre to the periphery; from the imperial past of the two Castillas and western Andalucía to the less grandiose but more realistic future of the coastal regions of north and east.

## COLONIAL WARS

Wealth was still believed to be gained mainly from trade and the exploitation of overseas colonies. The Crown continued to rely very heavily on revenue from the trade monopoly with the Indies and to ensure its growth it had to invest very substantially in the maintenance of this monopoly. By now the terms of trade between the metropolis and the colonies had probably deteriorated beyond repair with Spain unable to supply the manufactured goods required by a growing colonial market. But it was universally felt that naval power could prevent foreign goods from reaching the American shores, to the benefit of Spain's manufacturers and the Royal Fisc.

Felipe V started to make plans for the restoration of the Spanish navy and the strengthening of colonial defences immediately after 1714. Unfortunately his dynastic interests in Italy, or rather the aspirations of his two Italian wives, Maria Luisa Gabriela of Savoy and Elisabeth Farnese, to obtain suitable appanages for their children, dictated his foreign policy for the first half of the century. With the restoration of the Spanish Bourbons in Parma, Piacenza, Guastalla and the Two Sicilies (Naples) and the final pacification of the area in 1748, the Spanish Crown could turn its undivided attention to colonial matters. Building on Don José de Patiño's great contribution to maritime and commercial development in the 1720s and 1730s, every effort was made in the 1750s to regularise the system of *flotas* (New Spain – México) and *galeones* (Tierra Firme – Perú), to enforce Spain's monopoly over the Atlantic trade, to promote metropolitan exports, and to extricate Spanish commerce and industry from unfavourable commercial treaties.

The scope for success was rather limited. The terms and conditions of trade with the American colonies had already deteriorated to such an extent that the Spaniards had become trading agents of foreign producers. Spanish manufacturing industry was no longer capable of supplying the required goods, and the produce the Spanish fleets and galleons supplied with great difficulty was no longer wanted or could be obtained much more cheaply through the Manila galleon that plied its wares regularly from south-east Asia to Acapulco, the vast array of contraband traders swarming the American seas, or the English 'annual ship'. The latter '500-ton' concession, together with a licence granted to the South Seas Company to import slaves into America, were particularly crucial in that it not only gave the English a licence to make money but it also established regular contacts between American traders and English suppliers. In the final analysis, the failure and frustration of the colonial authorities in trying to regain control over the Atlantic trade was due to Spain's inability to satisfy the commercial requirements of the local merchants of Nueva España and Tierra Firme, rather than hostility to metropolitan control or the favourableness of the commercial clauses conceded to England in the Treaty of Utrecht. Local American merchants, for their part, having broken their economic dependence on metropolitan imports were very soon demanding political autonomy as well.

Nor was Spain's navy capable of regaining supremacy at sea, nor even in combination with the French. By the peace treaty of 1763, which concluded the Seven Years War, Spain lost Florida and all territories east of the Mississippi river and had to recognise the settlements of British logwood cutters in Central America (Honduras). She also failed to recover Menorca and Gibraltar and was forced to restore to Portugal, Britain's ally, the only territorial gains she had made during the war. At a great cost, therefore, Spain was able to recover Havana and Manila, which the English had taken in 1762. The full realisation of the economic and military weakness of the colonies finally brought home the need to apply urgent measures to try and salvage the situation. No longer in control of the Atlantic trade routes, the notion of free trade with the colonies gained universal acceptance as the only way to revive colonial trade.

## Carlos III

Forty-four years of age when he succeeded his half-brother Fernando VI to the Spanish throne, Carlos III (1759–88) came from Naples after twenty-five years' experience ruling that country. He brought with him a number of capable administrators (Grimaldi and Esquilache) and was a lavish patron of the arts. During his reign two new royal residences were erected, La Granja (Segovia) and the Palacio Real in Madrid, also the Prado Museum and the Puerta de Alcalá in the best neoclassical tradition of eighteenth-century Europe. His leadership in the cultural and scientific field found expression in the foundation of the royal academies and the support and encouragement given to the 'Economic

The Puerta de Alcalá in Madrid

Societies of Friends of the Country' which, modelling themselves on the *Sociedad Vascongada* of 1765, sprang up all over the land to promote agriculture and industry. He was endowed with a great deal of common sense and readiness to allow his most enlightened ministers to govern without too much interference; he is also remembered as 'the best Lord Mayor of Madrid' and his care and solicitude for his subjects and their capital city was recently celebrated in a retrospective exhibition to commemorate the anniversary of his death in 1788.

## FREE TRADE

Liberalisation, or rather the lifting of commercial restrictions with the colonies, was the policy to be adopted in view of the impossibility of maintaining a trade monopoly and careful check on communications with the Indies. The desirability or inevitability of that policy objective had been argued for some time, and in 1762 it was restated by Bernard Ward. The Irish polyglot had been commissioned by Fernando VI to travel extensively in Europe and report back with the fruits of his experience and knowledge gained from other countries. His *Proyecto económico* summed up the views and impressions of the *arbitristas* of the seventeenth century: freedom of trade and competition within and protectionism against foreign produce, financial and fiduciary flexibility as well as agrarian improvements, promotion of manufacturing industries, and scientific research.

On the main issue, free trade within the empire, full liberalisation took twenty years to bring about, from a limited franchise to the Windward Islands in 1764 to the Free Trade Act of 1778, applicable to Tierra Firme and extended to New Spain in 1789. The arguments in favour of these reforms were vindicated by the tenfold increase in exports from Catalunya from 1778 to 1789 but otherwise the impact on the productive capacity and enterprising character of the nation as a whole was minimal. Free trade was too little and too late; Spain had neither the manufacturing nor the commercial power to regain the American markets.

As for her ability to keep foreign interlopers out of American harbours, the time when Spain could regain mastery of the seas was long past. The treaty of 1763, and the ensuing negotiations between Britain and Spain in the mid-sixties to find an accommodation for some outstanding grievances, made it abundantly clear. If some sectors of Spanish opinion still believed that the new assertiveness of the enlightened monarchy could retrieve the position overseas, the crisis over the Islas Malvinas (Falkland Islands) hammered home the enormity of the task. Spain sent an expeditionary force from Buenos Aires to dislodge the British from Port Egmont in the spring of 1770. The mission was accomplished, but the spirited response from Britain and the prospect of a war, which France was not prepared to countenance, forced the Spaniards to climb down without adequate safeguards regarding the Spanish claim to the South Atlantic islands.

## RELATIONS WITH BRITAIN OVER
## THE THIRTEEN COLONIES

Relations between the two countries improved a little after 1771. Britain eventually decided to evacuate Port Egmont in May 1774, and while no indication was given that the move was in any way fulfilling a previous obligation, Spain was allowed to accept the evacuation as the realisation of hopes given to them in the past. The British conciliatory mood towards Spain came through in the negotiations over Vieques Island, near Puerto Rico (known to the British as Crab for the abundance of that crustacean), Balambangan (a small island north of Borneo), and the restraining influence upon Portugal in her response to the Spanish military campaign in the River Plate in the summer of 1776. The ensuing negotiations restored to Spain the colony of Sacramento (lost in the Seven Years War) and the seven missions to the east of the Uruguay river (Treaty of Limits of 24 March 1778). London's conciliatory mood was the result of the concern over the scale of the struggle in North America. Prime Minister Lord North was resigned to the inevitable, telling the House of Commons in January 1774 that eventually they would have to face the combined navies of France and Spain. The Bourbon powers would certainly intend to make the most of Britain's colonial conflict. France decided to come to the support of the Thirteen Colonies in February 1778 but Spain first offered Britain her neutrality in return for some of the outstanding claims: as usual Gibraltar came top of the list, followed by Menorca, Florida, Mosquito Shore (the Yucatan Peninsula) and the logwood-cutting establishment in Honduras.

The instruction to the Spanish ambassador in London with the offer of neutrality and mediation was dispatched the very day the Treaty of Limits with Portugal was signed. Britain's unwillingness to satisfy Spain led the latter into the war in June 1778. The peace treaty of 1783 brought a measure of satisfaction to Carlos III's foreign and colonial policy. Spain recovered Menorca and West Florida, but not Gibraltar which had successfully resisted a joint Hispano–French descent in 1782. She also obtained a precise definition of the British right to cut logwood in what is now known as Belize and the evacuation of British establishments along the Mosquito Shore. In the short term, the last years of Carlos III's reign were moderately successful in the field of colonial and international endeavour, but in retrospect it can be argued that Spain's contribution to the Thirteen Colonies' struggle for independence from Britain was a dangerous precedent for her own colonies and that the right of navigation in the Mississippi river inherited from the British gave the United States an ideal avenue of penetration into México.

## *The limits of Bourbon reformism*

The eighteenth century in Spain has been referred to as a great colonial century, a period of solid and substantial recovery from the exhausting legacy of Imperial Spain especially in the second half of the century during the reign of one of its most likeable and enlightened rulers, Carlos III. Those who hold this view blamed the incompetence of his successor, Carlos IV, and the disruptive pressures of the French Revolution for bringing the century to a disastrous end. Perhaps French historians, whose contribution to our understanding of the eighteenth century has been so important, tend to extol the virtues of a period when Spain seemed to be under the spell of French rationality and style, although it seems as if the modernising reformism generally attributed to the reign of the most illustrious Spanish Bourbon never progressed far beyond the drawing-board, or when implemented, compounded the misery it was intended to rectify. The momentous years between the execution of Louis XVI in 1793 and the independence of the Spanish American colonies in 1824 simply proclaimed the economic retardation of the country, the unwillingness of the ruling estates to respond to change, and the weaknesses of the reformists' power base.

The Crown's part in initiating this process of change remained fixed within the constraints of its limited sphere of power. The level and range of State or Crown expenditure in, for instance, 1731, 1788–92, 1817 and 1829–33, showed no appreciable improvement. As in the best years of Imperial grandeur between 65 and 75 per cent of public expenditure continued to be allocated to the defence of the realm. The financial resources of the Crown for promoting productive investment were therefore limited, and when aimed at spearheading the manufacturing capacity of the country the recipients were royal factories specialising in the production of luxury goods, such as glass, ceramics and tapestry, which were the only products with a market among the ten per cent of the population with the purchasing power.

Subsistence farming, the pattern of economic activity for 90 per cent of the population, was not likely to stimulate demand in the form of a mass market; nor was the transport system which, despite some positive efforts towards the end of the century, was slow and expensive. In the land-locked interior, apart from Madrid which saw the beginning of a real road network to supply the capital's needs and to connect the various royal residences, and some significant road improvements in the northern half of the peninsula, inter-regional trade was minimal and normally transported on the backs of mules and asses.

## THE 1766 BREAD RIOTS

The main inhibitions to growth and development were still to be found in the countryside: not always overt opposition from the privileged proprietors, but simply wilful acceptance of the 'reality' of things – pragmatism in the face of increasing land values and rising rents. Carlos III's first reformist measures proved counterproductive and those among the leisured and moneyed classes could argue that ill-conceived and half-baked ideas had brought famine and discontent to the land. On 15 July 1765 a royal instruction relinquished state control over the price of wheat in the belief that competition would make corn cheaper. Municipalities and townships were on the verge of starvation after six years of severe drought; by the end of 1765 Crown officials from all over Spain were urging the government to take emergency measures since the existing stocks of grain were being hoarded by the main distributors expecting to make a killing from the inevitable price rise, which in fact reached its peak in March 1766. The riots in Madrid, which terrified Carlos III out of the capital, spread like wildfire throughout the realm. It was a new wave of protest which, with increasing regularity through the eighteenth century, was to underline the incapacity of the system to feed its growing population even at a subsistence level.

## THE EXPULSION OF THE JESUITS

All shades of opinion were eager to capitalise politically on these events and the reformist ministers of Carlos III, while adopting very severe measures to reduce the riots and restore public order, used this opportunity to get rid of the Jesuits, who were considered too powerful in their control of education in universities and colleges and in their opposition to reform – a state within the state, placing their allegiance to Rome above their duty to their monarch. The opposition between the Church in general and the reformist administration related also to the expressed intent of the latter to disentail the Church's mortmain land. The ostensible reason for their expulsion from the Spanish territory was their alleged participation in the riots, inciting the populace to mutiny against the established authority. Since there is as yet no proof of their direct involvement, the decision to single them out for retribution was perhaps a reflection of the need to make an example of an institution clearly opposed to reform but not supported unanimously by other privileged sections of the community, and also to find a scapegoat to pacify the masses.

## ENLIGHTENED REFORMERS

The presence of one of the country's leading 'enlightened' aristocrats, Don Pedro Aranda, combining the presidency of the Council of Castilla (the supreme organ of government) and the military command of the region's capital, reinforced the reformist tendency within government circles. Aranda and Don Pedro Compomanes, general attorney of the Council of Castilla, found in Don Pablo de Olavide, the Peruvian land reformist, the enthusiasm and ability required to carry on with the programme of reform. From 1766 until his fall at the hands of the Inquisition in 1776, Olavide more than anybody else was the spearhead of reform, the practical exponent of its possibilities and limitations and the centre of all controversy. He put his hand to all aspects: state subsidies and storage facilities for corn to ensure adequate supplies in lean years; protection of agriculture against the encroachment of livestock; equitable distribution of municipal and communal land; free trade for entail and mortmain land; retrieval of municipal administration from the self-perpetuating local notables; and university reform to improve teaching and reduce the monopolistic control over chairs and government positions of the *colegiales mayores* from the established universities.

## REACTION FROM THE OLD ORDER

From 1769 support began to falter. Aranda ordered an enquiry into Olavide's administration of the Sierra Morena colonias and suspended him without warning. He was vindicated by the committee's report and reinstated, but a year later a new set of instructions restricted his sphere of action and his main anchor in Madrid, Campomanes, also lost his position as general superintendent of land reform. In 1774 the Inquisition started proceedings against him: by November 1776 he was in prison and in 1778 he was exiled from Spain. The backlash also claimed Grimaldi, the foreign secretary, for his involvement in the policy of reform and his defeatist attitude in the international arena.

As for Campomanes, documents sent privately to Carlos III sought his dismissal on grounds which amounted to a comprehensive indictment of his life's work. He held on to his position and became President of the sheepowner's association, La Mesta, in 1779 and the Council of Castilla in 1782. His 1795 summing up of the inquiry on the Land Reform Bill, which he had instigated in 1765, contained no more than a restatement of the free trade doctrine enshrined in the view that 'individual interest' was 'the first instrument of prosperity'; there was no reference to the structural changes which he himself had advocated in the past and Olavide had tried to bring about.

## The Count of Floridablanca

The secretary of state from 1776, Don José Moñino, Count of Floridablanca, appeared to keep up the thrust of reformism well into the 1780s. His considerable success in the international field secured his pre-eminent position as first minister of the Crown against the continuing opposition and intrigues of Aranda and other members of the upper nobility, who resented the social advancement of the lower nobility through the state universities and public service to the higher reaches of power still regarded as the preserve of the peers of the realm and their scions coming up from the *colegios mayores*. In this conflict between high birth and honourable endeavour in the service of the State we see a re-enactment of the social tension of the first half of the seventeenth century; rivalry between the upper nobility, i.e. the Aragonese faction surrounding Count Aranda, the senior military officer in the land, and the lower nobility aspiring to the high positions of the state administration, the judiciary and service abroad, through merit and enterprise. With their reforms the Bourbons, especially Carlos III, had revived the social prestige of the army, which brought the upper nobility back into service. In 1771 he also created a new Military Order to reward merit and enterprise; it still required applicants to be of noble birth at least on the father's side.

In 1787 Count Floridablanca established the *Junta de Estado*, which was in effect a permanent ministerial council which met at least once a week under his own chairmanship. To guide the cabinet in their deliberations an 'Instrucción reservada' was issued in July 1788. It started with a clear statement about the need to defend the Catholic faith and then there followed a comprehensive account of the programme of reform associated with the enlightened monarchy of Carlos III. If Floridablanca still held the progressive views of the 1760s, events across the northern borders in 1789 threw him unambiguously on the side of tradition and order. Carlos III's reign ended then on a note of rejection of the programme of reform intended to recover the country from the doldrums of the seventeenth century.

The end of the seventeenth century coincided with a rise in agricultural production which in turn stimulated population growth. The slow but steady increase in the number of mouths to feed continued to spur on agricultural prices and land values, and to bring marginal land under the plough. Since overall there was no substantial improvement in productivity and, the amount of land available to satisfy a rising demand was minimal, owing to the traditional restrictions on the transfer of land, the pressure to capitalise on the rising demand for agricultural produce was turned on the tenants and farm labourers, leading eventually to rural depression and the food crises of the latter part of the eighteenth century. Notwithstanding the brave and brilliant efforts of minority groups and the significant development of the Catalan region, the general picture of the country for the eighteenth century as a whole presented an image of little, if any, economic development and even less social progress.

## WAR AGAINST THE FRENCH REVOLUTION

From 1789 events in neighbouring France were the catalyst that forced Spain to respond to changing circumstances in the midst of a universal struggle where she had the most to lose. Spain was still in possession, at least nominally, of the largest colonial enterprise, coveted by the two main contenders for supremacy in Europe and overseas, France and Britain. Carlos IV and his son and heir Fernando VII played the monarchical roles: the former resigned and indifferent, the latter ('a repellent personality') timidly and full of duplicity, while their realm and colonies experienced the worst adversities of their long history.

In 1789–90 the fears instilled by revolutionary France among the established order were no doubt fanned by serious unrest among the population over food shortages throughout northern Spain from Barcelona to Galicia. Floridablanca posted soldiers along the borders, and the influx of refugees from France, including some 6000 priests, added to the counter-revolutionary mood of the country; there were those who advocated a crusade against French subversion.

While these incidents placed Spain in a most delicate situation, Carlos IV had already given proof of his lack of either purpose or resolve in public as well as in private matters. The arrival at court of Don Manuel Godoy caused the King, for the sake of his wife's high regard for the young and attractive guards officer from Badajoz, all in one year to dismiss Floridablanca, to bring in Aranda as a stopgap, and then allow Godoy to take supreme command of the army, and declare war on France when Louis XVI was executed. Carlos IV's regard for the French branch of the dynasty seemed to have the support of the established forces, who contributed money and, for the last time in Spanish history, sent their own private armies to the battlefields. The war found little echo among those who knew what the military and naval possibilities of the country were. Officially the Royal army in 1791 consisted of 50,000 men and 366 general officers; that is, one general for every 137 soldiers.

On the other hand, Godoy and those who believed that the French monarchy's demise implied the weakening of the French nation were soon to find out that the young French Republic could still count on the considerable wealth and strength of the country. By July 1795 the French national army had occupied several Spanish towns from Bilbao to Figueras and were approaching Miranda de Ebro. Spain had to rush to the peace talks at Basle to negotiate withdrawal of French forces from Spanish territory in return for Spain's half of the Caribbean island of Santo Domingo. Godoy was rewarded with the flamboyant title of *Príncipe de la Paz*, an outrage to traditional monarchists and to young Fernando, who as Crown Prince was the only one entitled to such honour. Peace was made with the French Directory and Spain returned to the traditional policy of friendship and alliance with France for the sake of her American colonies.

## WAR WITH BRITAIN

The result was twelve years of near permanent war with Britain, the loss of Trinidad in 1797 and the two disasters at sea which put paid to Spain as a naval or colonial power: Cape San Vicente in February 1797 and Trafalgar in October 1805. Central to this conflict was the renewal of the war between Spain and her western neighbour, Portugal. Godoy, whose wings were trimmed in 1798 as a result of the disastrous events of the first phase of the war with Britain, returned to his former pre-eminence to make war on Portugal in 1801-2. The Peace of Amiens in 1802 brought Spain some small territorial gain in Portugal and the return of Menorca, which the English had occupied at the end of 1798, enough to keep Godoy in Carlos IV's good books. But the resumption of the war at sea in 1805 reaffirmed British naval superiority. On land, however, Napoleon Bonaparte carried the day again with his brilliant victory at Jena over the Prussians in October 1806. Portugal was now all the more relevant to the implementation of his celebrated plan to set up a continental blockade against Britain's trade, the source of her prosperity and power. A year after Jena, Napoleon and Spain agreed that joint French and Spanish forces should invade Portugal, the closest ally Britain had on the continent.

The first phase of the operation was the transfer of French troops across Spain, but going beyond the terms of the agreed operation against Portugal, the French garrisoned important cities such as Pamplona and Barcelona, and in March 1808 Napoleon's brother-in-law, Marshal Murat, made his entry into the Spanish capital itself at the head of a powerful army. Meanwhile Godoy and the Spanish Bourbons, Carlos IV and Fernando, neglecting their responsibility to the nation, were vying with one another in their abject subservience to Napoleon for the sake of their own positions. Murat sent them all to Bayonne to sort out their differences. Napoleon made them renounce their rights to the Spanish throne and in July proclaimed his own brother Joseph King of Spain as José I. By now, though, the country was up in arms against the French invaders. On 2 May 1808, when the last of the royal family were leaving the capital to join the others in Bayonne, the people of Madrid rose against Murat and his soldiers. The shooting of Spanish patriots by Murat's firing squads on the following day is the drama that Francisco

Goya (1746–1828) immortalised in his famous painting, 'The Shootings of May 2nd'.

## *War of Independence against Napoleon*

The uprising swept the country, turning into a savage five-year war of independence. Napoleon himself had to go to Spain at the head of a 90,000-strong army, but no sooner had he arrived than he had to rush back to northern Europe where Germany and Russia were also rising in a war of national liberation against the foreign intruder. On the Iberian front, the British expeditionary force under Wellington continued to fight the French forces of occupation until the conclusive Battle of Vitoria in June 1813, while, in a truly popular struggle for their country, Spaniards of all persuasions sprang from the undergrowth in small bands of *guerrilleros* to fight the only type of war open to them: swift strikes at the edges of the large and well-seasoned Napoleonic armies followed by a quick getaway to the shelter of the familiar terrain; harassment of small detachments, food supplies, convoys, postal services and communications; and the creation of a climate of fear among French soldiers.

The social mix which sustained this insurrection has given some substance to the view that this was a nation at war, the first united action of all Spaniards against a common enemy. It is certainly true that this was the first appearance of the popular masses with a strong ideological direction from the Church and active participation from the clergy, especially in northern parts of the country like Navarra, Galicia and the interior of Catalunya. These *guerrilleros* were mainly from among the poor and deprived, and were eventually integrated into the regular army – the most successful guerrilla leaders being absorbed into its higher echelons, to turn up later in the century as crusaders of liberalism or happily sharing with the new political families the purchase of disentailed land which gave them entry to the style and ethos of the landowning aristocracy. On the other hand, the established nobility, the urban notables, administrative and political authorities, and even the regular army, having appeared to accept the new order at first, later on trickled back to the patriots' front, although the nobility at least never joined the *guerrilla* and would only agree to fight in the regular army when called up by the officers and the local juntas after the initial disruption.

When José I, *Pepe Botella* as he was known to Spaniards on account of his partiality to wine, left Spain in 1813 some 12,000 families of *afrancesados* (pro-French) went with him. The smallness of this figure may show how Spaniards, as in similar situations elsewhere, tried to survive and bent with the wind or even profited handsomely from troubled waters. Those politically or morally aware of the changing circumstances would have found it extremely difficult to read the signs accurately and to make a rational accommodation of their existence, especially when subservience to French ideas was identified with treason. Goya, who witnessed the events, portrayed some of the horrors and incongruities of the period in his drawings.

The French troops, for their part, did very little to endear themselves to the rank and file of the population; as well as their exactions on the countryside for provisions and supplies, they wreaked devastation on the productive infrastructure of the country. They were not alone in this: both British and French troops destroyed the textile factories of Segovia and Avila, the former obliterating the wool industry while the latter directed their fire against silk. Napoleonic soldiers filled their knapsacks with choice samples of Spain's artistic treasure. Goya himself was at one time instructed by Godoy to prepare a lot of fifty Spanish paintings to be transferred to France – an instruction which he apparently carried out to the best of his ability as a Spanish artist, that is by carefully selecting second-rate canvasses. José I took with him a rich collection of articles which his contemporaries referred to as 'King Joseph's impedimenta'. Marshal Soult, the besieger of Cádiz, was also notorious for his record as a plunderer of Spanish works of art; Spanish patriots nicknamed him *robacuadros* (picture-stealer).

## Las Cortes de Cádiz

While the *guerrilleros* took to the field, the towns that were not occupied by the French filled in the power vacuum left by the royal family with local juntas, self-appointed assemblies of the rich and influential, which

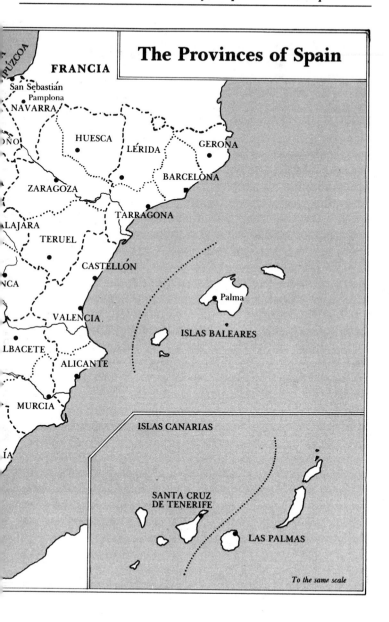

# The Provinces of Spain

FRANCIA

San Sebastián
Pamplona
NAVARRA

HUESCA
LÉRIDA
GERONA

ZARAGOZA
BARCELONA

TARRAGONA

LAJARA
TERUEL

CASTELLÓN

NCA

VALENCIA

Palma

ISLAS BALEARES

LBACETE
ALICANTE

MURCIA

ISLAS CANARIAS

SANTA CRUZ
DE TENERIFE

LAS PALMAS

*To the same scale*

not only organised the resistance against Napoleon but also outlined the principles of their own legitimacy. Given the renunciations of the royal family at Bayonne, sovereignty was now vested in the people at war against the foreign invader. Some juntas were more radical than others, but on the whole they contributed in their short existence to the formation of a strand of democratic thinking, embodying the views of the most progressive among eighteenth-century reformers and the constitutionalist opportunities presented to them by the abdications of the royal family. They laid the foundations for Spain's first attempt at constitutional monarchy.

Following Floridablanca's suggestion, the local juntas delegated their authority to a *Junta Suprema Central* which first assembled, under his presidency, in Aranjuez on 25 September 1809. Meanwhile the crushing defeat of the nationalist forces at Ocaña forced the Central Junta to retreat to Sevilla and then Cádiz, where on 24 September 1810 the executive Junta and the Regency Council, which continued to represent conservative authority on behalf of the empty throne, convened *Cortes Extraordinarias y Generales* to draft a constitution for governing the nation. The fruits of their deliberations were promulgated on 19 March 1812, the day of St Joseph – thus the nickname *la Pepa* given to the document.

The Constitution of Cádiz was a programme of action for a constitutional monarchy. The preamble of the instrument of government referred to national sovereignty and individual rights and liberties: the end of fiscal privileges, freedom of expression, abolition of the Inquisition, free primary education for all, and the establishment of a national militia to protect human rights and ensure universal application of constitutional principles. The new charter acknowledged the principle of separation of powers, ascribing the power to legislate to 'the Cortes with the King' and executive power to the Crown alone, and laid down the system for the election of deputies (one for every 70,000 inhabitants) to the single-chamber assembly representing the nation through indirect and universal male (over twenty-five) suffrage, with municipalities and provinces as the basic constituencies.

## THE CONSTITUTION OF 1812

The basic premise of the political philosophy behind the constitutional charter was the recognition of the citizen as the holder of rights and obligations and the protagonist on the political stage. The individual was to be freed from any restriction to the full untrammelled use of personal liberty and private property, that is freedom from the restrictions of mortmain, entail and feudal relationships. Thus, the realisation of this individual freedom meant the total dismantlement of the old fabric of society: the end of the old privileged order based on four highly differentiated estates, the abolition of guilds, and especially the abolition of private jurisdictions (seigniorial and ecclesiastical). The Crown would no longer be synonymous with the State but subject to very precise definition of its executive power. No self-respecting monarch, Wellington commented at the time, could inhabit such an edifice with dignity: least of all Fernando VII who, having exhibited a despicable talent for duplicity and treachery in 1808, from 1814 showed a highly inflated opinion of his own royal person.

This social and economic programme reveals a certain tragic grandeur, a nobility of spirit among those party to a future vision of society built in the rarefied and siege atmosphere of Cádiz, with Napoleon's troops literally charging against its battlements. But it also betrayed a signal lack of political realism, an Olympian disregard for the state of the nation, several stages behind the level of development that could have made their dreams possible. The geographical and military context of their deliberations helps to explain the inordinate range and ambition of their political aspirations. In the first place, Cádiz was still the centre of American trade and the melting-pot of traders and commercial agents from all over the world. Secondly, the occupation of most of the peninsula by the French made travel to Cádiz from the conservative centre difficult; representatives from the eastern, more liberal, periphery, on the other hand, found it easier to travel by sea. Furthermore, deputies from the Americas shared views which were likely to lead to devolution of power to the colonies. In all cases, where duly elected representatives could not reach their destination substitute deputies from among those present in Cádiz were delegated. And there were writers and journalists who contributed with their eloquent leadership to the general excitement and exhilaration of this historic moment. The liberal majority in the *Cortes Extraordinarias* was carried away by a tide of words, which only a very small percentage of the population were able to understand.

The majority view of the country was outside the Cádiz parliament. After the triumphant passage of the liberal flagship, which caught Church and nobility unawares and in disarray, the forces of reaction rallied to the defence of the Crown and the destruction of the presumptuous Constitution. The old establishment argued that the pedlars of French views and ideals were condoning a wholesale abdication of their national heritage to the foreign invader, thus identifying *afrancesados* and liberals. A solid formation of *serviles* (abject slaves of monarchy and tradition – which is how the liberals repaid their taunts about *la Pepa*), led by the Bishop of Orense, President of the Regency Council, emerged from the initial chaos and in the first election for the Cortes Ordinarias in July 1812 were well able to return a majority of deputies. By then Wellington had beaten the French at the Battle of Los Arapiles, near Salamanca, defeated them again in their retreat to the north in June 1813, and in combination with Spanish and Portuguese troops finally ejected them from their last important holding, San Sebastián, on 31 August 1813.

The newly-elected conservative majority pinned their hopes for an orderly restoration of the absolutist past on the transfer of the parliamentary assembly to Madrid, away from the atmosphere and circumstances that had made *la Pepa* possible. An outbreak of yellow fever in Cádiz aided them in this regard. The official opening of parliament was to take place in the liberated capital of the country on 15 January 1814.

## *Fernando VII, 'the Desired One'*

Meanwhile in December 1813 in Valençay, Napoleon agreed to restore Fernando to the Spanish throne. The latter's loyal servants were quite happy to view this personal transfer of kingship as a vindication of absolutist rule. Liberals, on the other hand, were equally adamant that the appointment of the chief executive of the nation was not the prerogative of a foreign ruler but a delegation of authority from the national assembly, subject to the incumbent swearing to honour and defend the Constitution. Fernando had no intention of accepting a conditional succession to the Crown. The crowds that welcomed him back as the 'Desired One' gave him their full and rapturous support. His loyal and trusted servants rushed to pay him homage and offer their unconditional allegiance. Prominent army generals like Elío and Eguía, as well as the British expeditionary force under Wellington and Whittingham, were also there to encourage him in his determination to govern as an absolutist ruler. So on 4 May 1814, six weeks after setting foot in Catalunya after the humiliations of Valençay, he issued his first decree as King of Spain, declaring the Constitution of 1812 null and void and restoring the Inquisition.

The twenty years that followed surely stand as the darkest period in Spanish history. Aided and abetted by an ever-changing caucus of disreputable characters, corrupt politicians, and arrogant and ignorant senior officers, he sustained a comprehensive policy of repression and terror to eradicate even the shadow of opposition to his ignominious rule. For a short while in 1820, when an important section of the army urged him to govern as a constitutional ruler, he had no qualms in quickly accepting a situation which negated his entire past record or in 1823 helping finance a French army to restore Spain to his oppressive and autocratic tyranny, which after that reached unprecedented depths.

## WAR DEVASTATION AND ECONOMIC DEPRESSION

Not only liberals and constitutionalists were hounded out of the country or annihilated in a systematic campaign of total war against dissent and opposition. The country at large suffered a severe economic recession: the slow but steady recovery of the previous century was petering out, the benefits from trade liberalisation coming to a sudden halt when Napoleon instigated a continental blockade to starve Britain of the sinews of war. It is easy to imagine the devastation brought on Spanish communications when Godoy decided to join Napoleon in his fight against Britain and in the process gamble away both Spain's navy and her colonies, not to mention the dire effects of shifting alliances and policy changes on both individuals and nation, and the sheer destruction wreaked upon fields and towns by large marauding bands and armies demanding victuals and plundering the country.

Unlike the War of Succession at the start of the eighteenth century, the War of Independence took a particularly heavy toll on the infrastructure of the country: cities razed to the ground, like Zaragoza, Badajoz and San Sebastián; manufacturing establishments distinguished for their technological investment, like textile factories and the Royal Porcelain Factory of *El Buen Retiro* (the showpiece of eighteenth-century monarchical endeavour), wilfully wasted; the network of communications badly impaired; and tree-felling, burning or stealing of crops and slaughter of animals severely depleted the capital stock of agriculture. In 1820 the incoming minister for agriculture in the first liberal administration reported to Parliament that wine, cereal and olive oil production in 1818 was 35 per cent down on that for 1799.

## *The Independence of the American Colonies*

The American colonies, in theory at least still under metropolitan authority, might yet have provided the seeds of recovery, if Spain had been prepared to acknowledge the growing demands for some form of devolution in keeping with their separate economic development and growing isolation. But again Fernando VII was even less disposed towards compromise. He could only consider a military solution: one final expeditionary force to reduce his rebellious subjects. The 10,000-strong army sent in 1814 had disintegrated through war and disease, inadequate supplies and lack of pay. In fact, it was the last army assembled for that purpose near Cádiz in 1820 that, in their refusal to embark for America and face hardship and disease, helped Comandante Riego to force the Constitution of 1812 on the arbitrary and faint-hearted ruler and helped to bring about the liquidation of the colonial past. When the end finally came in December 1824, Fernando VII's contemporaries may have pondered on the priorities of a monarchy unable to ensure a return of the colonies to metropolitan authority but ready to finance an army of 132,000 under French command to restore him to absolute power over his peninsular subjects in April 1823.

BETWEEN CARLISM AND LIBERALISM

Fernando VII's last years brought a dramatic twist to the history of his ill-fated kingdom. His determination to secure his own succession was as stubborn as he had been obdurate in stamping out all opposition to his authority. His fourth wife, the Neapolitan princess María Cristina, bore him his first child on 10 October 1830. Only now his die-hard supporters of the recent past stood in the way of his paternal ambition. The problem was that Infanta Isabel was a girl, and females were excluded from dynastic succession by the French Salic Law introduced by Felipe V in 1713, abolished by Carlos IV and endorsed in 1830 by Fernando VII himself. However, two years later the King fell seriously ill and his brother Don Carlos stated that he would not accept Isabel's succession to the throne. His own advisers were also of the opinion that a female succession was not viable.

Momentarily recovered from his illness Fernando proceeded to dismiss his government and to dismantle the Royalist Volunteers, a body of 120,000 men (twice the strength of the Army) which he himself had created as a bulwark against subversion, but which was now turning to Don Carlos as a more determined defender of 'God and Country'. Fernando and his wife unashamedly hastened to build up a body of opinion and support for Isabel among moderate liberals, who had been exiled or excluded from all political participation since 1823, and when Fernando died on 29 September 1833 his widow María Cristina assumed power on behalf of her daughter. The leading officers of the volunteer corps rose up in arms in support of Don Carlos' claim to the Crown; thus the name *carlistas*.

## THE FIRST CARLIST WAR

The war that followed has been described as Spain's first civil war in modern times, the embattled struggle between two irreconcilable visions of the country – between the old and the new, between the dark and obscurantist society of the past and the progressive and enlightened hopes for the future. Carlism had a very limited geographical base: the countryside of northern, mountainous Spain from Biscay to El Maestrazgo (Castellón), the very areas where the War of Independence against the French had been fought most fiercely. The release of communal and municipal land to the vagaries of market forces intensified the conflict; those northern regions where tenant farmers, shareholders and sharecroppers lost the use of the land or had to pay higher rents to the new urban proprietors were the populist element of the traditionalist movement. Since they were unable to establish any kind of governmental framework and never controlled an important town or city apart from Estella in Navarra, which they made their capital, guerrilla war was the only form of action they could wage on the *cristino* armies.

Considering that the army, the administration of the State and most of the country accepted Isabel as their lawful *Princesa de Asturias*, with her mother as the Queen Regent, the long war between *carlistas* and *cristinos* showed again the incompetence and weakness of Fernando VII's legacy. The scattered and highly mobile bands of Carlist fighters operating in a very difficult terrain could only be contained by a large, highly organised army. In 1832 the royalist territorial force had only 67,317 men in active service (of whom 17,000 were royal guards). To recruit, train and maintain an army capable of bringing the northern rebels to acknowledge Isabel's succession financial resources had to be found. The wholesale disposal of ecclesiastical property was to provide the means. In return the female line of the Bourbon monarchy had to make virtue out of necessity by accepting military leaders as the political arbiters of the country and pinning their colours to the liberal flag.

## Spanish Liberalism

What economic liberalism meant as embodied in the legislation of 1812 and 1820–3 was firstly the dissolution of the manorial system – that is to say, the abolition of private jurisdictions (personal ties, services and dues to the lord of the land); and secondly the introduction of market forces in the countryside, i.e. freedom to buy and sell land, to hire and fire labourers, or to negotiate free contracts, to use and abuse land released from the binds of primogeniture, entail and mortmain. Furthermore, the liberal agrarian reform aimed to parcel out the commons and municipal lands and bring them under private ownership, for only then would the land yield a higher return. As Campomanes said in 1795, 'individual interest was the first instrument of prosperity'.

Political liberalism hinged on the principle that the sovereignty of the nation resided with the Crown and a bicameral parliament: the former as the chief executive of the nation, the latter (Senate and Congress) as the main legislative chamber. Members of the Senate were appointed by the monarch, a system of representation which fixed the traditionalist line of Castilian constitutionalism (estates or *estamentos*). Liberal radicals (the so-called *progresistas*) accepted the Senate in the hope of redressing the balance in the future by gradually widening the political franchise to a single chamber. Except for a brief moment of transient hope in the municipal elections of 18 December 1868, the universal suffrage for males over twenty-five which the exhilaration of Cádiz had put on the statute-book on 1 January 1810 was until 1890 only a dream.

The nation was represented in the lower chamber (*congreso de diputados*) from an electoral roll of between 0.15 per cent (1836) and 5.7 per cent (1879) of the total population. This appeared perfectly natural to 'moderates', like Martínez de la Rosa, Marqués de las Amarillas, Donoso Cortés and Cánovas del Castillo. 'Doctrinaire liberalism' identified property, particularly landed, and political representation. Voting was then the right of those with a stake in the country and a few others with academic and professional qualifications; only those paying rural, urban or, from 1878, industrial contribution were entitled to exercise this political right.

The inability of the Queen Regent to reduce the Carlist uprising because of the lack of an adequate army led to the implementation of the liberal programme for agrarian reform. Mendizábal was brought in from twelve years' exile in London to sort out the finances of the land and produce the means to fight the Carlists successfully. He managed to obtain financial backing and most of the fire power from London, as well as a considerable land (12,000 men) and sea (one squadron) force. But the coffers of the State required a more substantial injection than adding to the national debt. Mendizábal turned to the well-tried recourse of expropriating municipal and ecclesiastical land, thus completing a long process which dated back to the very beginning of the growth of monarchical and nobiliary power in Castilla.

## DISSOLUTION OF PRIVATE JURISDICTIONS

The landed nobility were the first to benefit from the new dispensation.

The Royal Palace in Madrid

The Royal Decree of 26 August 1837, which aimed to free *señorío* land from primogeniture and entail, found the nobility in an ideal position to benefit from it substantially. In 1837 the Crown, in the care of the Queen Regent (her own position rather precarious on account of her marriage to a commoner only three months after Ferdinand VII's death), had to make concessions to the liberals for the sake of the struggle against Carlism. Nor did the lords of the land show any desire to support the Crown as they had done under Fernando VII. Perhaps the decisive factor in this change of heart on the part of the nobility was that the legal instrument of 1837, intended to bring jurisdictional *señoríos* under the authority of the State, exempted those in actual possession of the land from having to submit title deeds as to the nature of their holding.

The distinction between territorial and jurisdictional *señoríos* had never been made clear in legal texts and the nobility had shown no particular interest in helping to identify the nature of their landholdings, which were exploited in exactly the same manner – the returns from the land coming from rents, jurisdictional dues and taxes. But in the period prior to 1837 they had been most active in asserting that all their land was of the first category and therefore to be deemed as private property with unlimited title of ownership. Prescriptive rights or exemption from the burden of proof placed them in an unassailable position. No party in this new alliance between the old landowning aristocracy and aspiring new rich, who were buying land and wanted more, would care to investigate claims to property lest it should lead to conquest, usurpation and violence as its foundation. Other interested parties, such as towns, municipalities and tenant farmers who brought these matters to the attention of the Courts, very rarely managed to obtain redress from the judiciary.

## ECCLESIASTICAL DISENTAILMENT

In the short term, the onslaught on the patrimonial foundations of both the regular and secular Church was the least likely to raise serious objections from any sections of the community apart from the Church itself, whose members have ever since denigrated Mendizábal as the architect of that 'great robbery' (*inmenso latrocinio*). The 'moderate' politicians who cried out against the spoliation of the Church when in opposition were quite happy to let 'progressive' legislation run its course when in power. Disentailment of church property also meant the loss of jurisdiction and of fiscal contributions, like tithes and first fruits, which were now transferred to the State. The Vatican had come to terms with the new situation and eventually in 1851 signed a new Concordat which left the Spanish Church with voluntary contributions from the faithful, payments for specific services, and a substantial assignation from the national budget for the needs of worship and the requirements of the clergy (*culto y clero*).

On the whole, Mendizábal's legislation achieved its short-term objectives: it paid off part of the national debt and provided the funds for close to 300,000 men under arms to end the Carlist war, thus enhancing the political credibility of the 'progressive' liberals to complete Mendizábal's task. The alleged long-term objective of the reform, however, did not seem to have been advanced in the least. Mendizábal claimed to be bringing forth a 'large family of small landowners' to give social substance to the liberal cause. This important social objective seemed to have gone badly awry already; earlier disentailment laws under Carlos III, IV and Fernando VII, showed that the number of small proprietors in northern Spain had decreased from 50 per cent at the beginning of the eighteenth century to 36 per cent in the mid-nineteenth century, with a corresponding increase of insecure tenancies. Social unrest in Valencia in 1803–4, the war of the *agraviados* ('the aggrieved ones') in agrarian Catalunya in 1827, and indeed the Carlist insurrection of 1833 were desperate fights against a pattern of modernisation which brought them further misery and deprivation.

In 1839 the military were able to bring an end to a most exhausting and cruel war. On 29 August Espartero, the *cristino* general, and Maroto, Don Carlos' commander-in-chief in the north, signed the Convention of Vergara which recognised Isabel as the legitimate Crown Princess of Asturias and, most significantly for the future role of the army in Spanish politics, safeguarded pay and promotion prospects of the former Carlist officers. Navarra's special status was also acknowledged in the *Ley Paccionada* of 1841 (the Foral Pact), which enshrined to the present day the financial and legal autonomy of the province under the Diputación Foral (Regional Assembly). This conciliatory peace helped the old Navarrese kingdom to retain its individuality, with important economic and social consequences. Municipalities throughout Spain tried to resist losing their lands; but only Navarra was successful in opposing municipal disentailment. Unlike other parts of Spain, the towns and villages of Navarra have managed to retain a great proportion of their common lands which still provide substantial allotments for the local community and capital investment for economic promotion and public amenities.

## DISENTAILING LEGISLATION OF 1855

The second major stage of the liberal agrarian reform was the work of Madoz and his *desamortización general* of 1 May 1855, which provided for the sale of all lands not privately owned. The bulk of this huge operation took place between 1855 and 1867, and was virtually completed by 1876. Since Spain in the mid-nineteenth century was a predominantly agrarian community, this massive transfer of real estate from corporate to individual ownership completely transformed the country and lumbered it with a structure of power the consequences of which are still painfully obvious today over large areas. With the ecclesiastical, municipal and communal lands went also all forms of public benefaction, which from now on would have to come from a severely impoverished state. The safety net of the common lands which villagers had shared for centuries (hunting grounds, pasturing fields, the timber to make charcoal, cut firewood and repair their homes and farms) was pulled from under them.

As for the social objective, which Madoz as well as Mendizábal had claimed to be of paramount importance, the new dispensation, far from redistributing land among the poor peasants under a system of collective municipal use or long-term leases, reduced large numbers of small proprietors, unable to keep their holdings at a time of rising rents and prices, to the condition of landless peasants, with their physical labour as the only saleable commodity to bargain with for their living. A few voices, like Alvaro Flórez Estrada, had advocated a mortgaging system linked to a long-term secured tenancy, which might have enabled them to amortise their purchase over a long period; but such facilities as were provided benefited the existing rich and the owners of public securities. They could pay in bonds quoted well under par. Valuation procedures may not have been at fault but the acceptance of paper money in lieu of cash presented financial speculators with largesse the like of which Spaniards with liquid assets or government stock were never going to witness again.

The economic aim of this massive transfer of land from public or corporate to untrammelled individual ownership was to create competition that would bring more land under the plough and make it more productive. It showed no more prospect of realisation than the alleged redistributive objective so loudly protested by those hoping to benefit from it. Some ten million hectares were sold, equivalent to 20 per cent of the land mass and 40 per cent of arable land. Large tracts belonging to the Church or the Crown which had not been put to work in the past because of lack of capital or enterprise would now be brought under the plough by individual proprietors seeking to maximise returns on their investment. Agricultural production (cereals in the two mesetas and vines in peripheral regions) expanded, especially in the middle decades of the century, and more than kept up with population growth (from 11.5 million at the beginning of the nineteenth century to 18.6 million by the end of it), to the extent that in the third quarter of the century Spain was self-sufficient and exporting fairly large quantities of wheat.

The increase in production was no doubt a consequence of the increase of land under cultivation and rising demand. But there was no improvement in productivity: in fact, cereal yields per hectare fell. Once again the law of diminishing returns came into play when poor-quality land was ploughed in search of short-term returns, without capital investment. The severe crisis of the end of the century, when the disentailment process was over and Spanish wheat had to compete with cheaper produce from faraway countries, was to underline the continuing undercapitalisation and to expose the crude realities of a system of production which expanded only in response to high protective tariffs. The result was price increases which further depressed standards of living and impaired the competitive edge of exporters.

In conclusion, therefore, the social and economic potential for growth and stability in the countryside and in the Spanish economy in general was sacrificed willy-nilly to the short-term exigencies of an impoverished Fisc and a Monarchy under siege, with the moneyed classes well poised to pounce upon the wholesale alienation of 'bienes nacionales' (the national heritage) at bargain prices. When Carlism was defeated the new amalgam of forces behind María Cristina and her daughter Isabel II had to be gratified and firmed up against all challenge from the lower orders who, as the main casualty, were beginning to show the strength of their resolve against the most iniquitous features of the new regime. Defenceless as they were before the unlimited power of their landowners over the means of production and the political prerogative, the poor peasants and the landless labourers remained tied to an agrarian system for ever undercapitalised because of the availability of cheap and submissive labour.

## *Redefinition of the Structure of Power*

The new balance of power struck in the middle decades of the nineteenth century between the established landowners and the newcomers from industry, commerce and the service classes, proved extremely durable. It was based on centuries of undisputed social and economic hegemony, with the social climbers only too eager to underwrite and emulate by purchasing land and a title of nobility, or through marriage. The position of authority enjoyed by the landowning aristocracy could not have been lost on the aspiring social élites from non-agricultural sectors. The 1837 Act which exempted the landowners from having to show their title deeds was the first act of parliament under a liberal administration. It was not long before the upturn of the economy and the business, banking, railway and mining expansion of the middle decades of the century were to bring new men to wealth and high social status.

A text of 1822 published by the Catalan historian Josep Fontana shows in all candour the symbiotic relationship between cotton textiles from industrial Catalunya and grain producers from dry-farming Castilla, Extremadura and Andalucía. Once the American colonies had broken away, Catalan manufacturers depended all the more on peninsular protected markets: 'Is it not proper that we should eat the corn grown by our brothers so that they may consume our fruits and industrial products?' And so it was that the two main areas of economic activity remained locked in a non-competitive and retardatory economic embrace. Those, very few and far between, who might have been intent on furthering modernisation of the productive capacity of the nation on the basis of a wider political and economic franchise, were silenced by the conservative and respectable (*las fuerzas vivas*) who looked to France and saw ruin and devastation brought about by social subversion. They predicted a similar development for Spain if the foundations of the new state were not firmly laid.

## THE ARMY

The new establishment lost no time in drafting the military to head the new power structure and to oversee its operation. The task was urgent: the dissolution of the *señoríos jurisdiccionales* left most of the country without any recognised authority and the first half of the nineteenth century had more than its fair share of peasant unrest, bread riots, anti-fiscal insurrections and anti-seigniorial uprisings.

The civil and ecclesiastical lords, who had administered justice, taxes, municipal appointments and social services in their own territories from time immemorial, had been overrun more than once by the disaffected masses. The new authority of a civil society had to be defined and all the subjects of the new state had to be reached. Bearing in mind all the adverse circumstances which Spain was going through at the time, the efforts made in this direction were quite remarkable and could be achieved only in the context of a military hierarchy ready and willing to place themselves in the service of the leading economic forces.

The position of the army was both qualitatively and quantitatively central to the new structure of power. In the first place, the higher nobility had always figured very prominently in the upper echelons of the army. The *guerrilleros* who climbed through the ranks in the struggle against the French may have introduced a radical element, but whatever ideological differences may have existed within the army in the first decades of the nineteenth century, they were easily resolved – as shown by the Vergara accommodation between Espartero and Maroto in 1839 which brought the Carlist officers into the national army. The military, or at any rate the leading commanding officers of the period (Espartero, Maroto, O'Donnell, Narváez, Prim, Pavía, Martínez Campos, Don Fernando Primo de Rivera, Serrano, Topete) were the arbiters of Spain's political life.

The military were overwhelmingly present at all levels of the administration: in 1850, for instance, there were 153,977 men serving in the army, amounting to 88.33 per cent of the people employed by the State, with 55 per cent of the national budget. In comparison, there were only 267 judges for the whole country. Through marriage, land purchase and titles of nobility, the generals at the top of the military pyramid were all integrated into the new amalgam of financiers, speculators, landowners, prosperous lawyers and political families. Of the 2450 nobiliary titles in Spain at the end of Alfonso XIII's reign in 1931, some 1400 had been created in the preceding hundred years, and the army, certainly in the middle of the nineteenth century, figured very prominently among those elevated to the highest status. Furthermore, the policing of the countryside and the enforcement of the new property laws and land enclosures were entrusted in 1844 to a new paramilitary force, *la benemérita guardia civil*, to replace all local security services of the past. After some attempts to establish the force as a civilian organisation accountable to parliament and government, it emerged as a section of the army as regards recruitment, training and promotion prospects of the officer corps. Its regular and spectacular growth has no parallel in contemporary Spanish history: from 5501 'numbers' at its inception to 19,105 in 1898, garrisoning 514 stations in 1846 and 2179 in 1897. By 1939, when it took over frontier posts from the *carabineros*, *la guardia civil* had extended its 'beneficent' sway to the furthest reaches of Spanish territorial and maritime boundaries. As a highly-structured, endogamous force, living on the margin of civil society in their *casas-cuarteles* (living quarters) in close co-operation with the municipal authorities, they have epitomised among the lower orders the worst features of the new Spanish order. The urban landscape of countless municipalities bears imposing witness to the solid formation of the ancestral home (maybe a medieval castle or a fortified manor house) of the local landowning aristocrat, the parish church and vicarage, the town hall, and the *casa-cuartel de la guardia civil*, lining up along the main square.

## 1868: 'La gloriosa revolución septembrina'

The dominating position of the military in Spain's political life was made abundantly clear in the eventful years between Isabel II's fall and flight from Madrid on 30 September 1868, and the restoration of the Bourbon monarchy in the person of her son Alfonso on 29 September 1874. The general officers who rose against Isabel II's 'intolerable' rule, including General Francisco Serrano, the Queen's former lover, were the protagonists of the 'pronunciamiento' (coup) of Sagunto (Valencia) of 29 September which brought her son Alfonso XII to the Spanish throne from Sandhurst where he was a cadet. The only exception was General Juan Prim y Prats who was assassinated on 27 December 1870 soon after bringing a new monarch from Savoy to occupy the vacant throne. The Savoyard Amadeo I was actually elected in Cortes on 16 November 1870 but abdicated on 11 February 1873, quite unable to cope with an impossible situation. Between 11 February 1873 and 19 September 1874 Spain drifted into its first republican experience, having to contend with a Carlist uprising, the first Cuban insurrection against Spanish rule, and a Cantonalist revolt in Cartagena.

With the generals' leave and in the name of Alfonso XII, on 31 December 1874 Don Antonio Cánovas del Castillo formed a civilian government and reinstated a form of parliamentary rule with two chambers (Congreso and Senado) and a British-inspired two-party rota system, formalised in the constitutional charter of 30 June 1876. However corrupt and restricted (property or professional qualification were required to exercise the right to vote), the electoral system provided a venue for political debate and offered some avenues for the widening of the political franchise. In the circumstances it was a step forward which brought some stability and economic growth until its collapse in 1917. The military were quite happy to return to their barracks. Together with the peers of the realm, the high-ranking officers were, of course, members of the Senate in their own right.

In fact, until quite recently nothing politically significant has ever happened in Spain without the active participation or tacit acceptance of the most senior army officers. By commission or default army generals have dictated Spain's incidental history and their interests and views have always been adequately safeguarded from factionalist upheavals. They claimed to be the saviours of the nation and the custodians of the liberal state as represented by its social and economic forces. In their support for the Crown, though, they proved to be quite pragmatic; to their cost both Isabel II in 1868 and her grandson Alfonso XIII in 1931 discovered that high-ranking officers, no matter how close to the throne, were prepared to bring about or countenance their departure for the sake of social peace and the unity of their army.

# CHAPTER SIX

# Growth without Stability

## *The Start of Industrialisation*

From the low ebb of Spain's economic and political prostration of the early decades of the nineteenth century, the middle years witnessed a wide range of change and advance in the economic infrastructure of the country. Mail-postage was introduced in 1849 and optical telegraphy came into operation between Madrid and Irún in 1850 and then extended to Cádiz. Electrical telegraphy followed in 1852. The years 1855–6 signalled the great step forward in this direction. Communication services were opened to the public, the main phase of disentailing legislation was passed and the legal and financial framework for the building of the railways were laid in the Railway Act of 3 June 1855 and the Banking and Finance Act of 28 January 1856.

Controls and communications dominated the thinking of the period as the first stage on the move towards industrialisation. From the point of view of Spain's poor performance thus far, foreign capital, technical instrumentation and expertise from abroad were essential. No progress looked possible without an adequate system of transportation. The first railway line came into operation on 28 October 1848: it ran 29 kilometres between Barcelona and Mataró. By 1865 there were 5478 km of track, and twice that number by 1901, reaching a total of 17,071 km by 1931. The almost exclusive dedication to the building of the railways proved to be excessive from the start. The first phase came to a halt in 1865 because of serious financial crises caused by poor profits due to low demand for the service. A different layout might have attracted more goods and passengers, or an adequate road service could have enhanced the scope and reach of the system, and thus the level of utilisation. But the roads had suffered badly since the times of Carlos III and no attempt was made to improve them or build new ones until the end of the century. In 1880 there were 19,500 km of road; 8000 km were added in the next ten years and they reached a total of 56,885 km by 1931, when Spain was the fifth largest European country in terms of the number of motor vehicles on the roads. Local bus lines completed the system from 1918, but the road-building of the early decades of the twentieth century was not paralleled by adequate efforts to keep the railway system in good operational order, thus creating severe bottlenecks in the transport of goods and passengers and underlining over the years the lack of a comprehensive policy for the country as a whole.

## RAILWAYS AND MINING

The railways were running ahead of the economy. Large capital investment was crowding out other areas of productive investment such as manufacturing or heavy industry. In the heyday of the railway construction boom the financial facilities and franchises granted to the foreign companies amounted to more than 60 per cent of the total capital invested at the time. This excessive capitalisation may have been conditioned by the high profitability of the construction rather than the use of it once built. The largesse of foreign capital which made the construction of the first phase possible came mainly from France and Belgium. It was the start of a permanent feature of Spain's model of industrialisation, sacrificing the future requirements of her economic development to the short-term aspirations of foreign, speculative and commercial capital.

The layout and the rail gauge chosen also pointed to short-term considerations on the part of the Spanish authorities. The mountainous terrain of the Spanish peninsula, it was said, necessitated a rail gauge wider than that prevailing in Europe so as to provide sufficient base for heavier and more powerful locomotives. National security also had a part in this decision, for after the past experiences of foreign armies parading their military might across the peninsula the peculiarity of the Spanish system could help isolate the country from foreign armies and foreign goods. The layout was dictated by political considerations rather than economic ones. Like the spokes of a wheel, it radiated from the hub (Madrid) to the periphery, leaving interregional communications to an uncertain future. Even today the industrial centres of the north continue to suffer from those short-sighted decisions.

Nor did nationalistic considerations appear any more consistent in the context of those who argued in favour of protection for Spanish industry. The financial framework for the railways was thrown wide open to foreign investors and national speculators. Spanish capitalism favoured the cosy world of state priming and protection. The same may be said of the legal and financial framework devised for the exploitation of the subsoil of the country which from Roman times had provided Spain with a vast wealth of mineral riches. In this area of economic endeavour the multiple effect of the extractive industry on the surrounding countryside was even less significant. The Mining Act of 1868 made Spain into the bargain basement of the world for copper, lead, iron, mercury, zinc. For £20 a mine could be established. British companies were the bulk buyers of these essential resources and Río Tinto was the flagship of the mining bonanza. It was purchased in 1873 and fifteen years later was considered to be one of the richest mines in Europe, from 1897 to 1911 yielding to British and Spanish investors an annual average of 70 per cent on capital invested. The copper pyrites were extracted and processed in open-air furnaces according to the most advanced technology and then taken by rail directly to British ships anchored at the port of Huelva. The spin-off of the industrial enclave for the host country consisted only of several thousand jobs for the famished and destitute southerners who were still attracted to the industry despite the lowest wages in Spain and the highest level of contamination. It was the atmospheric pollution that caused the mining population to erupt on several occasions, especially in 1888 and 1920, into some of the most savage industrial conflicts of the period. The conniving and repressive attitude of the Spanish authorities outraged even a conservative deputy from the area, who reported to parliament the massacre that followed a peaceful demonstration before the Town Hall of the municipality of Minas de Río Tinto in 1888.

Rising population growth and growing diversification in agricultural production, technological advance, capital accumulation, and financial and commercial flexibility, were all there to prime the general move towards industrialisation and modernisation of Spain's productive forces. To judge only from purely quantitative indicators, growth and development proceeded unabated until the 1930s. The long and steady process, however, was neither balanced nor equitable. The hundred years separating the death of Fernando VII in 1833 and Alfonso XIII's hasty flight to safety in 1931 were constantly interrupted by economic, social and political crises, usually a combination of all three. Spain is certainly different from other European countries with whom Spaniards like to be compared; she has had the most climactic past. In the century from 1833 for instance the following dates could be singled out as dramatically critical: 1833–43, 1847–8, 1866–1876, 1886, 1898, 1909, 1917, 1923, 1931 and the final catastrophe of 1936.

## Economic Growth and Uneven Development

The new patterns of promotion and exploitation of the natural resources of the land were not bringing material prosperity for the large majority of the population, nor even relief from the cyclical demographic disasters of the past. Nor was the solid amalgam of old and new forces contributing much to a new feeling of unity of purpose among the historic regions of Spain. The 'invertebration' of the Iberian peninsula was a deeply ingrained social and economic reality which had to be reconciled within the framework of a less intransigent version of the unitary modern state. Intent only on retaining central control of the nation, the controllers from the centre failed repeatedly to encourage converging forces and centripetal and interregional tendencies in the search for cohesion between regions and individuals.

The most obstructive feature in this respect was the chronic failure to create a national market which would have stimulated the whole of the economy through newer and bigger demands. Since Spain was still eminently agrarian, it was the failure in the countryside that impeded progress. Traditional agriculture continues to hold the key to the understanding of this unsteady pace towards the future. By far the most important of Spain's three main cultures, wheat, olives and vines, was cereal production. It occupied more than 50 per cent of all arable land, including almost all the two Castillas, Extremadura and Andalucía. Until 1931 it represented twice the total value in money terms of all other agricultural production, and five times coal, iron and steel production put together.

## CEREALIST AGRICULTURE, VINES AND OLIVE GROVES

The formal introduction of the capitalist ethos to the countryside made no difference either in ownership patterns or exploitation systems. Average yield per hectare throughout the first three decades of the twentieth century stood still, at half the French or German yield, with the province of Almería just about managing a quarter of the national average. The structural weaknesses of cerealist, dry-farming agriculture were thrown into dramatic relief by agronomic improvements abroad and the transport revolution. Steam-engines brought highly competitive wheat from the USA prairies to Europe: the severity and speed of the impact has been seen in the arrival route of cereals at Barcelona – in 1884 60 per cent of the imported total was arriving by rail, presumably from the interior of Spain, but by 1886 only 11 per cent came that way; 89 per cent was arriving by sea. The official solution was higher import duties; there was no other, according to Prime Minister Cánovas del Castillo, in spite of a spate of inquiries, speeches and printed words which did very little to assuage the suffering of the people or to raise the yield of the land.

The primitive cereal cycle – drought and poor harvests, high prices bringing marginal land under the plough, overproduction, and low prices leading to withdrawal of land from cultivation – was still in full flow and relatively safe from interference from the state authorities who sent the army and the *guardia civil* when the peasants had the effrontery to publicise their misery and disaffection.

The other components of the Mediterranean triad were not so violently subject to the vagaries of weather or international market fluctuations, nor were they so crucial to the overall situation of the country. Nevertheless, on a few occasions they contributed a fair measure of disruption to the countryside. Wine, the most valuable cash crop of the peasant, continued its long, uninterrupted march into cereal land, reaching its peak in international competitiveness at the very time when wheat production was being shaken to its foundations by cheap imports from overseas. Spain increased its wine and brandy exports tenfold and effectively monopolised world markets between 1882 and 1892. France was the first to suffer the blows of phylloxera in the 1870s but the plague eventually came across through the eastern Pyrenees, taking a heavier toll on Catalan vineyards which did not quite recover until 1915. The Catalan tenant farmers, whose tenure was linked to the life of the vine, saw their contracts in danger of being reduced in line with the shorter-lived vines imported from America to replace the phylloxera losses. Their conflict with landlords over the length of their tenure became one of the essential ingredients of Catalan politics, which flared into violent protests when landlords tried to weaken tenants' rights in the early 1890s, in 1918 and in the 1930s.

Olive-oil production also expanded continuously from the middle of the nineteenth century around the main producing areas, Teruel, Lérida, Tarragona, Córdoba and Jaén. It was a classical crop, well suited to dry-farming agriculture, but it also presented problems in that there was great variation in the size of the harvest. One such dramatic fall in production (1931) was part of the backdrop to the advent of Spain's Second Republic. The effect on the social temper of provinces like Jaén, where it was almost a monoculture, helps to explain the particular virulence of social conflict there.

In the early decades of the present century there were also persistent efforts to escape from too much reliance on the basic produce of the land through diversification and irrigation. Between the 1840s, when the first crates of oranges were exported to Britain, and the 1930s citrus fruits were developed along the Levantine provinces, mainly Castellón, Valencia, Alicante and Murcia, to become together with wine the basic Spanish export. The loss of Cuba, Puerto Rico and the Philippine Islands in 1898 was followed by the spectacular expansion of sugarbeet which transformed the irrigation areas of Sevilla, Granada and Zaragoza. From then on these new crops, together with wine and olive-oil, have earned Spain the foreign currency needed to pay for foodstuff imports, manufactured and production goods. They also contributed to the general prosperity of certain areas, but in the process widened the existing gap with traditional cultures, sharpening social and regional differences between the lush and highly populated Levantine huertas of Valencia, Murcia and Mataró, and the empty, parched tableland of the interior.

## HEAVY AND MANUFACTURING INDUSTRIES

These regional variations became even more marked as the process of industrialisation continued without due regard for possible linkages between the different sectors of production. In most cases conjunctural factors simply firmed up the localisation and development of particular industries. It is quite unique in the industrial history of the West that the iron and steel works should be located where the iron ore was (Biscay) rather than next to the coal mines (Asturias). Asturian coal was, in fact, expensive to produce and of low quality and, perhaps most decisively, difficult to move. Railway and road transport planning did not seem to have taken into account the significance of these linkages between the various sectors of the economy. Asturian coal was in the unfortunate position of having to travel by sea to other parts of the country.

As for the Biscayan iron and steel industry, its spectacular growth took place in the shadow of the British industrial empire, as a peripheral supplier of cheap iron ores for British manufacturing factories. Iron-ore production increased seven times from 1875 to 1900 but only one-tenth was processed nationally. Apart from the profits of unequal exchange between cheap raw materials and expensive manufactured goods, the benefits of transport in both directions accrued also to British ships. The proceeds from the sale of iron ores were still quite massive and made the fortunes of some of the leading Basque families, who founded iron and steel works in the late 1880s and gained a firm hold on the Spanish banking system. After 1900, when British imports began to fall, Bilbao industrialists and industrial bankers turned their proceeds from the previous sale of iron ore and repatriated capital from the last overseas colonies towards manufacturing for internal markets. Like all other economic interests in the country, protectionism was the way to ensure those markets. Indeed, Basque manufacturing exports did not really take off until the 1930s.

Unlike the Asturias or Biscay, Catalunya's industrialisation had a much longer pedigree having proceeded from the latter part of the seventeenth century on a balanced and steady course. By the end of the eighteenth century agricultural development, a fairly equitable distribution of the land, international competition and colonial markets had produced a considerable degree of interaction between the different sectors of the production system. The great commercial expansion of the latter part of the eighteenth century had been closely linked to colonial markets. The loss of the last overseas possessions in 1898 underlined the level of dependency. Catalunya had also been very heavily reliant on imports of raw materials, energy resources and financial services. Steam power was eagerly seized upon when it first appeared and from 1890 electricity was produced in ever-greater quantities by the hydro-electric plants built to harness the power of the Pyrenean rivers. This lack of primary resources placed a heavy premium on imports both in terms of cost and security of supply, and conditioned growth in the direction of consumer goods (cotton and woollen textiles), cork, furniture, building materials, paper and publishing, lifts and tramways, to accommodate demographic growth. With Bilbao and Madrid, Barcelona was the fastest-growing city in Spain.

Bearing in mind the general contention that 'the low consumption level of the country as a whole and the sharp income differentials of its people' was a determining factor in shaping this model of industrialisation, Catalan industrialists might have endeavoured to encourage the development of Castilla's agricultural and pastoral farming and transport facilities. Despite their leader Cambó's efforts in this direction, Barcelona had no direct railway or road link with the industrial north. Notwithstanding the fact that the two railway companies operating in northern Spain were 60 per cent French-owned, passengers and merchandise had to change at Zaragoza, because *Madrid-Zaragoza-Alicante* belonged to MZA while the trunk line from Vigo to Barcelona belonged to *Norte de España*.

## PROTECTIONISM

In conclusion, therefore, the dominating feature of capitalist Spain was until quite recently protectionism – that is, high import duties to keep out foreign competition and retain a monopoly situation over internal markets. Protectionism is intrinsically self-defeating, and in the Spanish case it was married to a liberality on the matter of foreign capital and production goods from abroad verging on extravagance. At the time, free trade was the ideal of the liberal politicians. However, practical considerations as to why free trade ought not to be applied in some special circumstances always managed to carry the day. In 1869, for instance, Don Laureano Figuerola, the finance minister, tried to legislate for a gradual reduction in import duties in his famous Clause 5; but under pressure from Catalan industrialists, Prime Minister Prim prevailed upon him to raise tariffs by 35 per cent. One of the first measures of the 1876 Restoration government under Cánovas del Castillo was to suspend Clause 5 altogether.

From then on tariff walls grew higher and higher in response to pressure from sectional interests as they were particularly affected by some individual crisis. In this respect, at least, there was a wide consensus among all the economic interests: the old landowning aristocracy and the new landowning bourgeoisie, foreign capital, Asturian mining interests, Basque industrialists and Catalan textiles. When the law of diminishing returns came into play, the economic establishment could still retain and even enhance their share of the country's wealth by turning the screw on the labouring majority. In that regard the possibilities were endless, since continuing demographic growth in excess of resources and proletarianisation of the lower orders of society contributed masses of surplus labour in no position to demand adequate wages for their exertions.

## *Demographic Changes, Geographical and Occupational Mobility*

By western European standards the growth of human numbers was very moderate. Starting from 11 million in 1800, the first third of the nineteenth century had been racked by civil wars, famine and disease, including yellow fever and cholera. There followed a fairly rapid increase in the middle decades, slowing down towards the last quarter when civil and colonial wars, famine, disease and emigration decimated the population of the country yet again. In the south people were still starving to death in 1880–2; the 1885 outbreak of cholera took more than

100,000 lives; there was famine and devastation in 1904–6 and 1917–21, and the 'Spanish' flu of 1918 could still raise the already high mortality rate to over thirty-three per thousand. Between 1886 and 1913, 1.5 million Spaniards opted for voluntary exile to Latin America.

The new century heralded a dramatic change in the rate of growth, especially in quality and distribution. Between 1900 and 1930 the population rose from 18.6 to 23.5 million, a growth rate nearly double that of the preceding forty years. Although birth rates came down quite noticeably, from thirty-six per thousand in the latter part of the nineteenth century to twenty-nine in the 1920s, many more people lived longer, thus confirming the underlying tendency of the country away from the seasonal rhythms of the traditional agrarian society to a 'modern' demographic pattern, at least in the more prosperous areas of the land.

The traditional move away from the rural areas to the urban centres was also gathering momentum, both as cause and effect of the social and economic modernisation of the country. In 1900 there were only six towns with more than 100,000 inhabitants (Madrid, Barcelona, Sevilla, Valencia, Málaga and Murcia) and by 1931 there were five more (Zaragoza, Bilbao, Granada, Córdoba and Cartagena). Madrid and Barcelona far outstripped the rest of the country, from over half a million in 1900 to 750,000 in 1931. When in the 1910s overseas destinations became less receptive to newcomers from Old Spain, escapees from rural misery together with repatriates from the last colonial enclaves crowded into the industrial areas of the north and east, Barcelona, Madrid and Bilbao. In the 1930s municipalities of less than 10,000 still contained 57 per cent of the population.

Occupational mobility along the various sectors of the productive system replicated the pace and direction of the rural exodus. Until 1910 agriculture represented two-thirds of the active population of the country, with very little variation since the 1880s, but by 1930 it was 45.5 per cent of the working population; Catalunya witnessed a much stronger shift. For Spain as a whole the drift from the land went to services and industry in similar proportions. The industrial population did not grow especially fast. In 1845 the French economist Blanqui wrote that Spain offered the rare spectacle of a country moving from the heart

The Palace of the Bishop of Astorga in León, built by Gaudí

of the nation to the extremities, leaving behind in the middle of the desert a large conurbation (Madrid) of consumers, and civil and domestic servants. In the early decades of the twentieth century Madrid could boast that it was mopping up a large surplus of unskilled labour from the rural surroundings servicing the building trades; building labourers were the main component of the Madrid working class. Only Catalunya and the Basque provinces, and Asturias to a lesser extent, could be said to have a truly industrial working class.

The demographic face of Spain was changing, but at a much faster rate than economic development. Regional variations in wealth creation and distribution continued to grow sharper. Individuals escaping from the misery of the countryside to the hopeful prospects of mining and industrial towns found little accommodation for their dreams. The main poles of attraction for this impoverished and unskilled mass of uprooted peasants grew and grew beyond the confines of their old walls. Living conditions generally did not improve much. Overcrowding and poor hygiene contributed to the spread of disease. Literacy rates were not improving either; when referring to the brilliant literary and cultural life of the early decades of the century, undeniably a true rebirth from the long sleep of past centuries, Tuñón de Lara points out that more than half the population of Spain could not read or write, and the number of state secondary schools hardly moved between 1900 and 1920. What urbanisation and industrialisation, however imbalanced, brought with them was a greater concentration of working men and women becoming more aware of their plight and waking up to their potential, as a movement in the struggle for better working conditions and a more equitable distribution of wealth.

## WORKING-CLASS MOVEMENTS

Prior to 1868 social unrest was normally an agrarian phenomenon related to subsistence crises which, with monotonous regularity, especially in the south, assailed the lives of the small peasants, unsecured tenant farmers and landless labourers through hunger and disease. It took the shape of land seizures in times of political crisis. Land distribution (*reparto*) was the battle-cry; they usually claimed lands they felt had been illegally and fraudulently appropriated.

With the growth of cities, the emergence of sizeable groups of workers living together through the same experiences led to more militant attitudes. Quite typically, the workers' movement initially expressed its rejection of the new working conditions by setting new machines alight, striking spontaneously, and finally setting up self-defence associations. Barcelona witnessed the first stirrings of this workers' agitation in the mid-nineteenth century; as to the political content of their struggle it would seem that their early feelings and attitudes owed a great deal to the utopias of French socialists such as Fourier and Guesde. The introduction of Bakunin's ideas by the Italian Giuseppe Fanelli added a new dimension. Availing themselves of the freedom of association granted by the 'Glorious Revolution' of 1868 Barcelona's textile workers organised a regional branch affiliated to the First International and established a federal executive council. In Madrid a group of 'federalists' set up joint action committees. In these early rumblings the final objective, as stated by Farga Pellicer in Barcelona and Anselmo Lorenzo in Madrid, was anarchy.

This commonalty of aims did not last long. French repression after the Commune forced Marx's son-in-law, Paul Lafargue, into Spain where he managed to influence the leading group of Madrid militants, Pablo Iglesias among them, away from Bakuninist ideas. As a result they formed a new federation which sent Lafargue as its delegate to the congress of the First International at The Hague. The great majority of federalists were led by Farga Pellicer in support of the anarchistic ideas of Bakunin, while the small group from Madrid stayed close to Marx and authoritarian socialism. These leading workers represented only a very small minority in the country and for the most part they themselves were artisans and craftsmen. Agricultural workers and agrarian problems played no part in their activities: nor did miners and industrial workers from the Basque Provinces and Asturias. Given the widely differing rates of economic change and its highly localised position, the fragility of the First Internationalists and the excessive weight of Catalan textile workers were not surprising. Nevertheless, these ideological divisions were to play a major part in shaping the future of the Spanish labour movement.

The restoration of the authority of the State in 1874 meant the dissolution of the First International and years of clandestinity. In the south the next thirty-five years saw great anarchist advances among the rural population. The destitute and illiterate proletariat of the great Andalusian and Castilian estates were ideal sowing ground for the 'apostles' of the Millennium, who could easily lead them to violent rebellion against their oppressors, culminating in the famous insurrection of 1883. By then, the Andalusian branch of the *Federación Regional de Trabajadores de España*, set up in Barcelona in 1881, had exceeded Catalan membership.

## *The Tragic Week*

The Catalan countryside gave expression to a separate form of political activism. The wine crisis of the 1890s elicited a more determined and better organised protest from the *rabassaires* (tenant wine growers). They were as violent in their actions as the peasants from the south, but much more successful in their fight for a greater security of tenure for their individual vineyards and therefore not interested in collectivist propaganda. They entered the twentieth century as a privileged association of peasant quasi-proprietors who would play a dominant role at the centre of left-wing Catalanism after 1909.

Catalan industrial centres, on the other hand, still subscribing to Bukunin's brand of anarchism, were also moving towards 'propaganda by deed'. From the anarchist Pallás' attempt on the life of General Martínez Campos in 1892, a long chain of violent individual acts and equally violent retaliatory action from the State set the scene for the brutal events of the *semana trágica* in Barcelona in July 1909. The 'tragic week' started simply as a general strike against the call-up of reservists for the war in Morocco. This was a very old bone of contention among the popular classes: a heartfelt opposition to military service, to serving overseas under appalling conditions when the rich and influential could be exempted from this honorary endeavour through payment of a redemption fee. Feelings ran very high and the protest spread to other Catalan towns in a very confused and chaotic manner, without leaders or stated objectives, and with the usual mixture of barricades, church burnings and workers' revolutionary committees. One of the lessons the Catalan workers learned from their costly failure was the need to strengthen their organisation.

## UNIONS

The start of this new organisational phase of Spanish anarchism was the foundation in 1911 of the *Confederación Nacional del Trabajo (CNT)*, which included a large majority of industrial workers' organisations from Catalunya as well as agricultural societies from the eastern provinces. In 1919 it was joined by the mainly Andalusian *Federación Nacional de Agricultura*. Numerically, the CNT dominated the Spanish workers' movement until 1936.

Meanwhile, Marxist-inspired authoritarian socialism plodded along in the care of Pablo Iglesias, the son of a poor washerwoman, who from the base of the Madrid printers' craft guild originated in 1888 both the first Socialist Party (PSOE) and the first Socialist Union, *Unión General de Trabajadores* (UGT). Until 1909, despite the Freedom of Association

Act of 1887 which authorised the formation of trade unions, the Socialist movement was not much more than Pablo Iglesias and his printers' guild, trying to 'improve working conditions' for its members. Apart from Madrid, only Biscay and the Asturias and, to a lesser degree, Catalunya seemed to have reacted in any significant manner to Iglesias' undoubted reputation as a man of great integrity and moral fervour.

In line with the anarchist movement, PSOE and UGT reoriented their policies after the 'tragic week' with a view to greater solidarity with other labour and political organisations. This policy brought them their first parliamentary seat in the 1910 general elections. Membership for the two organisations grew considerably, still coming mainly from the capital and Biscay and Asturias. The policy of co-operation with Republicanism contributed also to reinforce the gradualist approach to parliamentary socialism, with the arrival of intellectuals like Professor Julián Besteiro and moderates like Indalecio Prieto, 'the political realist'.

To sum up, the variety and quality of response to economic circumstances at the turn of century can be understood in the light of internal differences in landownership systems, diverging patterns of urbanisation and industrialisation, variable growth rates, ideas and ideals from current socialist thinking abroad and, last but not least, the personalities involved and the type of reaction meted out to insurrectionary or disaffected workers by employers, landowners and the State. Spain encompassed a great variety of countries and peoples who have resorted repeatedly to violent confrontation as the only acceptable way of resolving their irreconcilable differences. The structural, social and economic changes of the early decades of the present century contributed hardly anything towards the bridging of those differences. In addition, the conscience of the nation was badly shaken by the total liquidation of the imperial past in the loss in 1898 of the last overseas possessions, Cuba, Puerto Rico and the Philippines, in an ignominious war against the United States of America.

## *The long crisis of 1917*

World War One galvanised the Spanish productive system into a short period of spectacular gains from exports to both sides in the European struggle. The export drive sent home retail prices soaring and the low-earning groups of the country saw their income whittled away by spiralling inflation. Then the sudden collapse of exports and the accumulation of unwanted stocks which followed the German blockade of the North Atlantic from 1 February 1917 turned the passing bonanza into severe recession and generalised conflict. The massive gains from neutrality were not ploughed back into productive investment but extravagantly wasted, and when the slump came companies turned to the State for subsidies and protection. But the State was in no better shape than companies or workers to introduce reforms or alleviate the fall: from 1912 the war in Morocco had been making ever-increasing demands on the Treasury and attempts to tax neutrality profits failed lamentably in the face of a well-orchestrated campaign led by Cambó. The whole nation was shocked out of the false sense of stability of Restoration politics. Unlike the 'tragic week' of 1909, which was contained by the army, on 1 June 1917 it was the army itself that sounded the alarm about their own particular predicament and the shock waves of unrest and discontent reached in all directions.

The political formula devised by Cánovas del Castillo, the Constitution of 30 June 1876, had exhausted the little chance it had of containing social and economic development within the twin poles of growth and stability. The challenge from large sections of the country looked for a moment as if a new form of consensus politics and wider participation in the process of regeneration might have been afoot. In the early summer of 1917, in the midst of Spain's severe economic dislocation, news of the Russian Revolution and the USA's entry into the war, and a heated ideological debate as to the European model Spain had to follow to catch up with the twentieth century, workers' organisations, military juntas, political forces and the industrial and commercial bourgeoisie toyed with the idea of joining forces to relaunch Spain on a course of regeneration away from the corrupt and restrictive practices of the Restoration oligarchs. The Catalan industrial and commercial élites identified the landowning and financial interests from the centre as responsible for all the ills of Spain, and the attempts to tax the profits of neutrality was resisted by Catalan industrialists as a Castilian attack on their liberties.

## THE ARMY TO THE RESCUE OF THE RESTORATION SYSTEM: CONSERVATIVE CATALANISM

The prospect of such a coalition of forces was only a mirage. If there was ever any serious desire for it, the general strike of 13 August threw the army and the leading economic forces of the country into the arms of their natural partners, the Crown and the political establishment. The government of the day had no difficulty in delivering the strike committee to prison and, with the help of the army, in putting down all signs of unrest within ten days. The Catalan parliamentarians, who had been assembled in the Town Hall of Barcelona since 5 July when the national Cortes was dissolved, lost no time in declaring themselves in no way connected with the workers.

The main casualty of the 1917 crisis was the contractual arrangement of liberals and conservatives to succeed one another in an orderly share out of the spoils of power. The Restoration alliance of landowners and commercial bourgeoisie had to accommodate new economic interests and restore the social and economic position of the army. The latter's protest came mainly from the middle ranks of the officer corps, colonels and majors, whose incomes had been hard hit by inflation; but it was also, they argued in their own defence, the expression of their wounded pride over a colonial war which they could not win without adequate support and recognition from the State. Since their interests and aspirations were not adequately represented at the centre of power, they came forward to seize it. From the moment the general strike came to an end the army, with the full authority of its supreme commander Alfonso XIII, exercised direct control and was present in all government coalitions.

Catalan parliamentarians, Barcelona's industrial and commercial bourgeoisie and Prat's *Lliga Regionalista* were equally scared by the threat of social revolution and easily lured by a greater degree of participation in the running of the country. Cambó, their leader in Madrid, moved now towards a greater share of power for Catalunya, content to strengthen 'the secret pact', by which (according to Gerald Brenan) Castilla became the economic tributary of Catalunya whilst Catalunya remained the political tributary of Castilla. Seen as the Lliga's defection to the centralist enemy, it fed into republican radicalism which came to dominate Catalan politics in the 1930s. As with the army, increased Catalan representation became a permanent feature in the governmental reshuffles of the next five years while the reinforced political establishment tried to salvage the semblance of monarchico-parliamentary rule.

The army and the economic interests and political aspirations of the Catalan bourgeoisie were thus easily reconciled, but failed to restore a measure of order to the country. All the luminaries of the old regime (Maura, Romanones, Cambó), with the explicit support of Crown and army, could not form a viable government. Meanwhile, reformist and radical republicans, socialists and workers' organisations refused to submit quietly to a reinforced alliance of conservative interests and Restoration politicians without due regard for constitutional legality. Workers' militancy reached a new pitch as living conditions and wage levels worsened, with the full impact of the post-war recession filtering through to all parts of the country. Workers flocked to UGT, and especially CNT, which by 1919 had 700,000 members, over three times as many as UGT, which also saw its strength trebled. It was at this point that Socialism started to make some gains among agricultural workers in the south, who until now had turned to anarchism for spiritual comfort and hope of liberation.

## 'THE TROUBLED YEARS' 1917–23: AFRICAN DISASTERS

The years after 1917 were among the most conflictive periods in Spanish history. Short of civil war, it was a full-scale confrontation of all the social forces of the country. Political authority in Madrid disintegrated in crisis after crisis. In Andalucía the peasants rose against the large estates in a series of revolts and land seizures known as the 'Bolshevik triennium' (1918–21). In Barcelona the 1919 strike of the *Canadiense* (the Canadian electrical company of Catalunya) started four years of political assassinations which claimed 700 victims, among them Prime Minister Dato and Salvador Seguí, the moderate union leader who tried to restrain the most violent elements of Catalan anarchism. The streets of Barcelona were the scene of a war of reprisals between union and employers' federation gunmen, strikers and strikebreakers.

Not even the army, not yet anyway, could restore law and order. They were deeply involved in a very expensive and unpopular war against the Riff tribes. Spain had accepted the protectorate over Morocco from Britain in 1912, to keep France from the coastline opposite. From the first moment public opinion was very critical of this colonial adventurism, costing taxpayers' money and poor people's lives for the sake of some politicians' mining interests and the army's personal ambitions and imperial revanchism. In the middle of a country torn apart by a brutal class war, only twenty-three years after the total destruction of the Spanish navy in an equally hopeless struggle to hold on to the last remnants of Spain's imperial past, bang came the news of a military débâcle, which severely tested the confidence and identity of the nation. On 21 July 1921 General Silvestre, his general staff and some 14,000 conscripts were massacred at Annual in a panic retreat before a smaller force of Moorish tribesmen under Abd-el-Krim. Some 7000 soldiers followed the same fate when the military stronghold of Monte Arruit had to be surrendered. The town of Melilla was all the army of Africa could salvage from the ruins. It is easy to imagine how the leading classes of the nation were submerged into a sea of recriminations and mutual accusations in quest of 'responsibilities' for the moral and political perdition of the country.

## *Don Miguel Primo de Rivera: The Iron Surgeon for the Regeneration of the Fatherland*

The cry for a full inquiry into the disaster threatened to bring not only the army but also the Crown into disrepute for alleged corruption, mismanagement and favouritism. On 13 September the Captain-General of Catalunya, Don Miguel Primo de Rivera, with the full support of the Catalan bourgeoisie and the consent of Alfonso XIII, pronounced himself head of a 'military directorate' ready to 'save the nation' from the machinations and vices of decadent politicians. The Restoration edifice came tumbling down like a pack of cards. There was not one single or corporate voice to champion its survival. It was highly appropriate that it should fall to Don Miguel to sign the demise of the system which his uncle Don Fernando, Captain-General of Castilla la Nueva, had helped to introduce in December 1874.

The country, including the old political establishment, must have given a great sigh of relief, for it would have been difficult to imagine anything worse than the record of the thirty-three previous governments from 1902 to 1923. Don Miguel Primo de Rivera was deemed to embody the authoritarian style and interventionist approach required to restore order and reset Spain on a forward course. The notion of the strong man, 'the iron surgeon' who would need to cut through political factionalism and economic self-interest, had been in the air since the shattering disaster of 1898. Don Miguel had shown courage and independence of mind, and was endowed with a directness of manner and cavalier spirit which endeared him to the people. Even his nocturnal escapades won him the affection of many who would have loved to share in those pursuits had they enjoyed the power and position of their idol.

The first years of his rule were quite successful. The economic upturn of the 1920s offered him relative prosperity and industrial growth which helped restore the financial situation of the state and even initiate major public works. With the co-operation of foreign capital large companies were founded, thus emphasising the propensity of earlier decades to monopolistic enterprises and foreign dominance in key production areas such as electricity, public utilities and mining. The 'social climate' also improved very considerably. Despite record population growth and a faster-than-ever rate of migration from the countryside, workers' living conditions improved. Primo de Rivera reinstated some of the social legislation of the last years of the Restoration to cajole the socialist trade union (UGT) into a 'social pact', while maintaining the full rigour of the law in his dealings with CNT (the Anarcho-Syndicalist Confederation). Leading socialist trade unionist Largo Caballero collaborated with the Dictator in the creation of compulsory arbitration boards and parity committees.

Socialist collaboration with the interventionist state of Primo de Rivera was made feasible when the most militant sections of the movement broke away in 1922 to start a separate Communist Party (PCE), which won its main supporters in the industrial north and the Levant. UGT also broke its unity of action pact with CNT in 1920. Largo Caballero's collaboration with the forces of order gained him the opprobrium of CNT membership and made any co-operation between the two main streams of trade unionism virtually impossible in the future. It was not surprising, since CNT was bound to interpret this unilateral decision on the part of UGT as a means of strengthening their position among the workers at their expense. In any case, Don Miguel's social surgery, as most of his other half-hearted and half-baked programmes of political and economic reform, was very limited in its range and application. His social legislation did not extend to the countryside, and far more important agrarian issues were totally neglected.

The futility and pretentiousness of this military solution began to be apparent in 1926. Without substantial structural changes to improve the revenue-earning ability of the State and its budget management, capital expenditure in major public works proved well beyond the possibilities of the heavily indebted nation. No number of regulatory bodies to control and promote key sectors of industry could resolve this basic discrepancy between ends and means. His policy of import-substitution and his nationalisation of petrol distribution in 1927 alienated foreign capital, which began to leave the country. Severe devaluation of the *peseta* fuelled inflation and led to unemployment and a general deterioration in living standards. The number of strikes and demonstrations climbed back to pre-Primo days. In 1929 the UGT refused to collaborate any further.

Don Miguel's unprofessionalism, his chaotic private life and his overbearing and despotic manner did not win him new friends and the old ones withdrew their misplaced affection. The political bosses of the Restoration became resentful for their ostracism from politics. Catalan conservatives, who had encouraged him to seize power, were bitterly disappointed when the dictator suspended the *Mancomunitat* in 1924 and launched a provocative and derogatory campaign against their flag, their language and their *sardana* (national dance). He also managed to antagonise the intelligentsia of the country and the university student body. But most fateful of all, overconfident after his victory in Morocco over Abd-el-Krim at Alhucemas Bay in 1926, he dared take his blunted scalpel of reform to the artillery officer corps, and in so doing attempted to make changes against the 'harmony of the military family'. On 26 January 1930, without consulting the King, he appealed for support directly to his military peers, eliciting a very lukewarm response. On the

30th he tendered his resignation to Alfonso XIII, who was eager to comply lest the general wind of disaffection against the whimsical and cavalier autocrat should also blow the monarchy away. Don Miguel Primo de Rivera escaped to Paris, where a few months later he died apparently broken-hearted. The state hotels in historic buildings (*paradores de turismo*) scattered among some of the more picturesque spots of the Spanish geography are a fitting reminder of his passage. To this day the older generation remember him nostalgically as the only ruler who made Spanish trains run on time.

## THE THIRD DEFECTION OF THE BOURBON MONARCHY

After two unsuccessful attempts by General Dámaso Berenguer and Admiral Juan Bautista Aznar to restore the situation to the 'status quo ante' Primo de Rivera, Alfonso XIII felt forced to vacate the throne on hearing of the first results of the municipal elections of 14 April 1931. He had ascended the throne in 1902, and during his long reign he managed to acquire a well-earned reputation for constitutional impropriety, political and military interference and involvement in speculative business ventures. As the conflicts and contradictions of the country became more acute, the position of an interfering monarch was also bound to suffer. In the last analysis Primo de Rivera's coup in 1923 was perhaps staged to spare the army and the Crown the embarrassment of an investigation into the Moroccan massacre. Unlike his father, Alfonso XII, who was a jealous defender of the army's ways and privileges, Alfonso XIII had ridden rough-shod over some cherished military conventions. His stock with the political élites was not very high either. His glum acceptance of Primo's 'pronunciamiento' and apparent readiness to allow parliamentary appearances and constitutional politicians to be by-passed cost him their support. By 1931, apart from a handful of people, who included some political notables and key general officers, no one was prepared to champion a monarch who had shown such contempt for constitutional decorum and military sensitivity.

# *Spain's Second Republican Experiment*

The King's flight in the evening of 14 April 1931, when only part of the electoral returns had come in, justified their worst fears. When in difficulties the Bourbon monarchs had shown their readiness to flee to the safety of self-imposed exile, leaving the country to fend for itself. As in 1868, the leading forces of the nation closest to the source of power again exposed their willingness to sacrifice a particular monarch as the price for the appeasement of the verbal tide of Republicanism and popular clamour in the streets of the main cities. The military's refusal to intervene in 1931 goes a long way towards explaining the advent of Spain's Second Republic. A contemporary British observer, H.W. Buckley, saw it as a 'negative pronunciamiento'. But the general 'abandonismo' (withdrawal symptoms) of the established forces and the feeling of outraged surprise point also to a political lockout, in the manner of Classical Persia when, after the death of the ruler, there followed several days of total anarchy so that the ruled would see salvation in the restoration of authority and order by the new holder of power. Meantime, the new system of government would have to be watched and guided from within. Don Miguel Maura, the eleventh-hour Republican and son of the leading Conservative politician of the first quarter of the century, was the one to install the Provisional Republican Government in the Home Office, while Alfonso XIII was setting off for Cartagena bound for London.

Provisionally, then, Spain engaged in a second Republican experiment, which was to prove as transient, confused and violent as the one that followed the 'Glorious Revolution' of 1868. To be viable the new Republic, *la niña bonita*, had to create an entirely new structure of power. The person of the king may have been removed from the driving seat but the institution of the monarchy was much more than the monarch himself; it was the kingpin of the economic and political fabric of society. Very quickly the 'living forces' of the nation got over their initial surprise and disarray, and proceeded to regroup and climb back to their 'natural' places in society by any means at their disposal. That implied the eventual restoration of the Crown at the top of the pyramid, as in 1814 or 1875. Indeed, for the President of the Provisional Government, Don Niceto Alcalá-Zamora, 'the ideal Republic would have been the monarchy without a king.'

The forces of reaction had no difficulty in finding ground for dissent or revolt; not even total inaction from the provisional government would have prevented clashes with the old order. To carry out a minimum programme of reform, the new political élite had to address some fundamental tenets of Spanish society and challenge social forces which were ready and willing to take pre-emptive action against any such attempt or to sabotage the workings of the system. As observed by a distinguished Republican supporter, the new form of government could draw some comfort from the fact that it had not come as a result of yet another *militarada* (military jink). But it was too early in the day to trust to the new legitimacy of popular consent when, apart from the upper surface of the political apparatus, the administration of the nation remained intact.

On the very day the country rejoiced, full of hopes and expectations over the arrival of *la niña bonita*, one of the serious bones of contention of Spanish society burst onto the scene, laying bare the precariousness of

Gaudí's Parc Güell in Barcelona

the minimal agreement that had brought anti-monarchical forces together. Companys hoisted the Republican 'tricolor' on the balcony of the Barcelona Town Hall and Maciá, the leader of the triumphant Republican Left (Esquerra), declared Catalunya to be a separate and autonomous state, an integral part of the Iberian Federation. On 18 April three ministers rushed to the Catalan capital to make Maciá withdraw his declaration of independence and stick to the terms agreed by the Republican Action Committee in San Sebastián on 17 August 1930 – that is, to draft a statute of autonomy for submission to the Catalan electorate and ratification by the national parliament in due course.

## CHURCH, AGRARIAN REFORM, REGIONAL AUTONOMY AND EDUCATION

The storm over regional aspirations was barely settled, or simply driven into sidings in order not to wreck the Republican coalition, when an old and even more divisive issue confronted the inexperienced politicians of the left and centre of the coalition with a shattering test to both the question of aims of the new dispensation and the question of means to achieve those ends. The challenge to the provisional government came heralded by the strong banner of tradition and belief, the organic conjunction of institutional forces under the battle-cry of 'God, Country and King'. Relations with the Church could not be easy, especially in the context of rather extravagant, hasty and impolitic promises of religious freedom and lay education. On 1 May 1931 Cardinal Segura, Archbishop of Toledo and Primate of Spain, expressed in no uncertain terms what the Church thought of the Second Republic. Don Fernando de los Ríos, the provisional Socialist Minister of Justice, saw Segura's letter as a declaration of war.

On 10 May the Monarchist Club in Madrid held a meeting well attended by prominent members of the propertied classes, who made no bones about their hostility to the new system and their intention of working for the restoration of Alfonso XIII. The popular protest against the meeting escalated into a series of riots and burnings of convents and churches throughout the peninsula which predictably were manipulated by traditionalist circles as clear vindication of their fears for the safety of the Church and the maintenance of public order. Relations between

Church and State deteriorated further with the publication of plans to remove religious images from schools, secularise teaching and cemeteries, legalise divorce, prohibit such public functions as Easter in Sevilla, withdraw financial contributions to religious orders, and expel the Jesuits from Spain. The hot summer of 1931 came to the boil on 8 October when parliament proceeded to debate the diminished role of the Church in Republican Spain. The excited and intemperate week that followed was an indication of the extent to which the lines were drawn. The issue was central for the credibility of the new regime: at stake was no less than the socialisation and ideological control of the young. Nothing short of total restoration of the confessional state would have satisfied Catholic opinion. The new legislature passed the controversial articles of the Constitution but the government coalition was split asunder in the process.

In the early hours of 14 October, immediately after the conclusion of the parliamentary debates on the religious issue, Alcalá Zamora, President of the Governments, and Maura, Minister of the Interior, tendered their resignations; the Agrarians and the Basque–Navarrese block withdrew from the Cortes for the remainder of the constitutional debate; and Lerroux's Radicals, who abstained over the religious issue, chose now to distance themselves from their uneasy alliance with the Socialists and Azaña's Republicans. The second-largest party in parliament, with 89 seats to the Socialists' 117 out of 470, the Radicals refused further collaboration with Azaña in the formation of a government, on the grounds that they could not countenance Socialist participation. Azaña was a capable politician and a distinguished man of letters, exerting a considerable influence among intellectuals and professionals, but his own parliamentary group (*Acción Republicana*) could only muster 27 votes. The support of the leading intellectuals of the country, organised through the 'Agrupación al servicio de la República' and represented in Cortes by José Ortega y Gasset and Miguel de Unamuno, was also showing severe signs of strain. Their high hopes for the democratic regeneration of Spain did not stand up to the hustle and bustle of parliamentary life.

The general election of 28 June 1931 had given the Republicans a more emphatic mandate than the municipal polls of 14 April, but the Radicals' withdrawal from the parliamentary coalition in December weakened them beyond repair and put paid to any progressive legislation.

The next and, to all accounts, most crucial undertaking, both for the future of the country and the Republic, was the modernisation of agriculture and the installation of some measure of order and equity in the countryside. Over the previous hundred years there had been no significant improvement in either type of crops, culture systems or landownership and exploitation patterns. Structurally, then, agrarian Spain could still be severely hit by underproduction and overproduction. The drought of 1930 ruined the olive crop, throwing a province like Jaén into total destitution. The unexpected bumper cereal crop of 1932 and the equally excellent harvest of 1934, on the other hand, sent wheat prices plummeting, dramatically disrupting the subsistence economies of large numbers of small proprietors, shareholders and leaseholders of Castilla la Vieja. The world recession that followed the 1929 financial crisis of Wall Street did not help either. Spain's traditional customers for the horticultural produce of the Levantine *huertas* (Britain and France) returned to import quotas and protectionist tariffs. Unemployment was rising, especially in the south among the young, because of the high birth rate and restrictions on emigration.

The situation in 1931–2 for a general agrarian reform was less propitious than it had ever been, even assuming a genuine interest on the part of those who claimed to be sincerely committed to bringing Spanish agriculture into the twentieth century. The technical problems of a genuine transformation of the countryside were plenty: it had to encompass totally different agricultural conditions obtaining in different parts of the country. Early commentators on the impossibility of legislating for the whole of the country expressed dismay at the one-sidedness of the intended reform which seemed to concentrate almost exclusively on the problems arising from the latifundia of the Deep South (Andalucía, Extremadura, La Mancha, Salamanca and Toledo). The problems there were particularly acute – one million landless peasants living on the brink of starvation – but not unique. Whatever the difficulties of initiating change, however, even the minimum programme was defeated in parliament in the committee stages of the bill and never reached the Statute Book.

In the context of the balance of parliamentary forces described above and the legal, technical and political implications of the very serious issues involved a small but determined group of so-called 'agrarian deputies' could wreak havoc with the bill, not surprisingly considering that those expected to be in favour of a modicum of social justice for the countryside were conspicuous neither by their attendance nor their participation in support of the bill when the crucial debates took place from mid-March 1932.

If that were not enough to wreck any chances of getting any agrarian reform bill through, the Catalan Autonomy Bill came before the House in accordance with Article 3 of the Constitution, which described Spain as 'an integral state, compatible with municipal and regional autonomy'. Unlike the Agrarian Reform Bill, whose lack of progress was due as much to poor support as to the strength and resourcefulness of its opponents, the question of devolution encountered an even more determined opposition from all sides of the House, including some leading intellectuals (like Unamuno and Ortega y Gasset) who had been returned to parliament on a Socialist ticket. The cross-lines of political attitudes to the two bills were a measure of the serious obstacles in the way of a consensus on any social or political change.

These issues dragged on through the summer of 1932, wasting a great deal of parliamentary time. Had it not been for General Sanjurjo's rising on 10 August, these two bills crucial for the credibility of the government might never have seen the light of day. The failed coup shocked the government into action. Prime Minister Azaña seized upon the new mood of apparent unity to lend his personal weight to the debates. On 9 September the two bills were rushed through, Azaña himself being the first to admit that General Sanjurjo's action gave him the means to instil some substance into the provisions of the Agrarian Reform Bill. Some 90,000 hectares of land were expropriated without compensation from the aristocratic landowners involved in the coup. In terms of the land available for resettlement the Act was no more than a punitive measure against twenty-seven grandees involved in Sanjurjo's conspiracy.

In the field of education the first Republican administration managed to make a considerable impact. Expenditure was doubled in 1931 and

1932. The number of teachers increased by 5000 a year and their level of remuneration was also greatly improved. The cultural and educational brilliance of the period exceeded all expectation. The percentage of children attending school, for instance, rose from 40 in 1931 to 55 in 1932, and educational missions and school colonies were set up to reach the most deprived and remote parts of the country. Federico García Lorca (1898–1936) was one of the foremost writers, taking Spain's classical theatre to the four corners of the peninsula with the group of itinerant actors 'La Barraca'.

But the intended aim of providing schools for the totality of the population, thus replacing the Church monopoly, was well beyond the wildest expectations as to the financial possibilities of the State. Some 30,000 new schools were required but only 6000 were built between 1931 and 1933. Again the southern half of the country was the last to benefit from those improvements; it had to survive under subhuman conditions, deprived of any spiritual or physical sustenance, with an illiteracy rate of 44 per cent. Twenty years later, in 1950, Jaén's was still 36.9 per cent, and the lowest rate for Extremadura and La Mancha was Toledo with 25.4 per cent.

## *1933–4: A Turning Point*

The people who stood to gain from the promised changes grew restive and their frustration gave rise to increased militancy, strike action and land occupations. For their part, the propertied classes, although not seriously challenged in their wealth and privileges, felt nevertheless threatened and retaliated by withdrawing the land from cultivation, refusing to benefit from irrigation works built at the taxpayer's expense or to co-operate with government authorities, and victimising workers involved in trade union activities. The lack of social progress, coupled with a deteriorating economic situation in the country as a whole, which pushed unemployment to record levels, and events abroad (general depression and the rise of Fascism), made 1933 into the most conflictive year of the Republican period. The number of strikes were double that of 1932 and many of them developed into full anarchist risings, especially in the most depressed sectors of the economy – agriculture, mining and the building industry. Fatal confrontations between workers and the Guardia Civil were the order of the day. The Republican administration, caught between its regard for constitutional legality and concern for law and order, on the one hand, and the rising expectations of those whose votes placed them in power on the other, never enjoyed a moment's peace to take stock of the situation. Always overtaken by events, they governed from the start with the aid of emergency powers, willy-nilly adding to the confrontational situation in the country. By the summer of 1933 the credibility of the government with the workers' organisations was wearing very thin.

One of the many violent incidents between labourers and the forces of order culminated in the massacre of Casas Viejas (Cádiz) on 12 January 1932. An apparently isolated and localised outburst of anger and frustration from a small community in Andalucía brought down the full force of the Law, costing the lives of twenty-one defenceless peasants. Azaña was held to be responsible for this act of state terrorism; after all, this time it was the Assault Guards, specially created by the Republic to reduce their reliance on the Guardia Civil for maintaining law and order, that seemed to have exceeded all sense of proportion in meeting social unrest. Any electoral favour the anarchosyndicalist movement may have shown the government coalition in the early months of the Republic turned to violent confrontation. The movement was now under the control of the Iberian Anarchist Federation (FAI), which was committed to anarchist purity and revolutionary struggle and centred mainly round Barcelona and Zaragoza, although still strong in Levante, Málaga and the Lower Guadalquivir.

Large areas of southern Spain turned to organised labour as the best way in the political circumstances of the new republic to advance their claims for social justice and land distribution. A new organisation, FNTT (National Federation of Landworkers), set up in 1931, claimed half a million members by July 1933; it was affiliated to the UGT, contributing nearly half its total membership. The large influx of land-hungry, highly frustrated peasants from the south radicalised both the union and the socialist party (PSOE). On 23 July the UGT leader, Largo Caballero, explained to the Socialist Youth movement that his reformist illusions had been shattered by the intensification of the social conflict:

socialist aims could not be accomplished within a bourgeois democracy.

## CONFEDERACIÓN ESPAÑOLA DE DERECHAS AUTÓNOMAS (CEDA)

Chronologically, the rise of CEDA paralleled the growing militancy among working-class organisations. The latter were the product of growing frustration over a system of government which had raised their expectations sky high, while the former was the response to the threatening 'socialist' republic. The main thrust for this new organisation came from Catholic and cerealist Spain. We have referred on different occasions to regular crises in Spanish traditional agriculture; the early 1930s were one such critical period. In the spring of 1931 the provisional government, with socialists Largo Caballero as labour minister and Fernando de los Rios as minister of justice, issued a series of decrees that looked like shifting the protection of the law for the first time in Spanish history from the rich and powerful to the poor and humble. They added up to a considerable improvement in working conditions and levels of remuneration for the land workers. But for the employers it meant rising labour costs in a period of price contraction, particularly in 1932 when a bumper crop followed arrangements made for substantial imports of grain from abroad. It was easy to blame the then minister of agriculture, Marcelino Domingo, for the awful mess.

The idea of a new 'electoral organisation of social defence' came from a priest, Angel Herrera. In view of the disarray among monarchist groups, it was essential to create a nucleus of resistance to fight the new elections. The appeal was sufficiently broad to attract a wide range of support. Agrarians, Carlists, monarchists, employers' and Catholic organisations flocked to the defence of the Church and the social and economic status quo. José María Gil Robles, a young lawyer of Carlist parentage from Salamanca and Herrera's protegé, became its leader from its beginnings in April 1931. The Vatican was right behind the movement. In fact, when in March 1933 it rose fully-fledged from its first national congress as CEDA, it acknowledged the leadership of the Church of Rome in all politico–religious matters.

The general election of 19 November 1933 brought in a new coalition of forces from the right of centre to the extreme right. The Radical

Party emerged as the political protagonist of the new legislature and on 18 December its leader, Alejandro Lerroux, announced a government almost exclusively Radical. But their numerical strength in the polls was rather deceptive: their victory owed a great deal to electoral arrangements with CEDA, which actually was the biggest party in parliament. In the previous two years the Radicals had been able to hold the Socialist–Republican coalition to ransom. Now they found themselves in the same position, with CEDA calling the shots. The Radical Party in government had to pursue or agree to extremely reactionary policies to keep their marriage of convenience with CEDA, but in so doing alienated a substantial section of their own followers.

For his part, despite his maiden speech to parliament formally announcing that CEDA was in politics not to defend a particular form of government but to watch over 'the contents' of any form of government, Gil Robles seemed to be interested mainly in manoeuvring himself into power. For two years, while the wind of reaction swept away the small social advances the previous regime had made, Robles pushed the opposition into a corner, playing cat and mouse with Lerroux. The result was eleven government reshuffles in just over two years. CEDA was in and out like a yo-yo, withdrawing support to bring the government down over President Alcalá Zamora's delay in ratifying the amnesty for the August 1932 conspirators or over the government's decision to commute the death penalty on seventeen Asturian miners or over a forlorn attempt to introduce the mildest of tax reforms in a country where the wealthy were hardly touched.

Meanwhile, all signs of progressive legislation were eradicated from the Statute Book. In December 1933 the peasants of Extremadura were expelled from the estates occupied in 1932; the Municipal Boundaries Act, which ensured that labourers in a municipality would be given employment before bringing in workers from outside, was repealed in May 1934. Vizcon de Eza wrote then that there were 150,000 families in southern Spain lacking the bare necessities of life. Catalan autonomy was clipped over a new act to enable winegrowers to purchase the land held in lease after some years of cultivation. Basque autonomy, which had been endorsed almost overwhelmingly by Vizcaya and Guipúzcoa, was referred back for a further plebiscite by the dissenting province of

Alava. And all the time the Minister of the Interior, Salazar Alonso, engaged in a wholesale 'preventive brutality' (Paul Preston) to dislodge all socialist and trade union members from town councils and local organisations. The general strike called by FNTT in June 1934 was savagely reduced and the 'National Federation of Land Workers' decimated. Any semblance of 'social catholicism' there may have been in CEDA's early programmes was well forgotten. A fleeting reference from a CEDA minister of agriculture, Giménez Fernández, who contemplated the notion of creating a property-owning peasantry in line with the alleged social objectives of the Church, elicited the comment from an agrarian deputy that, should Rome's encyclicals attempt to take away his land, he would turn heretic. 'It is hard to write calmly of the utter lack of responsibility which these classes showed at such a critical period of Spain,' commented a British journalist posted in Madrid at the time.

## THE INSURRECTION OF ASTURIAS

By October 1934 the labouring classes of the country were at the end of their tether. But they feared much worse if CEDA actually formed a government. The prospect of it happening caused a wave of protests throughout the land. A general strike called by UGT and the Socialist Party fizzled out very quickly; in Catalunya there was a new attempt to resume and enlarge their autonomy as a separate and independent state within the Iberian Federation; and in Asturias the miners took up arms against the reactionary republic. The situation in Asturias was serious enough to necessitate the ferrying of colonial troops from Morocco all the way round to Gijón, and all the expertise and commitment of one of the most prestigious and capable young officers in the Spanish army, Don Francisco Franco. The repression that followed vindicated their worst fears. War minister Gil Robles threw the whole weight of the state against dissent of any kind. Azaña himself, who was in no way involved in the protest movement, was also harassed and persecuted in an attempt to destroy the smallest remnant of opposition.

The Asturian revolt may have been an isolated and hopeless struggle but it showed that the reactionary republic could not assert its authority without the full force of the colonial army, thus foreshadowing 1936 and the three years of war that obscurantist and reactionary Spain had to fight to turn the clock back. It also forced working-class organisations and left-wing republicans to come into an electoral alliance to win the next election. Azaña, now much stronger politically because of the campaign of vilification waged against him, was the first to see the folly of going to the country separately in November 1933 and worked hard to bring the democratic forces together so that they could regain power and continue the work of the first biennium.

# CHAPTER SEVEN

# The Civil War and its Sequels

## The Popular Front General Election of 16 January 1936

The very broad electoral alliance forged by Azaña brought victory to the forces of the left. The Socialists re-emerged as the largest majority in the Cortes, representing just under a quarter of all the seats in parliament; with Catalan *Esquerra*, Republican Left and Republican Union, they commanded an absolute majority under the leadership of Azaña. On 19 January an all-Republican government was formed, the Executive Committee of the PSOE having decided prior to the signing of the electoral alliance that they would not participate. Without the Socialists no government coalition was safe.

The opposition was dominated by the extreme right (CEDA), with the second largest majority but no Radical support. In fact, one of the interesting aspects of this election was the total annihilation of the middle ground, if that were the position the Radical Party was occupying at the time. Not even its erstwhile leader, the flamboyant and wily survivor Lerroux, was returned to the Cortes. The growing polarisation of the political forces of the country, together with an electoral system which greatly favoured coalitions, contributed to this sharp chasm in the legislative chamber. Outside, in the constituencies, political allegiances were evenly divided: of the 72 per cent who went to the polls (considerably more than in 1933) the two broad political alliances, extreme right and moderate left, collected 67 per cent, with only one percentage point difference between the two electoral groupings. The debate about the significance of the last Republican general election and the distorting and divisive effects of its electoral system as a contributing factor towards the final military solution is purely academic. The die was already cast and Spain was sliding swiftly towards violence and chaos.

Political ambitions and personal animosities played an important role in Spanish politics. The institutionalisation of the political process was just beginning; there was as yet no formal recognition of political parties as the main protagonists of political participation. In any case parliamentary democracy was already fatally wounded; from left and right there was ample evidence of increasing reliance on extraparliamentary activity seeking to subvert the system. Street fighting was escalating into gang warfare, reminiscent of the worst excesses of the early part of the century. The mixture of impending disaster and radical fervour reached its climax in July. To avenge the death of one of their comrades, on the 13th a group of Republican police officers assassinated the new leader of the opposition, Don José Calvo Sotelo. This was the detonator that set the country ablaze. A group of young army officers who had been conspiring for some time under the nominal direction of Sanjurjo (in exile in Portugal since the previous plot of 1932) decided to use the shock of Calvo Sotelo's violent death as the moral spur for the *pronunciamiento*. The signal for the uprising came from the army in Morocco on the 17th, and from there it spread to the mainland with varying degrees of success.

## A CUSTOMARY SOLUTION: BACK TO THE TRENCHES

The rising of a few officers under General Sanjurjo, the most senior army commander, was in the best military tradition. Intended as a replay of Don Miguel Primo de Rivera's successful *pronunciamiento* of 1923, the main actors expected acceptance if not support from the main garrisons on the mainland and the forces of law and order, for the sake of the 'harmony of the military family'. As the custodians of the 'essence' of Spain the military were coming to the rescue of the country from moral and territorial disintegration at the hands of anti-Spain and the depraved agents of international communism and freemasonry. The chief objective of the insurrectionists was to restore law and order. Their main political allegiance was to the Crown.

Most of the wealth of the nation and the contacts and influence abroad rested with the Alfonsine monarchists, who advanced the financial sinews of the uprising. The only populist element present in the initial stages of the 'nationalist movement' came from Carlism, mainly Navarra and Alava. Apart from the colonial army of Africa and the Carlist contingent (70,000 volunteers for the whole of the war), the territorial alignment of both loyalist and insurrectionist Spain to a great extent replicated the wide regional disparities of the country: traditional, subsistence agriculture against horticulture and industry; centre and south against northern and eastern periphery: rural backwardness against urban growth; and also rich against poor and centralist against regionalist. Such violent contrasts and struggles, however imbedded in the past, burst to the surface in specific circumstances with their own conditioning momentum. The long view from the future endows the past with an air of inevitability but contemporary perception of events might well have regarded their incidence as accidental, and therefore susceptible of conscious management by decision-making powers. And then there was chance, that improbable force which blots the copybook of the historical continuum.

By September of 1936 the geographical alignment of the warring Spains was quite predictably similar to the voting-behaviour patterns and growing polarisation of the body politic of the Second Republic. Nevertheless, there were random contingencies that explain that Zaragoza and Sevilla, for instance, were on the side of the insurrectional movement from the start. While Guipúzcoa and Vizcaya, on the side of the loyalists for the sake of their regional aspirations, pursued none of the Catalan revolutionary pathways and, until their surrender to the 'nationalist movement' in the summer of 1937, lived relatively uneventfully according to principles no less conservative and ultra-Catholic than those which some generals and colonels were seeking to restore.

Not only whole regions or large towns and cities went fortuitously one way or the other, but families were also swept about in the maelstrom of civil strife or caught up on the wrong side of the territorial divide. Unlike foreign wars that bind a country together in the face of an alleged or recognised external enemy, internal strife leading to a long and protracted war of attrition where both sides were determined to impose their exclusive interpretation of the social and economic shape of civil organisation tears the country apart for generations.

## From 'pronunciamiento' to civil war

The first two months of the conflict threw into sharp relief the wide social and territorial divisions which had brought the Iberian peninsula to this sorry state of affairs. While the loyalist side muddled through to restore the authority of the State internally and to organise its defences against the military rebellion, the dissident forces strove to bring their fight to the centre of power. Their objective was Madrid. But first they had to ferry their Moroccan army across the Straits of Gibraltar. This operation was made possible by the early intervention of Italy and Germany in the form of air transport and by the inability of the Republican navy to patrol Mediterranean waters effectively. Its ships' cruising range and fire-power left a lot to be desired, and denial of refuelling facilities in Gibraltar and Tangier rendered them useless.

The battle for Madrid in the autumn and winter of 1936 was the first pitched encounter between government forces and the insurgents. Five months of fierce fighting set the pattern for the long, all-out war of attrition Spain was going to endure. There was no quarter given from either side. The people of Madrid gave ample proof of their resolve and courage and found comfort and inspiration in the knowledge that there were friends abroad coming to their aid, even if Britain and France, who might have been expected to supply arms and equipment to a democratic government at a reasonable cost, preferred to remain outside while turning a blind eye to the open intervention of Italy and Germany on the side of the insurrectional forces. The only major power prepared to help the Spanish Republic to survive was Russia. The first Russian tanks were seen in action in the outskirts of Madrid on 24 October and the Russian fighters appeared against the skyline a week later.

International communism also helped enormously in raising the moral consciousness of the world's intelligentsia and working classes to the plight of the social and democratic Republic, and recruiting a large and enthusiastic army of freedom fighters from all walks of life. The Paris International Exhibition of 1937 was the venue for prominent artists

'Guernica' by Pablo Picasso © Dacs 1990 from the Museo del Prado, Madrid

from Spain to canvass support for the Republic. Pablo Picasso brought there his indictment against the bombing of the civilian population in the small market town of Guernica, symbol of Basque nationalism. Joan Miró, Salvador Dalí and sculptor Julio González were also represented. Equally expressive of the artistic and intellectual weight of support for the Republic was the gathering in Valencia in July 1937 for the Second International Congress of Anti-Fascist Writers of literary personalities from all over the world.

On 14 October 1936 the first foreign volunteers arrived in Albacete to be trained and dispatched to the Madrid front the day before the insurgents launched their general attack on the capital. Altogether some 35,000 volunteers (including 10,000 French and about 2000 British) are believed to have fought in the International Brigades between 8 November 1936 and 15 November 1938, when they were disbanded at a military parade in Barcelona in their honour where Dolores Ibarruri (*la pasionaria*) told them in a farewell speech: 'You may go proud. We shall not forget.' Very heavy casualties bear witness to their personal commitment and individual courage, and their contribution to the battle of ideas abroad was immeasurable. No other conflict in the twentieth century has so forcibly caught the imagination of writers, poets and film makers and their testimonies bear witness to the honour and glory of these people who, in the 'Battle of El Jarama' (6–27 February 1937), brought their faith, heroism and their lives, but also the hopelessness and tragedy of the struggle, to the cause of freedom and social justice.

But in a large-scale civil war with half a million combatants on either side personal daring and individual courage were much less momentous than financial resources and technical equipment, military know-how and unity of purpose. On all these counts the odds were heavily weighted in favour of the forces of reaction. The initiative rested all along with the insurgents, and the Republicans were forced to respond the best they could, cutting losses, reducing the lines of defence and hoping against hope for a negotiated settlement or a general outbreak of hostilities in Europe.

## THE INSURGENTS

By the end of August 1936 the boundary line between the two Spains ran from the west of Málaga in a vast semi-circle round Madrid to the east of Zaragoza and the Pyrenees, and to the north-western corner of the country (Galicia). Between Navarra and Galicia stood Asturias and the Basque provinces. The insurgents' authority covered only a third of the territory and less than a third of the population but commanded the main wheat-producing areas of the country. Their military superiority was based on the army of Africa (some 25,000 Moroccans and legionnaires in the first instance). General mobilisation of the areas under their control followed instantly and the population of military age from the middle and upper classes were promptly recruited and trained as non-commissioned officers to man the lower levels of army command. In addition, by January 1937 there were 22,000 Italians, 20,000 Portuguese legionnaires, 6500 Germans and a few thousand volunteers from other parts of the world.

The strength and resolve of the rebellious army chiefs left no doubt as to the ultimate source of power and firm direction of the 'nationalist movement'. On 1 October 1936, at the behest of the Air Force Chief, General Kindelán, military command fell to General Franco who happened to be the man in charge of the main professional army corps. His military credentials as a professional soldier were unexceptionable; equally excellent were his political qualifications as a defender of law and order and staunch upholder of traditional values. He was not committed to any particular ideology, which made him particularly suitable as an arbiter between the various political formations.

Supplies and technical equipment of the best quality arrived easily and largely on credit. Portugal's Salazar was most sympathetic to the rebellious officers, helping with the transfer of weapons to the insurgents. Germany and Italy recognised Franco's regime as the sole legitimate government of Spain on 18 November 1936, ten days after the start of the siege of Madrid. But it was not only from Germany, Portugal and Italy that the insurgents received constant and substantial help from beginning to end of the conflict. 'Nationalist' agents and envoys were able to purchase on credit in the sterling–dollar area services and equipment that the Spanish government could only obtain with great difficulties through cash payments.

## *One Leader, One Party*

Once in control of the armed forces Franco did not take long to assert his authority over the political ingredients of the 'nationalist movement'. Prominent Alfonsist civilians and the majority of the rebellious officers were of the view that the restoration of royal authority would have to be deferred to the requirements of war; it was not the time to contemplate political compromises which would obstruct the military objective. The ideological coherence of the uprising was soon given the best possible fillip by the Church, which lent its weight of centuries to the 'crusade' against the infidel, the anti-Christ, the godless Republic of 'Jews, Masons and Communists', the unholy alliance of the enemies of 'authentic, eternal Spain'. The loyalist stand of the Basque and Catalan ecclesiastical hierarchy did not seem to exercise them unduly, nor indeed the initial prominence of the Moors, as main participants in the reconquest of the Iberian peninsula. The tactical pragmatism of the military leaders of the 'movement' experienced no serious difficulty in absorbing the political organisations channelling civilian militancy. Carlists and Falangists had political aspirations of their own but their chances of installing themselves in the top echelons of the chain of command were very slim.

On 18 April 1937 Franco decreed the foundation of the one civilian formation to incorporate all the 'respectable' political forces of 'eternal Spain': FET y de las JONS (*Falange Española Tradicionalista y de las Juntas Ofensivas Nacional Sindicalistas*. The 'T' (for Navarrese Traditionalism) stood discreetly among the initials representing the 'crusading' spirit of Catholic, conservative, agricultural Castilla la Vieja (the enterprising core of Imperial Spain now aiming to relive the glorious past with the help of the tail-end of colonial Morocco). The architect of this amalgamation, Serrano Súñer, Franco's brother-in-law (*el cuñadísimo*), was well positioned to conclude later on that 'the centre of gravity of the regime, its true support, was and continues to be the army'. On the surface, the ideological baggage containing the 'Nationalist Movement' derived from José Antonio's Falangist programme of 1934. It offered a modern-sounding discourse which related to Mussolini's Fascism and syndicalist aspirations at the same time, thus updating the recent proclamation of Javier Pradera in *The New State* for a corporatist structure based on the natural, 'organic' social forces of the nation. 'Nacional-sindicalista' was the new denomination intended to create the orderly framework of relations for the different strata of the productive system.

## REPUBLICAN SPAIN STRUGGLING TO SURVIVE

Where the insurgent forces were soon coalescing into a block of destruction, strongly defined in social, economic and political terms under the authoritarian control of a professional army, Republican Spain retained the economic and regional variations that had militated for centuries against social cohesion and political unity. Republican Spain was both agrarian and industrial, and the social dreams and aspirations arising from the inequitable and imbalanced growth of the preceding century were compounded by the reassertion of regionalist aspirations.

The composition, chain of command and resource situation in the government forces encapsulated the insurmountable obstacles in the way of a concerted effort to beat the challenge of the insurrectionists. What characterised the development of a Republican army, their strategy and tactics, wrote its English historian Michael Alpert, were the sorry tale of their continuing shortages and the disrupting effects of constant interferences from national and international political tensions. However, despite this background of intrigue and strife between political formations, revolutionary goals, military exigencies and regional disjunction, Republican Spain managed to bring its dispersed forces under centralised military control, albeit at the expense of the revolutionary gains of the first year of the war. The sacrifice of these gains on the altar of military efficiency for the sake of final victory has been the subject of heated arguments among the vanquished ever since. Whatever the personal enmities and antagonisms of the Republican leaders and their genuine thoughts and aspirations on the question of the model of civil society they were fighting for, short of unconditional surrender, the overwhelming and isolated presence of Russia's aid, paid for in advance and in solid gold, was decisive for the continuation of the war.

The interests and ambitions of the western powers did not help Republican Spain very much either. The lack of support from western democracies 'aided Franco as decisively as if [they] had sent arms to him' (Jill Edwards). For instance, British appeasement towards Mussolini for the sake of an agreement in the Mediterranean encouraged the latter to play a prominent and overt role in support of the insurgents. In fact, in the midst of a great deal of self-interest on the part of the various European powers involved in the Spanish question, only Italy provided human and military resources in a generous and undemanding way and when the conflict was over showed a great deal of forbearance and understanding in settling war debts with Generalísimo Franco.

REPUBLICAN EPILOGUE

By the summer of 1938 the 'nationalists' had reached the Mediterranean and the Pyrenees between Jaca and Andorra cutting off Barcelona from Valencia and separating it from the hydro-electric plants of the northern watersheds that supplied its energy. The Republican forces could just about hold the line of defence but it was only a matter of time before the final offensive would come. Prime Minister Negrín continued to negotiate on all fronts, hoping for the outbreak of a general European war over Czechoslovakia, which did not come. Britain's surrender to Hitler's plans at Munich on 29 September 1938 occasioned Russia's withdrawal from Republican Spain and the resumption of German deliveries to enable Franco to launch the final offensive against Catalunya on 30 October. No longer a match for the advancing 'nationalist' armies, the Republicans were routed towards the French border. Barcelona fell on 25 January 1939; the war was nearly over.

Britain and France were the first to come to terms with the new situation. The increasing threat of a European war obviously made the foreign policy-makers of those two countries realise the crucial strategic importance of the Iberian peninsula as long as it was in the 'right' hands. It was imperative to work on Franco to keep him from his former supporters. They did not wait for the fall of the capital to recognise the nationalist forces as the sole government of Spain on 27 February 1939.

The conflict dragged slowly on to the bitter end the way it had started. After all, the two sides of the embattled struggle were part of the same whole. The presence of the Republican government in Barcelona from the end of 1937 caused endless friction between the centralist authority and Catalan susceptibilities. While Azaña and Negrín to the end of the war looked upon Catalunya as a state within the State, not fully contributing to the war effort against the common enemy, Catalans felt that the central government was constantly seeking to erode their autonomy and regional identity. And Madrid in the last weeks before its fall on 28 March 1939 witnessed a military coup against the Communists, intended to facilitate a negotiated settlement with Franco.

The Spanish Civil War was, in the first place, a class war which the 'right' sections of the community won because they had on their side the unity of principle and firmness of purpose to reassert their vested interests and reaffirm the integrity of the nation. The defenders of democracy and of a more equitable civil society lost their fight because the nature of their cause was both complex and volatile. Local idiosyncrasies, widely differing models of social organisation and regional disparities fragmented the war effort and gravely impaired the fighting spirit of the people. Spain was a divided country condemned to resolve her differences by war. The hardest lot of the contest fell upon the Republican mix of social and political groupings which not only embodied all the strife and discord of the previous century but also had to contend with an international situation not at all interested in Spain's second republican experiment in liberal democracy.

## *The New Spain: 'España, una, grande y libre'*

After the celebrations of Victory Day, 1 April 1939, the new masters of Spain proceeded to apply the iron rod of their military rule to the vanquished territories. Not the slightest dissent was to be countenanced. Total restoration of social order and political authority was the minimum goal of the new dispensation. The whole of Spain was reduced to the single and absolute authority of the new head of state. The triumphant nation was an 'organic totality' with no private jurisdictions or separate identities. Those individuals, groups or regions who in any way collaborated with the 'reds' (all Republicans) were meted out a very short shrift purported to obliterate even their memory. Those who had not fallen before the mortal wheels of the war machine (like Lorca who was shot in his native Granada in the early days of the war), or did not quite manage to flee to the relative safety of foreign lands (like the poet Antonio Machado who died from mental and physical exhaustion on 22 February 1939 in a small French town close to the border, soon after his narrow escape through the Catalan Pyrenees), were put through the ordeal of death by summary execution, long prison sentences in labour camps or, for the least unfortunate, total deprivation of any basic civil rights, ostracised from public life and stripped of their social and occupational skills.

Among the first measures of the new order there figured a total revision of teaching materials, overhaul of secondary, university and primary education, and a ruthless purge from the teaching establishment of all Republican sympathisers and collaborators. Six thousand secondary teachers were shot and some 7000 imprisoned. The intellectual and artistic élites of the country were made to leave or chose to exile themselves from the rickety world of ideas and mental attitudes of the new regime.

Wholesale retribution and physical and mental annihilation were the only means to return to the natural order of things, eradicating for ever Marxists, Jews and freemasons who had conspired to destroy the very essence of eternal Spain. The atmosphere of repression was blurted out in the regular press. A Falangist publication, appropriately called *Redención* (Redemption), encouraged the nation to denounce the traitors in their midst and signalled the way to contrition through pain. Prison was not enough to cleanse political sins. The film by Basilio Patiño, *Canciones para después de una guerra*, recaptures the mental deprivation and garish entertainment of these years, a far cry from the intellectual brilliance and daring experimentation of the pre-war decades.

## RESTORATION OF THE SOCIAL ORDER

The religious orders were entrusted with the education of the young who were rich and socially sound enough to benefit from private education. In this function they were complemented by Falangist and Carlist youth organisations and the compulsory period of military service which completed the process of assimilation into the totalitarian whole. The family, which sealed the marriage between Church and State, was firmly placed under the authority of the former. Divorce was made illegal (23 September 1939) and a religious wedding ceremony obligatory (10 March 1941). The Spanish catechism to be used in all religious instruction, the 'New Ripalda', enumerated the modern errors condemned by the Church: 'Materialism, Darwinism, Atheism, Pantheism, Deism, Rationalism, Protestantism, Socialism, Communism, Syndicalism, Liberalism. Modernism, and Masonry.' And the rule prescribed to avoid these errors (from the 1944 version) was: 'Do not read any newspaper without the previous consultation and approval of your confessor.'

Carlists in Navarra and Alava, and Falangists in the rest of Spain were the foot-soldiers, the service class of the new politico-military edifice and the willing purveyors of the official state doctrine. The backbone of the national-syndicalist regime was the vertical trade union (*sindicato*) where employers and employees resolved their differences in a spirit of service and co-operation. The workers would benefit from the implementation of the social legislation of the early decades of the century while for the employers there was full recognition of private enterprise and property as the perennial sources of the economic life of the country. The administrative structures of this new version of corporatism provided jobs and sinecures for the new breed of servants of the State. The Syndicate (one for each sector of economic activity) was the most convenient medium for supervised collective bargaining and the channel for the resolution of industrial and labour disputes.

# *Don Francisco Franco Bahamonde, Caudillo de España*

The ideological exclusivism of the new regime was undoubtedly the offshoot of the prevailing desire for order, private property and Catholic orthodoxy. Nevertheless, it was Generalísimo Franco who was invested with all the powers of the State with the full backing and recognition of the two buttresses of society, the Military and the Church – the towering embodiment of the nation and subject to no earthly control, since his right to rule derived from victory over heathens and infidels 'to the greater glory of God'. After all, 'the Champion of the Crusade' had reconquered metropolitan Spain from the tail-end of the empire.

The Moors from Morocco, who played such a crucial role in the early part of the war, may have felt slighted by this slanted vision of the Spanish past. Some of them, of course, had honours heaped upon them for their loyalty to the cause: the Grand Vizier of Tetuán (the capital of the Moroccan Protectorate) was awarded (19 July 1936) the first *Laureada de San Fernando*, the highest military distinction of the realm, bearing the name of the great crusader himself, Fernando III de Castilla. But no matter, historical consistency has never been a serious worry to a victor in battle; the past could be refurbished to make it fit the new image.

One of the early English biographers of Franco ascribed the secret of his continuing hold on power to 'a careful, almost pharmaceutically measured blend of the political ingredients in [his] camp, so that none should be left out and none should be dominant'. There was no secret, but a single-mindedness of purpose and decisiveness in the execution of his plans which had made his reputation in the Moroccan wars from 1912 to 1927. There it was in 1927 that he won his promotion to be one of the youngest generals in Europe at thirty-three years of age. The same cold-blooded presence of mind he showed against dissenting officers came through again in his dealings with the main civilian ingredients of the counter-revolution: Carlists and Falangists. The Unification Decree of 18 April 1937 brought them together under his generalship (*jefatura*), and ever since until his death he showed ruthless determination and resolve in the face of opposition from whatever quarter.

In the protracted and no doubt painful struggle to retain the reins of power Franco devoured or cast aside most of the close associates of the early days but was able to make new friends and win fresh adherents to his personal calling. The pre-eminent role played by the Falange in the first eight years of his rule can be seen as evidence of his need to control a large body of men personally loyal to him. Falangist membership shot up from 75,000 in the summer of 1936 to one million by the end of the war, and Falangist militias, the paramilitary force reorganised in July 1940, were not dissolved until 12 December 1944. Equally, the press and propaganda service of the State was placed under the control of the party in 1941 and remained there until its transfer to the Education Ministry on 27 July 1945. Since Franco was able to survive the formidable coalition of forces urging him to give way to the restoration of the Bourbon monarchy, his alleged quip many years later that Spain was easy to govern must be taken as a genuine assessment of his own excellent suitability for the governance of the country and its people.

## EARLY OPPOSITION TO FRANCOISM

In March 1942 came the first and only real challenge to Franco's autocratic rule, and it came from his closest retinue, key social and economic forces and the top brass of the military, and at the worst possible time on the international front. The majority of prominent soldiers, aristocratic landowners and the upper reaches of the professional classes – in fact, traditional, conservative, Catholic Spain – expected a return to normality, that is the monarchy, in the person of Don Juan de Borbón, Conde de Barcelona (his father Alfonso XIII had died in 1941). The first nucleus of conspirators formed a committee for the restoration of the monarchy. To add to Franco's difficulties in having to bring to heel some of the more powerful people in the land, some of them famous soldiers like himself, the balance of power in Europe was starting to turn against the Axis now that the USA had joined the war.

On 8 November 1942 the Anglo-American offensive in North Africa was launched. A few days later Don Juan issued his first anti-Francoist manifesto from Lausanne. Although Franco was personally guaranteed by President Roosevelt and British foreign secretary Eden that the landing was in no way intended to interfere in Spanish politics, he was fully aware that the monarchists were banking on allied support to further the cause of monarchical restoration. It must have been an impossible position. On 5 June 1939 Franco had told the National Council that the impending war in Europe was going to require a great deal of 'cunning circumspection' on the part of Spain. His first reaction was neutrality, but when the German armies reached the Pyrenees in June 1940, appearing to be unstoppable, his policy turned to non-belligerency. A new foreign minister, Serrano Súner, the leader of the Falange, who was known to be very pro-German, took charge of the new policy on 17 October 1940. Two years later the regime was given a face-lift with the creation of a national assembly and in September 1942 Jordana returned to the foreign office and to the policy of neutrality, providing a number of facilities for the Anglo-American landings in northern Africa and for air and naval operations from Gibraltar. Serrano Súner, *el cuñadismo* (Franco's brother-in-law), who had been the most vociferous supporter of Hitler, faded away from national and party politics. Two weeks before the Normandy landings, on 25 May 1944, Winston Churchill told the House of Commons that Spain had rendered an important service at a time when 'Spain's power to injure Britain was at its very highest'. For those who were banking on British support for the restoration of the monarchy, he warned that the internal political problems in Spain were a matter for the Spanish themselves.

It was this policy of benevolent neutrality towards the allies that enabled Franco to diffuse the monarchical opposition to his person, while maintaining a copious correspondence with Don Juan trying to fend him off with vague promises. But the pretender declared in an interview in January 1944 that on no account would he agree to a restoration based on the principles of the 'national uprising'. One by one Franco scattered the opposition through exile, dismissal from office or imprisonment, and by the end of 1944 he seemed to have established his authority beyond question. But the most formidable trial in this tug of war with monarchical tradition was yet to come. The prospect of victory over the Axis dictators was euphorically viewed by all opponents of the new regime inside and outside Spain as the sign of liberation from Franco's iron fist.

## A Different Image

During the autumn of 1944 and the spring of 1945 monarchist officers, conservative interests, moderate republicans and socialists in exile rallied round the restoration of the exiled monarchy as the plausible return to normality under the auspices of Britain and the USA. Spanish communists and left republicans in France, who had so actively contributed to the resistance movement against the German occupation, crossed the Pyrenees through Val d'Aran in September 1944. Their frontal attack failed but considerable numbers continued their struggle against Franco in small guerrilla units ('maquis' from the French 'maquisard') which operated throughout the north, Extremadura and Andalucía until 1951. On 19 March 1945 Don Juan restated his inherited right to return to Spain to reconcile all Spaniards. Even the Church, or at least the Primate of Toledo, Cardinal Plá i Deniel, expressed certain ambiguity in his support for the Francoist regime when he called for a wider political participation with stable political institutions, while the Holy See's legate in Washington, Monsignor Cicognani, had secret talks with socialist leaders Indalecio Prieto and Luis Araquistáin.

On the ninth anniversary of the 'glorious uprising' (18 July 1945) Franco tried to stem the tide of his critics by removing the most objectionable symbols of Falangist totalitarianism and appointing a new government (his third) more presentable to the western democracies: 'more in the nature of a military dictatorship traditional to Spanish-speaking peoples' and more akin to the Christian Democratic groups emerging in Germany, France and Italy. A Bill of Rights (*Fuero de los españoles*) was decreed, the high-sounding clauses purporting to institutionalise basic human rights, and the Church's role was brought to greater prominence. The years after 1945 were a period of intense clericalism through Eucharistical congresses, revivalist missions and Sunday campaigns for the propagation of the faith among non-believers (Domunds). The new men to project the new image were mostly members of a lay Catholic association founded by the Jesuit Angel Herrera (the guiding light behind CEDA in 1932) at the beginning of the century (ACNP: *Asociación católica nacional de propagandistas*). People like Alberto Martín Artajo and his successor Castiella at the Foreign Office, and José Ibáñez Martín and his successor Joaquín Ruiz Giménez at the Ministry of Education, filled important positions in the education, information and censorship services.

These signals to international opinion did not take the edge off the ground swell of opposition against the last of the western dictators. After victory over Hitler had been celebrated with the brief honeymoon between East and West, and the foundation of the United Nations at Potsdam on 2 August 1945, world leaders gave way to this swell of anti-Francoism. France initiated the campaign by closing the frontier on 1 March 1946. On 12 December the UN general assembly passed a resolution inviting all members to withdraw their embassies from Madrid. Spain was also excluded from all organisations set up to help with the recovery of western Europe. Considering the way some of the countries now clamouring for Franco's blood had contributed to his victory, their official anti-Francoism could be seen as a case of bad conscience. And it was this feeling, perhaps, that drew support for Franco from unlikely quarters when they saw this international condemnation as directed against all Spaniards, for the UN resolution contained neither economic sanctions to bring him down nor recognition of the republican government in exile. Nor, indeed, did Britain and the USA actively support the restoration of the Bourbon monarchy, on which most opposition forces were still pinning their hopes for a possible return home and general reconciliation.

For his part, Franco was quick to capitalise on these feelings with further indications of wanting to soften his grip. On 26 July 1947, after overwhelming endorsement by the nation, he formally declared Spain to be a kingdom. This plebiscite was claimed to be an endorsement of Franco's rule for life, especially when in August 1948 Don Juan de Borbón agreed with Franco to have his son and heir, Juan Carlos, educated in Spain as the intended successor when the time came. A new legitimacy had been carved out of victory and the inexorable defence of traditional and conservative values and beliefs. The world, or the parts of it which counted as far as Franco was concerned, was beginning to come round to his way of thinking. He had not been the 'Champion of the West' for nothing, while others were fraternising with communism. The implications of Spain's strategic position in the western Mediterranean were too obvious for the military and diplomatic establishment of the United States. The French frontier was reopened in March 1948 and successive visits from US naval officers paved the way for the treaty of military and economic co-operation signed on 26 September 1953. The same year Spain also signed an important treaty with the Vatican, thus enhancing Franco's sway over his Catholic subjects beyond any reasonable doubt, and in November 1955 the UN rescinded its 1946 resolution.

## FRANCO'S ARMED FORCES

Franco's sway over the country was therefore firmly and uncompromisingly established by the early 1950s. An accurate measure of his own position as the ultimate arbiter of Spain's political course was the way in which he kept the army throughout his rule. The new generation of high-ranking officers were either his personal followers or newcomers who owed their promotion and command to the Generalísimo. The State provided endless opportunities to satisfy their economic and social aspirations: for instance, a third of the ministers between 1938 and 1969 came from the military. There were also jobs and sinecures aplenty for all the excombatants and military ranks. In 1946 the budget for the armed and security forces accounted for 50 per cent of all state expenditure. In a highly bureaucratised and sedentary army the limited demands on career soldiers left plenty of room for other gainful occupations. For the young officers and professional soldiers who hankered after a modernised army, the military agreements with the United States promised updated equipment and training facilities in modern warfare techniques.

The social responsibilities of the State normally associated with the running of a modern society came a very poor second. As for the management of the economy, the Francoist State did not go far beyond the full and total restoration of property rights to the victors. In the context of internal struggles for a share of power, the European conflict, the subsequent quarantine placed upon Franco's regime and a series of disastrous harvests from 1946 to 1948 left the new order no room for manoeuvre. Making a virtue out of necessity, Franco's economic advisers were claiming to be operating a system of economic self-sufficiency which in any case seemed to concur with the strait-jacket of a siege economy, a return to the social and economic past, and total condemnation of any form of political or ideological dissent.

## THE HUNGRY YEARS

Cut off from the economic world outside, the first decade of Francoist Spain has been aptly described as 'the hungry years'. There is no dearth of examples, especially south of Madrid, of the scale of scarcity and deprivation unparalleled in Spain's living memory. The long-suffering mass of landless peasants were not even allowed the forlorn hope of escaping to the towns and cities. During those years it was the people from the towns who tried to move back to the country, in the hope of at least procuring the basic means of subsistence. One of the foremost economic exponents of the new regime wrote in 1941 that the per capita income of the population had sunk to nineteenth-century levels. Despite food rationing from 1939 to 1951 even the basic necessities of life, such as bread grain, were in dire need. In the 1940s half the active population of Spain was still labouring in the agrarian sector, agricultural produce representing a quarter of total production and accounting for two-thirds of total exports.

In the midst of this deep-seated agricultural depression the main beneficiaries, the large landowners of central and southern Spain, continued to prosper, strengthening their hold over the land by turning to direct cultivation, encouraged by the profits to be made from starvation wages, subsidised prices and the thriving black market in basic commodities. A network of corruption and graft enabled them to make the best of the state interventionist stand in prices, and to have first access to fertilisers and to agricultural implements when the exodus from the countryside, which started in the late 1950s, compelled them to mechanise. They could now pose as profit-minded farmers shaking off the opprobrium of centuries as a parasitical class living off land values rather than agricultural production. The structural changes of the 1950s were yet to bring to them a period of plenty, especially for wheat, wine and rice producers who could rely on highly subsidised prices, with little control from the State as regards either quantity or quality.

The mass of landless peasants was consequently enlarged with new recruits from among small proprietors, leaseholders and shareholders who had to sell or vacate their plots to those who had sole access to the capital accumulated under these conditions or were reclaiming their own land for direct cultivation. The alleged ruralist bias of the 'nationalist uprising' was no obstacle to these developments. Lip service was paid to irrigation and technical modernisation, expropriation and redistribution of large estates, colonisation of uncultivated land, and concentration of the twenty-two million fields of less than two hectares in the poor dry lands, still the most intractable problem of Spanish agriculture. By 1970 landless labourers and subsistence and middling peasant farmers, a total close to three million people, had left the land. The massive displacement of people from the countryside well exceeded the human losses caused by the civil war, subsequent repression and exile.

The industrial landscape of Franco's Spain in its first phase was equally grim. All levels of production, consumption and investment fell to pre-war levels in a general process of retardation without parallel since the darkest hours of Fernando VII's reign. Countries like Italy, Greece and Yugoslavia doubled their industrial production in the five years after the war. Even the worst industrialised nations initiated their recovery quite quickly. It is true that they had US aid programmes to help them, but Spain did not suffer as much devastation from her own war either in the fields or in the cities. Republican militias may have burnt churches, but not factories; and the worst of the fighting had taken place in open country along the lower Ebro. Transport and livestock were not very badly affected. The victors themselves claimed that the work of reconstruction had been completed by 1945. Agricultural depression in a predominantly agrarian society failed to bring the resources and demands that fuel industrial growth. It was not entirely a coincidence that the first signs of industrial recovery should appear in 1951 after the best grain harvest for a decade. The harvest of 1945 had been the worst of the century so far.

## A SIEGE ECONOMY

The crude mixture of interventionism and traditionalism, dressed as self-sufficiency, compounded the abyss of fear and deprivation. It was a form of 'economic paternalism' not basically different from what had gone on before: import substitution and protective tariffs. The regulatory excesses of the State, without any overall pattern other than protecting the social and economic structures of the nation, and the lack of human and technical resources to guide the economy or promote growth led to fear and uncertainty, which discouraged enterprise and stunted labour. Whether out of virtue or necessity, self-sufficiency caught the Spanish economy in a vice the grip of which could only be released through trade liberalisation and opening the productive processes of the country to international markets.

An economic policy of slow or no growth in the short term suited a closed system of societal organisation. The Francoist regime made development and growth very difficult. The inadequate administrative framework inherited from nineteenth-century liberalism was actually further reduced and weakened so as not to interfere with private interests. In all areas where the State is assumed to play a prominent role, the function and scope of the Spanish administration grew smaller, with fewer resources, both human and financial. The seemingly parodoxical nature of Franco's new order may be characterised by its unique blend of ideological exclusivism and economic anarchy. As a percentage of the national wealth, State revenues fell sharply from 18.61 in 1935 to 11.12 in 1955. Furthermore, in the early 1970s 55–60 per cent of public income was still coming from indirect taxation collected from goods and services, while income tax levied on earnings and property accounted only for 33 per cent. Between 1945 and 1953 the level of wages of the working classes in the urban areas was around 50 per cent of the pre-war level. In one of his more perceptive moments Franco himself confessed to a situation in which the crusade had been 'the only war in which the rich became richer'.

And yet a system of societal organisation so desperately seeking to wind the clock back could not stop internal and external forces from propelling the country along the avenue of industrial growth and economic development at the expense of the staid and regressive features of the recalcitrant past.

The painful regression of the dark years of Francoism looked as though the country was taking a leap back into the past the better to move onto the greener prospects of the future. Between 1951 and 1973 Spain underwent a total transformation which some western European societies had taken a whole century to achieve. The speed and depth of the changes were all the more remarkable when seen against the low ebb of post-war repression, international isolation and utter misery and deprivation for the large majority of Spaniards. Even within the inner circle of the Francoist oligarchy there had soon been advocates of change. Manuel Arburúa, the trade minister in Franco's fourth government (1951), initiated his term of office with a series of measures purporting to introduce a modicum of order in the management of the public sector, to liberate the economy from the more obnoxious forms of state intervention, open up markets and encourage free enterprise. The same wind of change breezed into the ministry of agriculture under the aegis of energetic and enterprising agronomist Rafael Cavestany; he too brought to the Spanish countryside some relief from state intervention, letting agricultural prices drop in relation to industrial prices, and encouraging modernisation through capital investment.

## US AID

Capital gains from starvation wages and protected agricultural prices began to feed into banking institutions and industrial investment. To judge from Franco's determination to reach an agreement with the United States at whatever cost, the Head of State himself, though primarily perhaps for the sake of his own survival, acceded in theory to those liberalising views of the economy. In addition to the military agreement, the 1953 Treaty provided some financial and economic aid, together with recommendations to move closer to an international market economy – i.e. monetary and financial stability, relaxation of trade controls and public sector restraint.

The economic and financial aid assigned to Spain in return for the establishment of several US military installations on Spanish soil was preceded by private loans from banking organisations which set the scene for a constant and massive flow of US dollars to the present day. US aid must figure as one of the prime motors of Spain's economic development. The Catalan economist Joan Sardá Dexeus wrote of the first aid from across the Atlantic that it was to the Spanish economy like water to a desert. It enabled the authorities to stop food rationing and to purchase badly-needed cotton, soya-bean oil, animal fodder and fertilisers. In the very short term it helped stabilise prices until 1954, and industry started to expand. In the medium term, however, this input of foreign capital acting upon a low-productivity and tightly-corsetted economy sent the already strong inflationary trend into a spiral which led, from 1955 to 1959, to a trade-balance deficit five times the corresponding annual average of 1945–9 and suspension of foreign debt payments.

## On the Brink of Bankruptcy

It was a very serious financial and economic crisis, but not surprisingly it came in the wake of a serious relapse into acrimonious feuding between the political families within the regime, and the growing challenge from industrial workers and disaffected students to the model of economic development and political stagnation. In addition to the new treaties with the USA and Rome in 1953, Spain also became a full UN member in 1955. But the joy of her reconciliation with the main debating chamber of the world was soon dispelled by a very frosty start to the year 1956 and subsequent hurricane winds and dramatic flooding in the Levant in 1957. Industrial workers had returned to life, from the fear and starvation wages of the 1940s, under the umbrella of Catholic workers' organisations and were greatly encouraged in their consciousness by student dissent. The first serious strike (public transport workers) occurred in March 1951 in Barcelona; there followed a similar stoppage in the important shipyards of Euskalduna in Bilbao in December 1953, and widespread industrial action in the spring of 1956 in Catalunya, Asturias and Pamplona.

In 1954 the government tried to overcome some of the problems relating to excess production in some industrial sectors (such as textiles) by increasing the purchasing power of the consumers through wage increases. In the circumstances these rises could not fail to give another twist to the inflationary spiral, further eroding workers' income and fuelling industrial militancy. Some of the workers' demands were met: on 24 April 1958 a limited instrument of free collective bargaining was introduced – the government retained the power to mediate between employers and employees with a 'compulsory settlement'. The regime seemed to have lost the initiative in industrial matters, but in no way, as we shall see, did it mean to lose political power.

## OPUS DEI: A NEW STYLE OF GOVERNMENT

In characteristic fashion Franco turned now to a new team that could cope with the more technical problems of the 1960s. They came from a semi-secret Catholic lay order, the secular institute of Opus Dei. Their prominence in cultural and scientific fields had started with the appointment by the ACNP minister of education Ibáñez Martín of José María Albareda Herrera to CSIC, the only research council in Spain, which provided funds and congenial atmosphere for young scholars to study at home and abroad. By the late 1950s the Opus Dei numbered among its members powerful business leaders and university professors. Their aim was to marry Catholic orthodoxy with the management techniques and conservative neoliberalism of US business schools. Their book *Camino*, the vade-mecum for a happy and successful life in the world of business and politics, stressed discipline and leadership, and recommended discretion as to their link with the order. In fact, different degrees of association permitted large numbers of people to join them whatever their walk of life or level of commitment to the Institute. But quite obviously, given their main objective of exerting a powerful influence in public life, they proselytised most resolutely among élite elements of society and promising university students.

These were the men who presided over the years of growth and rapid change. As university professors, financial specialists and businessmen they were believed to possess the expertise and technical know-how to lay the foundations for sustained growth and material prosperity. Furthermore, they brought to government from safe sectors of society a supposedly non-political preoccupation with economic problems which the regime could claim as evidence of the developmental character of the dictatorship. But these technocrats would have to administer very sharp medicine to the economic system before things could get better. Their remit, in the first instance, was the twin objectives of drastically reining in inflation and bringing the balance of trade deficit into surplus in the shortest possible time. Spain had to be made solvent before anything else. In the medium term the object of the exercise was to lay the foundations for sustained and balanced growth in the context of a closer integration with the international market economy. As practitioners of an orthodox neocapitalist philosophy and firm believers in the virtues of private

General Franco

enterprise and resource allocation through the market forces, their recipe for financial control and sustained economic growth, unequivocally endorsed by their foreign mentors, was a crude mix of fiscal and monetary instruments of stringent austerity which, in the view of the advising organisations (IMF and OECD), performed the trick.

## THE STABILISATION PLAN OF 1957–9

The first surgical instrument applied to the Spanish economy was the Stabilisation Plan of 1959, without doubt the most ambitious operation on the economic front. The first step in the new direction was to dismantle the discriminatory multiple rate of exchange set up in 1939, fixing instead a single rate at 42 pesetas to the US dollar in April 1957 (60 in 1959), as a move signalling the way for the lifting of restrictions to foreign trade and encouragement to foreign investment. The devaluation of the peseta, intended to make exports more competitive and to discourage imports, was followed by a number of other deflationary measures which cut dramatically into government expenditure and the public sector of industry, but also brought order and control to the financial markets and increased government revenues. To judge from the acceptance of Spain in international banking circles, by the end of 1958 the operation was well under way. The grand plan, like all important announcements in the Francoist period, was offered to the nation on the twenty-eighth anniversary of the 'Glorious National Uprising'.

The financial and monetary objectives of the Stabilisation Plan were achieved almost immediately. It was then time to look at the prospects for future development and this brought the World Bank mission to Spain in June 1961. In February 1962 Spain made its first application to join the European Economic Community, with very little success. On 3 August the World Bank team of economic experts made their report to the Spanish government. The encouraging and favourable nature of their views and recommendations clearly gratified their Spanish hosts, who made a considerable effort to publish it within two months. The pressure for political and economic modernisation was on, both from opposition groups within (Christian democrats and monarchists) and exiled socialists and republicans, who gathered in Munich to publicise their disaffection for the regime. This report was to become the blueprint for the four four-year development plans which emerged in the full blaze of publicity from the specially created planning ministry, to steer the economy through sustained growth and increasing prosperity. The first commissioner for the Economic Development Plan, stated in 1969 (the first year of the second plan) that a per capita income of 1000 US dollars would blunt all political opposition to the regime and ease social tension. The implicit bargain seemed to be that the nation would have to sacrifice individual freedom and political participation in return for balanced economic growth and rising standards of living.

## A Truly New Spain: Spectacular Growth and Social Transformation

Average national income trebled in ten years and all economic indicators registered a rate of growth which outpaced all capitalist economies except for Japan, Greece and South Korea. Admittedly these international comparisons are very misleading: Spain's point of departure was very low. The savage deflationary programme set off by the Stabilisation Plan actually brought the level of income per head down, but from 1962 it was always up: from 1961 to 1974 the average annual growth rate of national wealth was 7 per cent. The level of growth and the time-span were truly spectacular, especially against the background of barely one per cent cumulative annual growth rate from 1860 to 1950. Leading the industrial field were chemicals, steel, shipyards, car manufacturing and electrical equipment. Needless to say, television sets, cars and fridges far exceeded all other production; not for nothing was the planned growth based on the deliberate promotion of domestic consumers' rising expectations.

Agriculture, on the other hand, continued to lag behind in terms of both production and productivity. However, by 1978 Spain had become the world's leading producer of olive-oil and third in wine and citrus fruit, and the number of tractors increased fivefold from 1961 to 1974 while the use of fertilisers doubled. The improvements in productivity levels, mechanisation, diversification, distribution channels and managerial techniques would come in the 1970s and 1980s, when changes in consumption patterns and excess production of traditional crops in Europe yet again posed problems which the Castilian mesetas and the pastoral agriculture of the north-west were ill-equipped to cope with. Except for the horticultural produce of the Ebro valley, the Levant and Lower Andalucía (and even there citrus and early fruits, and wines, have to withstand very strong competition from north African and other Mediterranean countries), agriculture is still a deficit sector of the Spanish economy, importing expensive animal fodder from the United States, and meat and dairy produce to satisfy higher purchasing power and high-protein diets. Its diminished role in the productive system of the country does not help attract attention to its plight. The farmers' massive protest for more protection in 1976, for instance, while totally justified, commented the Banco de Bilbao's annual report, failed to draw an adequate response from the government since they only represented nine per cent of GNP, down from 30 per cent in the early 1950s.

Chronologically, agriculture was the first contributor of capital to industrial investment. It was an internal factor very limited both in quantity and scope; external sources, starting with the first US loans, were much more crucial. Furthermore, tourism and migrants' remittances provided the additional capital required to keep on fuelling growth while underwriting Spanish solvency. Since the awful prospect of insolvency in 1957 Spain's balance of payments has always been in credit with gold and hard-currency reserves worth $6.5 billion in 1973.

## INTERNAL MIGRATIONS

The most striking feature of these years of growth was the massive transfer of people from the land to the prosperous periphery and the industrial triangle of the north-east. Madrid, Barcelona, Valencia, Bilbao and Zaragoza were the main receptacles of this flood, which spilt over the suburbs, settling first in shanty towns (*chabolas*) and then high-rise blocks. Between 1950 and 1976 the people living off the land, as a percentage of the total active population, fell from close to 50 per cent to 21 per cent, a large proportion going to the services sector, which increased in the corresponding period from 25 per cent to 40 per cent. In other words, 12 per cent of the Spanish population (some three million people out of a total of 35 million in 1975) migrated, mainly from the south-western quadrant, with the provinces of Badajoz and Jaén representing more than 25 per cent of the total.

Escapees from the poverty of the 'frontier of underdevelopment' (Orense, Zamora, Salamanca, Cáceres, Badajoz and Huelva, along the frontier with Portugal) far exceeded the labour requirements of the Spanish 'miracle'. Fortunately, they were able to flee further afield, overseas or to France, Germany and Switzerland. In the 1950s there was a first phase of transatlantic migration of some 40,000 annually to America; but in the 1960s and early 1970s it was the industrialised nations of Europe that absorbed two million Spanish workers, hoping one day to return to their homelands with enough savings to build themselves a house and even purchase a small business. People may no longer starve to death, at least in western Europe, but they certainly get pushed around. Except for the very old and the very young entire villages were deserted.

This huge translocation of people from the countryside also meant total transformation of living styles and occupational activities. In the two decades between 1951 and 1971 Spain had changed comparatively much more than in the previous hundred years. Urban population increased at double the rate of the general demographic growth of the country. In 1960 38 per cent of the population lived in the eight more heavily populated provinces of Spain; it was fifty per cent in 1980. The massive concentration of population along the Mediterranean beaches, to the detriment of the rest of the country, is an excellent example of the staggering rate of expansion and the lack of co-ordination with other sectors of economic activity. The 2.5 million tourists visiting Spain in 1955 rocketed to 34.5 million, by 1973. They returned to a more reasonable level of 30 million from 1974 to 1976, only to rise again, to a maximum of 43 million in 1984, by far exceeding the local population. The income from this source doubled from 1979 to 1985, exceeding migrants' remittances and capital inputs from abroad combined.

THE SHORT CHANGE OF GROWTH

Spain's fast road to industrialisation and modernisation was paved with a number of hostages to fortune. Given the political make-up of the regime, it is questionable whether there was ever any chance of really guiding and monitoring this vast and disorderly shift of human and economic resources as long as the State continued to appropriate a very minor part of those resources. The revenues of the State did not appreciably increase during this period of growth. In 1974 its share of the national wealth was only 13 per cent, when in other European countries it was between 35 and 40 per cent. Evidently the ruling élites were not prepared to tax themselves or their supporters. The State could not therefore raise sufficient revenue to promote long-term investment in the country's infrastructure; state income continued to come mainly from the lower classes through indirect taxation – in 1974, for instance, indirect taxation contributed 60 per cent of the national budget. The State therefore lacked the resources to adopt a positive role in the economic development of the country, let alone redistribute wealth.

In an increasingly competitive and highly technological Europe, Spain at the end of a long and sustained period of remarkable quantitative growth was still spending in education and technical and scientific research much less than all her trading partners. The high level of dependency that made growth possible in the first place, therefore, did not decline. Quite the opposite. On 18 January 1979 the newspaper *El País* presented Spain as a collage of names like Ford, Zanussi, Rhone-Poulenc, Siemens. Underneath there was the legend, 'the world's tenth industrial power'. The World Bank had anticipated it was the price to be paid for development and modernisation. The heavy mortgage on the future of the country as a socio-economically balanced, independent and sovereign nation was not considered by the prophets of growth, who were instrumental in opening Spain to it not so much by what they did, but rather by what they stopped doing after the period of self-sufficiency of the first phase of the Franco regime. The critics of the imported model of growth claimed from the start that the country grew despite its political masters.

# CHAPTER EIGHT

# Contemporary Spain

## The End of Francoism

Since the State failed to produce an orderly and equitable model of growth and a wider forum of political participation, the deep-seated social and regional tensions of the country raised their head again, making Franco's last decade a long sequence of industrial stoppages, strikes, go slows and works to rule throughout the country. Where public order and the authority of the regime were concerned the Francoist State showed not the slightest sign of accommodation with any kind of opposition or dissent, whatever the source. All labour disputes were deemed to be political and therefore crimes against the State subject to the harsh penalties of Article 222 of the penal code. The usually uncompromising stand from the forces of order (martial law, state of emergency, police charges resulting more and more in loss of life) further escalated the level of violence and retaliation.

In addition to labour disputes and industrial conflict, the regionalist aspirations of the more prosperous provinces of Spain came to the surface again as a response to the repressive policies from the centre after the war. Severe cultural and political repression in Catalunya did not blunt their separate identity or desire for separate status and administrative autonomy. In the years of growth Barcelona became the most important publishing centre in Spain, with important ramifications in the Spanish-speaking world. The Catalan Church continued to foster cultural studies very prominently and set itself up as a Catalanist focus. In 1966 the Basque provinces also started reclaiming their rights, which they had enjoyed for a very brief period during the war. These provinces were probably even worse treated than the Catalans; Franco referred to them as the 'treacherous provinces'. ETA, the Basque separatist movement Euzkadi ta Askatasuna ('Basque Nation and Liberty') emerged now at the forefront of the armed opposition to the Francoist dictatorship, obviously with a wide basis of support both in the Basque country and other parts of Spain, which enabled them to continue their activities. In 1970 the famous process of Burgos against ETA militants raised widespread condemnation from international opinion and the government had to impose yet again a state of emergency in Guipúzcoa for six months. Even the Catholic Church was withdrawing en masse from the regime, seeking a separation between Church and State.

## DETERIORATING ECONOMIC CIRCUMSTANCES

The world economic situation was not helping Francoism either. From 1972 large price increases in basic commodities, together with oil price rises from October 1973 and disruptions in the international money markets, had a significant effect on the Spanish economy. Her weak industrial base, the restrictive obstacles from the recent past and the high level of dependence on energy resources from abroad made her specially vulnerable. World recession affected the very sectors of industry where Spain had been making the most advances in production. Inflation rose from 17 per cent in 1974 to 26 per cent in 1977; and unemployment was rendered considerably more serious by the return home of many whom the general depression had made unwelcome abroad. From the heady days of seemingly permanent and unlimited growth and prosperity, Spain was now having to readapt herself to a decade of barely one per cent rate of increase in the economic activity of the nation. And this was at a time when uncertainty over the political future of Spain was growing faster than inflation. In these circumstances it was unlikely that any minister of whatever political complexion would wish to take difficult or controversial decisions in the economic field. In fact, finance ministers came and went between 1973 and 1977, and eight different packages of economic measures were introduced to little avail.

While Franco was alive everything still hinged upon him and his ruling élites. Despite all the social and economic changes that had transformed the face of the nation, the dominating structures of the land remained intact and were not prepared to budge. The authoritarian and centralising regime pretended to give way over certain issues, as in 1966 with a new press law and a new definition of the State as an 'organic democracy', or in 1969 when, hoping to keep monarchists on his right side, Franco had Juan Carlos officially designated to succeed the Head of State as the future king of Spain. After all, Juan Carlos had been anointed by Franco and was therefore honour-bound to rule by the principles and values of the victors in the Spanish Civil War. A model of circumspection, Don Juan Carlos had given very little concern to the Francoist establishment. In retrospect his conduct and demeanour can be seen as a careful preparation for his future role as the master player of the nation's transition to democracy; but at the time his seemingly obliging attitude towards the principles of Francoism won him the nickname of Don Francarlos.

## *Admiral Carrero Blanco*

To ensure the continuity of the regime Franco could count on Admiral Carrero Blanco, his prime minister, but on 20 December 1973 he was assassinated in a most spectacular explosion in the middle of Madrid. Franco's apparent confidence in the future ('everything is signed, sealed and delivered') seemed utterly misplaced. He might have looked over his shoulder to his Portuguese neighbour Caetano, Salazar's successor, who was deposed by the 'carnations' revolution on 24 April 1974. There were not many of his comrades in arms and early companions left to project the spirit of his rule to another generation. With their plots and strident campaigns to block the passage of time, those very few still alive and active politically contributed to the crisis and uncertainty of the final phase of Francoism. On 12 February 1974 Carrero Blanco's successor, Carlos Arias Navarro, the first civilian prime minister in the thirty-six years of Franco's rule, seemed to be offering in a declaration of intent an olive branch and a glimpse of hope of reform to the millions of Spaniards clamouring for liberalisation, regional devolution, amnesty for political prisoners and urgent attention to the deteriorating economic situation. The system, though, could find no more reserves of strength or ability among its depleted phalanxes. It could still, however, mount a dangerous destabilising campaign in the spring and summer of that year to dispel any notion of a peaceful transition from within and prevail upon Arias Navarro to reassert Franco's principles.

The isolation of the forces of reaction was made clear in February when Arias Navarro tried to discipline Monsignor Añoveros, Bishop of Bilbao, over his appeal for the recognition of the cultural and linguistic identity of the Basque people, which had enraged the right. Arias Navarro had to beat a humiliating retreat which further accelerated the Church's withdrawal from the regime. They still proceeded with the execution of the Catalan anarchist Salvador Puig Antich and the Polish refugee Heinz Chez despite an uproar of international condemnation, and prevailed upon Arias Navarro to dismiss leading members of his cabinet who were in favour of carrying out the liberalising 'spirit of 12 February'. It was the last act of a totally spent play. *El Generalísimo* recovered, so it seemed, from the circulatory ailments that kept him under close medical supervision for most of the summer of 1974, but his public appearance on television on 30 December reassured the nation that his end was nigh. Spaniards waited with bated breath. Don Juan Carlos' circumspect attitude during the forty-six days from 19 July when he acted for Franco as Head of State continued to cause some apprehension. Some may have argued that his future role as a constitutional monarch was not to be taken for granted, nor his acceptance by the majority of Spaniards who might have looked upon him as Franco's creature. Perhaps his own father, Don Juan, was of the same view since he did not abdicate until 15 May 1977, a month before the first democratic election for a constituent parliament. The stock exchange seemed to provide the only clear indication of confidence and trust in the future: from the summer of 1974 to the end of 1975 share values rose by 7 per cent.

Notwithstanding the strenuous efforts of his legatees and beneficiaries to keep him in this world, Franco finally decided to part company with his frail body on 20 November 1975. Not even his closest advisers believed that he had definitely gone. It was generally rumoured in Spain that the first issue before the government was to decide who would have the audacity to tell him.

## *Don Juan Carlos I de Borbón*

On 22 November 1975 Don Juan Carlos was proclaimed King of Spain. The leader of the extreme right *Fuerza Nueva* (New Force), Blas Piñar, announced in *Cambio 16* on the 17th that there was to be no monarchical restoration 'but the installation of a new Francoist monarchy' with 'no other thought behind it than the Nationalist victory in the Civil War'. While chronologically correct this statement chose to ignore that the monarchy had a strong pedigree which had survived relatively unscathed through the long transitional period of the military dictatorship. It was Franco who, as early as 1946, had to prop up his own claim to power by formally declaring Spain to be a kingdom.

To a large extent Don Juan Carlos could feel that his own legitimacy preceded and conditioned Franco's. Nevertheless, short of embarking upon a revolutionary path the King had to accept his present predicament as the legatee of the dictatorship. Consequently, he would have to pay careful regard to the warning implied in Blas Piñar's assessment of his impending succession as a continuation of the immediate past. He could only escape from the constraints of that legacy by asserting his own legitimacy in the exercise of his kingly duties. His only chance of success and even survival hinged on his own tact and skill in steering the country back to constitutional normality. His predecessor on the throne, Alfonso XIII, had not left the sort of political memory that he could draw on. But his father Don Juan was advising him of the need to establish himself in the traditional role of arbiter in a pluralist democracy. Whatever his intentions, Juan Carlos would have to tread very lightly; to all intents and purposes he was now heading the Francoist establishment, including the president of the government Don Carlos Arias Navarro.

From the moment of his coronation several decrees signalled the way towards liberal democracy and constitutional monarchy. Within the Francoist establishment there were many who had come to terms with the wind of change and Juan Carlos I was wise to capitalise on existing

King Juan Carlos

institutions. Monarchical legitimacy was never questioned, nor was it defined; and when it was formally recognised in the Constitution of 1978, without debate or reference to the national will, it revealed in its wide attributes and powerful prerogative the full extent of that power. There was, therefore, no break in continuity: Franco himself had ruled as an absolutist monarch, and the succeeding monarch in the full and proper use of his powers, was entitled to seek political reform as an improvement on the existing system through the legal instruments of the Francoist regime. Article 56.3 of the Constitution of 1978 states that the monarch is inviolable and absolved of all responsibility for his acts. He was also the Commander-in-Chief of the armed forces and on the day of his coronation, after addressing the Francoist Cortes, he sent a reassuring message to them as defenders of Franco's Fundamental Laws.

## CARLOS ARIAS NAVARRO AND ADOLFO SUAREZ

1976 was not particularly propitious for political experiments. Arias Navarro's dilatory tinkering with the idea of a negotiated reform from above and his return to the worst repressive features of the Francoist dictatorship reinforced the opposition in their resolve to come together. The Communist Party, which had emerged as the vanguard of the fight against Francoism, was also prepared to drop its excessive demands for a full 'democratic break' with the residual authority of the Francoist oligarchy. That is to say, the call was still for a full reform with the cooperation of all political forces, including important reformist elements from the Francoist political past. The problem was, therefore, how to find a man who could reconcile the disparate elements in favour of reform, while minimising the danger of a full-scale confrontation with the *bunker* (ultra-right).

Reassured by the show of affection and support for himself during his triumphant visit to the United States in early June 1976, Don Juan Carlos gave notice of his intentions: Arias Navarro 'was an unmitigated disaster'. The president of the government resigned soon afterwards and on 3 July Don Juan Carlos invited Adolfo Suárez to form a government. His appointment annoyed those among reformist Francoists who might have entertained hopes for themselves, irritated the opposition who saw him as a man straight from the ranks of the 'nationalist movement', and surprised everybody on account of his youth and lack of experience. But it did appease the intransigent right and gave the breezy and articulate prime minister the space required to pursue the path of political reform before the forces of reaction could rally their efforts to stop it.

By then the opposition from the right had been weakened by massive defection to the side of reform, but they were still firmly lodged in the interstices of the institutions of power; furthermore, there were the armed forces that would require delicate handling. When the mood of a country is ready for a change of course, there usually emerges the providential man to take charge of the rudder. In retrospect Adolfo Suárez proved to be the man, cunning and decisive enough to make the passage through the heavily mined waters of Spain's transition from one of the most repressive examples of military dictatorship in western Europe to formal liberal democracy. But the crucial part in this political drama must belong to the monarch himself, for he was acknowledged to have the power to change course, to appoint the man at the helm and support him in the perilous journey.

## *Political Reform*

Despite the continuing deterioration of the economy and erosion of living standards, with unemployment and inflation topping the European league year after year (the former to a maximum of 21.9 per cent of the active population and the latter approaching 40 per cent in the autumn of 1977), the Spanish road to liberal democracy seemed fairly straight and relatively peaceful but not yet to be taken for granted. The first stage was the Political Reform Act of 18 November 1976, which the last Francoist assembly passed almost unanimously, thus disbanding themselves. In a referendum on 15 December the people gave it a resounding yes, 77.7 per cent of eligible voters taking part, with 94.2 per cent of the votes cast in favour of reform. On the 23rd the Spanish Socialist Workers' Party (PSOE) was legalised.

The next year nearly brought the whole pack of cards tumbling down. On 24 January five labour lawyers were assassinated in the centre of Madrid; two very prominent members of the political establishment were also kidnapped. On the one hand, the armed military wing of ETA kept up an intense campaign of violence, especially in the Basque provinces. Other not-clearly identified groups like GRAPO and FRAP added to the generally tense atmosphere in the first half of the year. But despite all the provocation from extreme left and extreme right the King and his prime minister went ahead with their task. The Royal Decree of 18 March 1977 called for the first free general election since February 1936, to be held on 15 June. After some tense moments and to-ing and fro-ing between the government, the Supreme Court of Justice and an important section of the army, the Communist Party under the leadership of Don Santiago Carrillo was also finally legalised on 3 April.

## THE FIRST GENERAL ELECTION SINCE 1936

The general election underlined the commitment and euphoria of the Spanish people. Of 23 million registered voters over twenty-one, 18.4 million (80 per cent) exercised their right. In terms of right and left, the results of 1977 were not unlike those of February 1936, the electorate tending towards a bipartisan system (UCD – Unión del Centro Democrático – and PSOE) and a broad measure of political consensus towards the centre. The modest results for the Communist Party, with 9.5 per cent of the vote and 20 seats (out of 350) in Congress, may be the offshoot of that desire to eschew what may have been perceived as an extremist option: even more modest were the results obtained by the self-styled 'civilised' right, as represented by *Alianza Popular* with 8.1 per cent of the vote and 16 seats. Many of those who might have been expected to throng *Alianza Popular* obviously cut their losses and moved over in a hurry to the governmental right. UCD was the phoenix rising from the ashes of the new party of government. To be fair, though, this defection to the new political 'centre' (UCD) of ex-Francoist leaders well integrated in the structure of power exposed a willingness to change. After all, Adolfo Suárez presented the UCD option as the party responsible for the democratisation of the country. The strength of the regionalist options in Catalunya and Euskadi was also a sign of continuity with political life before Franco.

In two respects, at least, the general election of 1977 endorsed a complete break with the recent past. There was no confessional force claiming a pre-eminent right to the vote of the faithful: the secretariat of the Bishops' Standing Conference issued a document a month before the election openly stating that no political party could pretend to be representing the Church. It is doubtful that it would have been able to exert any great influence in any case: the process of secularisation had taken giant strides in Spain in the last two decades. In the second place, there was complete unanimity as to the role and status of the Crown as the ultimate source of authority, the integrating force of the nation and its supreme arbiter. Juan Carlos I's father abdicated his historical right to his son a month before the first general election, and a year later the Carlist pretender, Carlos Hugo de Borbón-Parma, made peace with the King and was granted Spanish nationality.

## CONTINUING ECONOMIC DIFFICULTIES

The constituent Cortes had its work cut out for the following sixteen months. Its appointed task was to draft a legal instrument which would guide the nation through to the consolidation of the pluralist democracy within the formal context of a parliamentary monarchy. Deputies and senators faced very controversial issues which they would have to resolve in the only way possible – trust and reconciliation between individuals, groups and regions, as the King admonished in his opening speech. The nation and its political mandatories entered the second transitional stage. In October the government entered into a series of agreements with all political forces, known as the Moncloa Pacts after the President's official residence. Inflation dropped considerably, though still nearly twice the OECD average, but unemployment nearly doubled from 7 to 13 per cent over the next three years. For the time being workers were prepared to give the government the benefit of the doubt. Not so the paramilitary groups of left and right and senior sections of the armed forces that continued their destabilising campaigns.

The general consensus over economic and social policy was highlighted on 14 October by a full amnesty, which allowed people like the communist Enrique Lister and the anarchist Federica Montseny to return to Spain after years of exile. Amid indescribable celebrations in Barcelona pre-autonomy status for Catalunya was recognised with the re-establishment of the Generalitat. Slightly less favoured Euskadi was also allowed the constitution of a 'general Basque council' to prepare the statute of autonomy. And the third historic nationality, Galicia, was also permitted to draft a statute of autonomy to be submitted to a local referendum and then to Cortes. The official syndicalist organisation was finally dismantled and workers held their first free trade union elections in February 1978.

Increasing violence from ETA and the debates over regional devolution were watched with trepidation by senior army officers, who interpreted them as a concerted challenge to the territorial integrity of the State. The autumn of 1978 was full of rightist indignation over ETA terrorism and national disintegration, leading to military plotting against further reform in the so-called 'Operación Galaxia' on 17 November while Don Juan Carlos was scheduled to be in Mexico. It was a botched-up affair but it showed the strength of feeling among army officers and the ultra-right's willingness to resort to any means; and it also showed an alarming lack of urgency on the part of the government to deal with it before it was too late and to punish its main plotters adequately. Colonel Antonio Tejero, for instance, only served seven months' detention and was given another post in Madrid where he had plenty of time and opportunity to prepare the next plot, encouraged by civilian sycophants who had made him into a hero.

All things considered, the fairly calm and collected debates in the Cortes over devolution and the rather quiet way in which the people of Spain went to the polls on 6 December to give the new constitutional charter an overwhelming vote of confidence were quite remarkable. The subdued nature of the constitutional verdict exposed perhaps an inkling of despondency over electoral processes. The level of participation dropped thirteen points to 67.7 per cent as compared with the high mark of the constituent general election of 1977 with 80 per cent. Quite typically, remote and misty Galicia recorded the highest level of abstention, 51.46 per cent. Much more worrying as a serious fissure in the general consensus of the country over the constitutional work of the Cortes was the lack of interest in Euskadi. The Basque Nationalist Party (PNV) pulled out of the parliamentary debates on the constitutional draft and then, under pressure from the more extreme political formations from the area, abstained in the referendum. More than half of the eligible voters stayed away from the polls, and nearly 50 per cent of the Basques who bothered to cast their vote rejected the Constitution on the grounds that the previous existence of their rights or *fueros* had not been recognised. The nature of their claim to autonomy, they argued, entitled them to a pact with the Spanish State rather than mere compliance with a concession granted from the centre. The deeply divided nature of the Basque vote, ETA's continuing violence and the concomitant and persistent danger of a military coup, never far from the minds of the ultra-right, made the achievement of an accommodation with the regionalist aspirations of the Basque provinces all the more urgent.

## *The Constitutional Charter of 1978*

Despite the conditional support in the north, the constitutional charter approved in the plenary session of Congress and Senate on 31 October 1978, ratified by the nation on 6 December and sanctioned by the King on the 27th, provided a framework of guarantees to ensure 'democratic coexistence within the constitution and the laws of the country according to a just and fair social and economic order'. It was a pro-grammatic document and therefore more than adequately stocked with fine declarations of intent and wishful thinking which would have to be given substance through the subsequent legislative work of the Cortes. Nevertheless it represented a widely endorsed charter which has lasted extremely well. On 6 December 1988, the tenth anniversary of its birth, the country celebrated with approval and even explicit support from such quarters as the Basque left, Euskadiko Ezkerra, who in 1978 campaigned against it. Similarly, the one political issue that more than anything else might have exercised the consensus-makers of the country was implicitly accepted by all as the kingpin of tradition and development, that is the negotiated departure from Franco's author-itarianism of the recent past to the political pluralism of Juan Carlos I's constitutional monarchy.

Article 1 states that 'national sovereignty resides in the Spanish people from whom all powers derive', but then it goes on to define the political form of the Spanish State as a 'parliamentary monarchy' with an hereditary ruler as the head of state, 'inviolable and answerable to no one' (Art. 56), and empowered to sanction and promulgate laws (Art. 62). In this area of constitutional legality the nation was of the opinion that the question of the political form of the State was better left alone. Those who might have queried the dynastic legitimacy of a ruler reinstated in 1975 by a military dictatorship would eventually become reconciled to a king who was able to earn his own legitimacy by his clear commitment to democracy – especially at the time of the military coup of 23 February 1981, when he not only put himself on the line against those who embarked upon an armed challenge against the State on the implicit assumption that they had the King on their side, but also warned the political representatives of the nation that he never again wanted to intervene so directly in politics. His constitutional role as the titular head of the State had been made clear in his speech to the plenary assembly of the two houses on 27 December 1978: the monarchy as the supreme custodian of the democratic order and symbol of unity and continuity 'must be above temporary discrepancies and sectional differences'. He wanted to be the King of all Spaniards and the equitable interpreter of the national good. In December 1988 opinion polls gave him unreserved praise and support for his thirteen years as the King of Spain.

## El ESTADO DE LAS AUTONOMIAS

The most novel aspect of the Constitution of 1978 was the reorganisation of the Spanish territory as a semi-federal state of autonomous communities. Article 2 of the Constitution 'recognises and guarantees the right to autonomy of the nationalities and regions of which it is composed and the common links that bind them together'. In the early nineteenth century, as a unitary state firmly and unequivocally directed from the capital Madrid, the Spanish territorial base was divided into fifty-two provinces under military and civil authorities appointed by the respective ministries in the capital. From the late nineteenth century with economic growth and social development in northern Spain an irrepressible will to obtain a measure of freedom from this highly centralised structure of power emerged. This desire for autonomy was not equally urgent or similarly voiced by all interested 'nationalities and regions'. The nationalities most assertive in this respect were those whose history, culture and language had uniquely survived through the vicissitudes of imperial domination from the Castilian centre and repeated civil wars. Other regions with a lesser claim to a separate status were seeking self-government to promote and develop their own potential. Their expectations were widely different and their tactical approaches equally at variance.

From the capital of the country what appeared as a constant in this permanent struggle was the hostility of those in control of the State to

# Autonomous communities of Spain

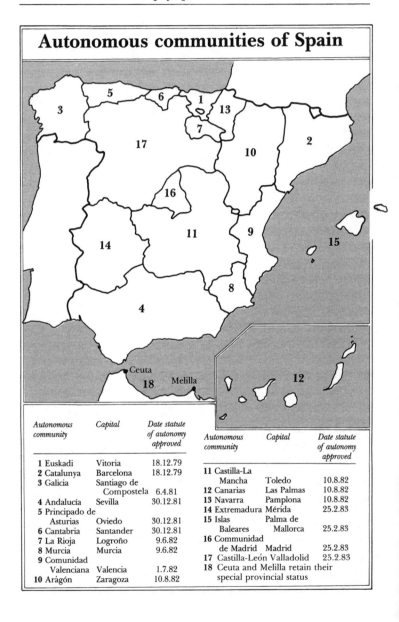

| Autonomous community | Capital | Date statute of autonomy approved |
|---|---|---|
| 1 Euskadi | Vitoria | 18.12.79 |
| 2 Catalunya | Barcelona | 18.12.79 |
| 3 Galicia | Santiago de Compostela | 6.4.81 |
| 4 Andalucía | Sevilla | 30.12.81 |
| 5 Principado de Asturias | Oviedo | 30.12.81 |
| 6 Cantabria | Santander | 30.12.81 |
| 7 La Rioja | Logroño | 9.6.82 |
| 8 Murcia | Murcia | 9.6.82 |
| 9 Comunidad Valenciana | Valencia | 1.7.82 |
| 10 Aragón | Zaragoza | 10.8.82 |

| Autonomous community | Capital | Date statute of autonomy approved |
|---|---|---|
| 11 Castilla-La Mancha | Toledo | 10.8.82 |
| 12 Canarias | Las Palmas | 10.8.82 |
| 13 Navarra | Pamplona | 10.8.82 |
| 14 Extremadura | Mérida | 25.2.83 |
| 15 Islas Baleares | Palma de Mallorca | 25.2.83 |
| 16 Communidad de Madrid | Madrid | 25.2.83 |
| 17 Castilla-León | Valladolid | 25.2.83 |
| 18 Ceuta and Melilla retain their special provincial status | | |

any loss of power to the provinces. Whatever concessions came from the centre, they were always reluctantly granted and severely hedged in whenever politically feasible. It always looked as if the central government, no matter what the social and economic forces in power might be, was giving away with one hand what it was trying to retrieve later on with the other. And quite obviously it was able to play upon the differing tactics and expectations of the claimants by sometimes seeming to concede too much or too little and always aiming to divide or dilute the regionalist aspirations of all. But the central government had to be seen to favour regional devolution, for any commitment to liberal democracy carried with it the implicit duty of disabusing the provinces which had been so savagely repressed before and after the war and to recognise their social, economic and demographic pre-eminence as well as the heavy toll they had paid in the struggle against Francoism.

Only after the attempted coup of 23 February 1981, which nearly destroyed Spain's hard-won democracy, was the party in power forced to come to an accommodation with the opposition in a joint com-mitment towards slowing down the whole process of autonomy in order to appease the army and the right. Apart from Catalunya, Euskadi, Galicia and Andalucía, the other regions seeking autonomy would have to settle for the slow route outlined in Article 143. The controversial LOAPA ('Law on the Harmonisation of the Autonomy Process') presented to the Cortes on 29 September 1981 was strongly opposed by those already enjoying their first regional governments after the first regional elections of March 1980 (the Basques and the Cata-lans); they referred the bill to the Constitutional Tribunal (the ombudsmen of the constitution), which froze at least the clauses which were trying to reverse the process of autonomy.

## THE FAILED COUP OF 1981

The attempted coup of 23 February 1981 was the catalyst that finally pushed the vehicle of democratisation and political liberalisation beyond the point of no return. The main political component of that process was the diminution of the centralist hold over the land, but it was this process of devolution which most upset and disturbed the armed forces, who saw it as the disintegration of the unitary state, the very essence of Spain. Violence in the north against the forces of order, which increased to a dangerously high level during the course of 1980, was the other immovable force in this head-on collision, with the ultra-right still centred round the army and the oligarchic interests of central and southern Spain. The events of 23–24 February 1981, viewed all over the world in all their tragi-comic splendour as Colonel Tejero brandished his revolver in the Cortes, put Spain's relatively peaceful transition to liberal democracy in the balance. Don Juan Carlos I earned his keep that long night of the 23rd; his decisive action as commander-in-chief of the armed forces was crucial. The army officers who plotted against democracy were assuming royal assent as the trump card in their action; when this was not forthcoming the failure of the coup was assured. The nation's rebuke for the action was meted out by a massive demonstration of support for democracy which took place in Madrid, with the leaders of all four main political parties at the head of the march.

The attempted coup was also instrumental in shifting large areas of support from the UCD to the socialist opposition, whose leaders were quick to capitalise on the windfall with protestations of political centrism and moderation, officially shedding their Marxist label, and of genuine commitment to satisfactory completion of the process of devolution and consolidation of democracy. The new and transient leader of the UCD, Leopoldo Calvo Sotelo, rushed parliament into joining NATO to pacify the military, but all the same PSOE was returned to power in the general election of 28 October 1982 as the only guarantee against reactionary attacks on the infant democracy.

Once in office the erstwhile opponents of the integration of Spain in the defensive system of the West were only too ready to find accommodation with the 'realities of power' perpetrating on their enthusiastic supporters a sleight of hand which even the Church castigated as a blatantly dishonest attempt to blackmail the electorate through a referendum on staying in NATO. The PSOE leadership under Felipa González could find comfort in the fact that *Alianza Popular*, the new opposition party rising from the ashes of UCD, recommended abstention when they had been so wholeheartedly committed to the

Atlantic Alliance before the election. The leader of *Alianza Popular*, Don Manuel Fraga, showed on this occasion that they put political opportunism before atlanticist convictions which they had preached as the national interest. The road to autonomy could now be travelled to its final destination.

The central issue of the new democracy for the next four years was therefore regional devolution and the various routes towards the new territorial organisation of the state. The first statutes of autonomy, for Euskadi and Catalunya, were approved on 18 December 1979, and separate status as an autonomous community was granted to Castilla y León, the seventeenth and last self-governing region to make up the new map of Spain, on 25 February 1983. There was still a long way to go until powers attributed to the various autonomies were officially transferred, but their new institutions were now in place and beginning to function. The range and complexity of the issues involved in the process of devolution were easily matched by the variety of routes to autonomy and the practical hurdles in the way.

## *Working Together with a Difference*

One thing was certain: the process of devolution added to the burden on the public purse, for a new layer of administration had been created and no corresponding savings at the centre had taken place. This was justified on the grounds that the messy state of affairs resulting from the original transfer necessitated co-ordination and repair work from the central administration. To which the regional agencies responsible for the devolved services responded that the shortcomings were due to insufficient resourcing and centralist constraints. The length list of laws and regulations referred to the Supreme Tribunal by the State or the Communities for further consideration is clear proof of the tug of war between the government and the regional parliaments. The most protracted legal wrangle was LOAPA which, if the Constitutional Tribunal had not come down on the side of the regions, would in effect have made their power to legislate in certain areas subject to the consent of the Madrid Cortes.

## CATALUNYA AND EUSKADI

The Inter-regional Compensation Fund (Art, 158.2 of the Constitution), intended to redress imbalances and to ensure solidarity between nationalities and regions, did not appear to have made much difference. It permitted people like the leader of *Convergencia i Unió*, Jordi Pujol, to strengthen his hold over Catalunya and severely dent socialist support on the bandwagon of right-wing Catalanism – with the exception of Barcelona, which remained the stronghold of socialist power in the principality, under a mayor no less creditable than Pujol himself as a Catalanist notable, Pasqual Maragall. Pujol, the President of the Generalitat, has been able to play on the fears of the Catalan middle classes of a backlash from the socialist power at the centre and their men at the Town Hall of the main city of the principality, while the Socialist Party in the central government fanned this fear by using every possible excuse to detain, delay or condition the transfer of funds, which the Generalitat claimed it needed to fund adequately the services devolved to the principality by Article 148 of the Constitution.

In Euskadi the balance of power between national and regional parties and between the three provinces, Guipúzcoa, Vizcaya and Alava, was much more fluid and the deterioration on the economic front was such that deadly inimical forces in the past were now prepared to talk among themselves and with Madrid. Heavy industry, which has traditionally dominated the northern landscapes, was the sector worst affected by world recession and changes in international specialisation; youth unemployment was amongst the highest in Spain. Modernisation of the productive system entails heavy capital expenditure and high technology. ETA's continuing violence against the institutions and forces of the Spanish State, more and more in their own territory, kept productive investment from the area. Socialist support had always been strong among the many immigrant workers in Bilbao and its industrial hinterland and in the inland province of Alava. The majority force in Euskadi as a whole, 'the Basque Nationalist Party' (PNV), had to enter into various pacts with the Socialists to be able to govern. Herri Batasuna, who in February

1988 tried to organise a campaign against the King's visit to Pamplona, had expressed unconditional support for the Constitution and the threshold of self-government contained within it. And even ETA-M (the military wing) appeared to want to negotiate terms and bring to an end the long-running sore which wreaked havoc in their own backyard.

As in Catalunya, Euskadi had a large residue of resentment and mistrust over certain features symbolising the centralising and repressive tendencies of the Spanish State. The party in power made no bones of their intention to go slow under the terms of Article 150.2. An example of this atmosphere of enmity and suspicion was the continued presence of civil governors in the autonomous communities, ostensibly to look after the interests of the central administration and to co-ordinate and liaise with its regional counterparts. Their function had been reduced to a minimum, and therefore, argued Catalans, Basques and Galicians, they should be removed from their midst for they no longer played any part, except perhaps as a permanent irritant and a reminder of their imperialist past. For its part the central government referred the matter of a Basque office in Brussels to the Constitutional Tribunal on the grounds that it amounted to separate diplomatic representation, which belonged exclusively to the State.

These and many other sources of friction, which the normally restrictive and prevaricating interpretation of the Constitution on the part of the centralist government brought to the fore, occasioned endless arguments between the centre and the periphery – not the most conducive atmosphere for a peaceful resolution of the outstanding problems regarding the nature and scope of the 'estado de las autonomías'. Notwithstanding all these arguments, it became a financial reality with most of their resources coming from central government, to the tune of 21 per cent of national public expenditure.

TWO KINDS OF AUTONOMY

However, in comparison with EEC countries, whether unitary or federalist states, the current level of budgetary decentralisation in the Iberian Peninsula does not seem particularly high; nor is it in the least equally applicable to the main five communities – Euskadi, Catalunya, Galicia, Andalucía and Valencia – who have a degree of self-government comparable with federalist states such as Austria, West Germany or the United States, and to the other twelve lagging well behind unitary countries like Denmark or the United Kingdom. But even the five Iberian communities, which enjoyed the optimum level of administrative freedom and resource allocation from the State, are not deemed to have reached a similar level of political decentralisation. Certain areas of community expenditure, like education and health, are still heavily controlled from the centre.

## *Private affluence and public squalor*

While resources and attention were lavished on issues pertaining to the territorial organisation of the State and the municipal, regional and national electoral processes, the economy of the nation continued to increase the gross imbalances between individuals and regions. Under a liberal democratic system and a socialist administration the State has not substantially improved or attempted to improve its ability to promote balanced and sustained growth. It has become more efficient as a tax-gatherer but less resolved to plough back a bigger proportion of the national product to fund public services or long-term investment, or to redistribute wealth. Relative increases in public expenditure are made possible by higher public deficits, which respectable State economists are the first to insist have to be kept within bounds.

In the mid-1980s Spain was Europe's star performer, with a 5 per cent yearly growth, nearly two points above the EEC average. In 1988 more than 54 million people, nearly one and a half times the native population of Spain visited the country, an increasing proportion of them to retire there. According to the Bank of Spain, company profits for 1987 doubled over those of the previous years. There were plentiful cash rewards, too, for bankers, financiers and property developers, political manipulators, lawyers, accountants, management consultants, media experts, advertisers, distributors, and the legal and economic experts of the growing state bureaucracy.

## GROWING DISPARITIES IN PERSONAL
## AND REGIONAL WEALTH

A substantial proportion of the population, according to an opinion poll of October 1988, condemned the intemperate regard for Mammon and believed there was growing corruption in high circles.

The battle for supremacy in the early part of 1988 between Banco Español de Crédito (BANESTO), one of the big banking cartels, and Cartera Central, a financial outfit who were also the main shareholders of BANESTO, fought out in the full glare of publicity, epitomised the prevailing philosophy. The point as regards profitability and productivity is that the conflict in BANESTO came to a head when the men from Cartera Central started to poke their calculators into not so much the high level of yearly profits for BANESTO, but the quality of those profits, which did not appear to have come from 'typical' banking services, that is financial mediation, lending and borrowing. Spanish money has usually been the dearest in Europe and so is the banking commission or differential between the cost of borrowing and lending. The Ministry of Foreign Affairs' Communications Office, in their monthly broadsheet for February 1989, referred to a French report on banking profitability in Europe, which duly highlights the fact that Spanish banks are the most profitable and expensive in Europe, goes on rather coyly to explain that this high rate of return arises from the high cost of money, monopolistic practices and dear services, lest some innocent reader should be induced to equate large profits with efficient management and competitive costing of banking facilities.

The excessive, some would say indecent, gains did not therefore go to productive or infrastructural investment. Nor was there any sign of a more equitable distribution of the much-vaunted wealth. Differentials in per capita or regional income continue to show the same wide discrepancies as before. With Ireland, Spain figured at the bottom of the European league as regards income per capita, with 900,000 pesetas per year. The Foundation for Economic and Social Research and the Banco de Bilbao studies on rent distribution point out that the gap between rich and poor regions is growing. In 1986 Spain experienced a growth rate of 3 per cent overall, but Andalucía, Galicia, Extremadura and the two Castillas lagged behind, while the Balearic and Canary Islands doubled their average rate of growth and Asturias suffered a recession of 0.4 per cent. The new feature of this pattern of regional disequilibrium was the Basque Country with only 1.5 per cent growth, coming mainly from the building industry and services. As regards personal income it appeared that 27 million Spaniards, the large majority of them, had to make do with an income well below the mythical per capita income mentioned above. Official figures based on research from the Banco de Bilbao refer to 30 per cent of Spanish households living in poverty, with a further 40 per cent between poverty and relative well-being, 20 per cent definitively well-off, and 10 per cent rolling in it.

### INADEQUATE SOCIAL SECURITY

These disparities were not addressed by the socialist administration in the 80s. Spain remained one of the worst performers in terms of social security expenditure. Another aspect of these disparities was the serious weaknesses in the area of employment, training and development of the workforce, and systems of production, a meagre 0.75 per cent of the national income devoted to research and development in 1987 for example, as against the 2.45 per cent European average. From the president of the 'Circle of Company Directors' (*Círculo de Empresarios*) also came the warning in February 1989 that the only areas of research and development in Spanish industry were taking place in chemicals, pharmaceuticals, electronics and information technology, all of them large transnational combines. After twelve years of losses SEAT, a subsidiary of FIAT and the main car manufacturer, only started to make profits in 1987 when taken over by Volkswagen. The main areas of investment for indigenous private capital, on the other hand, continued to be food, drink, textiles, hides and furs, and even in these areas the large retailing outlets were increasingly becoming foreign-owned.

## *The General Strike of December 1988*

On 14 December 1988 a 24-hour stoppage brought the country to a standstill. Official figures estimated 94 per cent participation of salaried

President González

employees or 7.8 million workers out on strike. The massive show of strength from all unions (headed by the socialist UGT and the communist CCOO) against the government's economic policy opened a new era not only in industrial relations but also in the political configuration of Spain's party system. The social democratic administration under Felipe González, lost all credibility with the workforce and the lower-earning groups. The United Left, led by the Spanish Communist Party (PCE), sought a closer relationship with both communist and socialist trade unions, while attracting members of PSOE who wished to reassert their commitment to democratic socialism.

The workers' organisations seemed no longer willing to be taken in by the government's blandishments or threats. They grew weary of the usual, and allegedly orthodox, remedies proposed by the economic ministers. Wage moderation, flexibility in employment and worsening working conditions had for too long been paid for by the workers' exertions and hardships. Labour costs were still among the lowest in Europe, which was why so much foreign capital travelled to Spain. While the increased wealth and its arrogant consumption was only too patently clear, the workers wanted a bigger share in the general prosperity. The crude monetarist policies said to be needed to maintain growth did not create jobs.

## SPAIN AND THE EEC

On the European front, Spain at long last was settling to a full and, hopefully, fruitful reconciliation with her European partners. The long years of economic backwardness and political ostracism were well behind. From 1986, Spain was officially part of the European Economic Community (EEC), and to make up for the years of isolation she projected a maximalist attitude towards further political and cultural integration.

From 1989 Spain had enjoyed her new international status as a member country of the European Union and, basking in the glory of the Presidency of the European Community, and entry into the European Monetary System and aiming to capitalise on the better than expected results in the recent European Elections, Spain's Prime Minister, Felipe González, went to the polls on 29 October 1989. He hoped for a renewed mandate for his economic programme and a 'stable' government to take Spain into the single European market in 1993. Felipe González and his Socialist Party were returned to the 350-seat Congress of Deputies (the lower chamber of the Spanish Cortes) with a majority of 175, exactly half the total number of seats in the Congress. Quite fortuitously, their overall majority was restored by the refusal of the four Herri Batasuna Deputies (the Basque separatist party) to take up their places in Parliament for the duration of that legislature. The tight parliamentary situation may have brought some moderation into government circles and a desire to accommodate their critics from the United Left Party (the main beneficiary of PSOE's losses) and the trade unions, whose opposition to the Socialist Party was so instrumental in bringing Felipe González to the hustings only three years after the previous General Election.

In March 1990 Spain joined the military Western European Union.

In the last week of October 1991, under the auspices of the USA and the institutional remnants of the Soviet Union, Madrid was also the venue for the Middle East Peace Conference; and in 1992 Spain firmed up her commitment to further European unifications as redefined in the Maastricht Treaty. She also became a non-permanent member of the United Nations Security Council, to start on 1 January 1993 for a period of two years, in the midst of a full-scale commemoration, on both sides of the Atlantic, of the 500th anniversary of the first European encounters with the Americas and the celebration of the Olympic Games in Barcelona.

## *The promised land, 1992*

As a celebration of past imperial grandeur Expo '92 was an unqualified success, and the Barcelona Olympic Games were also a resounding event, not least because of the unprecedented number of honours showered upon Spanish athletes for the first time in living history and the impression of unity displayed by the Royal Family, who have been successful in gaining respect both at home and abroad. But as Expo '92 drew to a close, there were all around worrying signs of Spain's poor economic performance.

Such benefits as might have accrued to the Spanish economy from capital imports prior to 1993, when one in every two share transactions was by a non-resident investor, could no longer be controlled, since deregulation of capital markets came hotfoot on the trail of economic liberalisation after Spain's full accession to the European Economic Councils.

The resignation of the former governor of the Bank of Spain in September 1992 was not the only case of suspected fraud. From 1989 onwards hardly a day passed without news of a member of the Socialist establishment involved in insider-dealings, pocketing substantial commissions in return for political favours, or setting up bogus offices for fictitious consultancy work in recognition of financial contributions to the party, culminating in the spring of 1994 with the prosecution of the former head of the Guardia Civil accused of a whole range of offences, the seizure of BANESTO (Banco Español de Crédito) by the governor of the Bank of Spain on the grounds of financial mis-management and corrupt practices, and four ministerial resignations.

While the comings and goings of the powerful and influential élites were paraded on the front covers of glossy magazines, general living standards, and sustainable and balanced economic growth did not seem to be making significant strides forward. The country had also been in the grip of probably the worst drought of the century: it had not rained at all in some parts of Spain for four years, with devastating effects upon large areas of agricultural production. Torrential rains and heavy snows throughout the winter months (1995–6) brought much needed relief to the parched earth and, with it, the prospect of a better harvest.

## *The General Election, March 1996*

The 1996 general election was held on 3 March with 78 per cent of the electorate turning out to vote. The Partido Popular (PP) won 156 of the 350 seats in the Congress of Deputies, thus falling short of an overall majority. The PSOE took 141 seats, IU 21 and the Catalan CiU 16. D. José María Aznar, leader of the PP, was able, only after protracted negotiations, to negotiate a pact with the right of centre CiU (as also with the Basque PNV and Coalición Canaria), which made possible his investiture as Prime Minister in early May. This pact with the CiU, which had not been without its problems, but which allowed its leader, D. Jordi Pujol, to negotiate growing areas of autonomy for Catalonia, was renewed in January 1998 until the end of the current legislature.

One of the administration's main priorities was the reduction of the budget deficit in order to qualify for membership of the single European currency. Several aspects of the government's policies, however, aroused intense opposition. A number of mass demonstrations and strikes marked the end of 1996 and early 1997.

More or less simultaneously, a number of corruption trials initiated under the outgoing socialist government came to their close. In March 1997 Mario Conde received a six-year prison sentence (commuted in February 1998 to four-and-a-half years), was fined 18m. pesetas and was ordered to pay 600m. pesetas in compensation to BANESTO. The Guardia Civil commander, Luis Roldán, was found guilty of fraud, embezzlement and tax evasion in February 1998 and sentenced to a total of 28 years imprisonment. In the summer of the same year, José Barrionuevo, former Minister of the Interior, and Rafael Vera, former Secretary of State for Security, received prison sentences still subject to appeal, for their roles in the so-called 'dirty war' against the Basque terrorist organization, ETA.

At the PSOE conference in June 1997, Felipe González, announced his resignation as Secretary General of the party after twenty-three years stewardship. He was succeeded by a loyal associate, Joaquín Almunia, although at the newly introduced primary elections for the selection of the PSOE's next prime ministerial candidate held in April 1998 he was defeated by José Borrell. His offer of resignation from the post of Secretary General, however, was rejected. This has led to some friction, still not wholly resolved, between the two men as to who actually leads the official opposition party.

## ETA CEASEFIRE

ETA continued its strategies of kidnappings and attacks on military targets under the new government and expanded these to cover local PP councillors, mainly, but not exclusively, in the Basque Country. The abduction of Miguel Angel Blanco, a young councillor in the Basque town of Ermua, led to an unprecedented outpouring of public outrage as a result of the cold-blooded way in which the young man was executed immediately after a 48-hour ultimatum on the relocation of Basque terrorist prisoners to the Basque Country expired. In the largest demonstrations since the attempted military coup of 1981, millions of Spaniards all over the country took to the streets. In response to public feeling, the Prime Minister vowed to intensify the government's campaign against ETA. The terrorists continued their campaign against local councillors. However, the terrorist organization began to suffer serious reverses in the second half of 1997 and the first half of 1998 on both the French and Spanish sides of the border in the form of multiple arrests and the capture of substantial arsenals. It would seem that these set-backs, increased public outrage and, to a point, the example of the peace process in Northern Ireland all led to the declaration of an indefinite truce on 16 September 1998, which is still in force. It now seems that José María Aznar's government will enter into direct negotiations with ETA.

## THE ECONOMY

Since 1996 the economy has grown more rapidly than in other European countries. Tourism continues to grow with 64.5m. visitors in 1997 (43.4m. tourists). Income from tourism was a record 3,920,800m. pesetas. The 1996 visible trade deficit was US$14,912, but there was a surplus of US$1,756m. on the current account of the balance of payments. This surplus increased by 70 per cent in the following year. GDP growth in 1997 was 3.4 per cent, the highest recorded since 1990. Annual inflation declined from an average rate of 3.6 per cent in 1996 to 2.0 per cent in 1997, the lowest percentage since the consumer price index was set up in 1962. Unemployment, still high, continues to decline. Government spending was projected to increase around 3 per cent in 1998.

Upon taking office in 1996, Señor Aznar declared his commitment to European economic and monetary union, so that considerable austerity measures had to be taken over this period to reduce Spain's budget deficit to below 3.0 per cent of GDP by 1997. This was achieved and Spain has qualified for membership of the single European currency which was introduced in January 1999.

# *The Eve of the Millennium*

On the eve of the millennium, Spain confronts the new century as a confident modern nation. Democracy is now, after twenty years, well established and Spain enjoys 'big country' status in the councils of the European Union. Economically, after demonstrating sufficient economic stability to join the first wave of membership of the Euro club, one of the current government's major difficulties is going to be proving that it is still sufficiently poor to merit the lion's share of EU development funds to the poorer members of the Union!

## SPANISH EXCELLENCE

The opening of the Guggenheim Museum in Bilbao only mirrors a lively artistic and literary scene with well established artists and writers such as Antoni Tàpies, Eduardo Chillida, Ricardo Bofill, José Camilo Cela, Antonio Buero Vallejo and Rafael Alberti as well as world famous performing artists such as José Carreras. Placido Domingo, Montserrat Caballe, Julio Iglesias, Antonio Banderas, Paca de Lucia and directors such as Pedro Almodóvar.

Spanish athletes have triumphed regularly at athletics meetings round the world since the Barcelona games and Spanish training centres for top athletes have become a model of their kind. In other sports, Severiano Ballesteros, Arantxa Sánchez Vicario, Alex Corretja, Miquel Indurain and Carlos Sainz are household names, while, amongst others, Spanish water polo, basket ball and of course football teams are amongst the best in the world.

Too many young Spanish scientists still have to follow in the footsteps of Nobel Prize winning physicist, Severo Ochoa, to the US or elsewhere to pursue their research, but a new generation of young scientists, still underfunded by European standards, are beginning to make a marked contribution to all areas of research from medicine to space exploration.

Spanish is continually growing in importance as a world language, while privileged relations with the Arab and Latin American worlds will ensure a role for Spain in Europe and the world for many years to come.

# Notes

# Notes

# Notes

# Rulers and Monarchs

## Visigothic Rulers

Under pressure from the Huns some 200,000 Germanic tribesmen invaded Roman Hispaniae in the autumn of 409 AD. The *Suebi* under Hermeric settled in the north-west and were later reduced (584) to the authority of the Visigothic Kingdom of Toledo.

The rest of the Iberian Peninsula was part of the Kingdom of Toulouse until 507, when Clovis I of the Franks forced out the Visigoths from south-eastern France. In 554 Athanagild moved his Court to Toledo.

Gesaleic: *507–510*
Athanagild: *551–567*
Leovigild: *572–586*
Reccared: *586–601*
Swinthila: *621–631*
Recceswinth: *649–672*
Wamba: *672–680*
Evigio: *680–687*
Egica: *687–702*
Witiza: *700–710*
Roderic: 710–711

## Muslim Spain

al-Andalus was governed from 711 to 756 as a province of the Emirate of Ifriqiya (North Africa), part of the Umayyad Empire of Damascus:

Tariq ben Ziyad: *710–12*

Musa ben Nusayr: *712–714*
Abd al-Aziz ben Musa: *714–6*

Yusuf ben Abd al-Rahman al-Fihri: *747–756*

## UMAYYAD INDEPENDENT EMIRATE

Abd al-Rahman I: *756–788*
Hisham I: *788–796*
al-Hakam I: *796–822*
Abd al-Rahman II: *822–852*
Muhammad I: *852–886*
al-Mundhir: *886–888*
Abd Allah: *888–912*
Abd al-Rahman III: *912–929*

## CALIPHATE OF CÓRDOBA

Abd al-Rahman III: *929–961*
al-Hakam II: *961–976*
Hisham II: *976–1009* (al-Mansur, his all-powerful minister, governed in his
   name until 1002 and his son after him)
Muhammad II: *1009*
Sulayman: *1009–1010*
Muhammad II: *1010*
Hisham II: *1010–1013*
Sulayman: *103–1016*
Alí ben Hammud: *1016–1018*
Abd al-Rahman IV: *1018*
Al-Qasim ben Hammud: *1018–1021*
Yahya ben Alí ben Hammud: *1021–1023*
al-Qasim ben Hammud: *1023*
Abd al-Rahman V: *1023–1024*
Muhammad III: *1024–1025*
Yahya ben Alí ben Hammud: *1025–1027*
Hisham III: *1027–1031*

## TAIFA (PETTY) RULERS: FIRST BREAK-UP

From 1031 to 1110 when the Almoravids from Marrakesh restored political
unity to al-Andalus, the Caliphate of Córdoba broke up into twenty-four
separate territories

## ALMORAVID EMIRS

Yusuf ben Tasufin: *1061–1106*
Alí ben Yusuf: *1106–1143*
Tashufin ben Alí Yusuf: *1143–1145*
Ibrahim ben Tashufin: *1145*
Isahq ben Alí: *1145–1147*

## TAIFA RULERS; SECOND BREAK-UP

From 1147 to 1172 there were eleven petty kingdoms which gradually fell under the domination of the new masters of Marrakesh, the Almohads.

## ALMOHAD CALIPHS

Muhammad ben Tumart: *1121–1128*
Abu Muhammad Abd al-Mumin: *1128–1163*
Abu Yaqub Yusuf I: *1163–1184*
Abu Yusuf Yaqub: *1184–1199*
Abu Abd Allah Muhammad: *1119–1213*
Abu Yaqub Yusuf II: *1213–1223*
Abdalwahid al-Makhlu: *1223–1224*
Abu Muhammad Abdallah al-Adil: *1224–1226*
Yahya al-Mutasim: *1226*
Abu-l-Ala Idris al-Mamun: *1226–1231*
Abu Muhammad Abdalwahid al-Raschid ibn al-Mamun: *1232–1242*
Abul-Hasan Alí al-Said al-Mutatid: *1242–1248*
Abu-Hafs Umar al-Murtada: *1248–1266*
Abu-l-Ala al-Wasiq: *1266–1268*

## THE NASRID KINGDOM OF GRANADA

Abu-Abdallah Muhammad I: *1238–1272*
       II: *1272–1301*
       III: *1301–1308*
Abu-l-Djuyusch Nasr ibn Muhammad II: *1308–1313*
Abu-l-Walid Ismail I ibn Faradj: *1313–1324*
Muhammad IV: *1342–1332*
Abu-l-Haddjadj Yusuf I: *1332–1354*
Muhammad V: *1354–1358*
Abu-l-Walid Ismail II: *1358–1359*
Abu Said Muhammad VI: 1359–1361
Muhammad V: *1361–1390*

Abu-l-Haddjadj Yusuf II: *1390–1391*
Muhammad VII: *1391–1407*
Abu-l Haddjadj Yusuf III: *1407–1423*
Muhammad VIII: *1423–1427*
Muhammad IX: *1427–1429*
Muhammad VIII: *1431–1444*
Muhammad X: *1444–1445*
Sad al-Mustain ibn Alí:*1445–1446*
Muhammad X: *1446–1453*
Sad al-Mustain ibn Alí: *1453–1462*
Abu-l-Hasan Alí ibn Sad: *1462–1482*
Muhammad XI (Boabdil): *1482–1483*
Alí: *1483–1485*
Muhammad XII: *1485–1486*
Alí: *1485–1486*
Muhammad XI (Boabdil): *1486–1492*


Granada surrendered to Isabel and Fernando on 5 January 1492


### Northern Domains

While al-Andalus declined politically and militarily into a number of weak
principalities, easy prey to ambitious warriors from the north, Christian Spain
started as a motley array of family fiefdoms along the Cantabrian coast and the
Pyrenean border. It was only when Muslim fragmentation allowed them to
expand southwards that the northern seigniories and counties began to define
themselves territorially and politically against the Muslims as well as against one
another.


### RULERS OF CASTILLA AND LEÓN

Fernando I de Castilla (*1035–65*) and León (1037–65)
Sancho II de Castilla: *1065–72*
Alfonso VI de León (*1065–1109*) and Castilla (*1072–1109*)
Urraca: *1109–26*
Alfonso VII: *1126–57*
Sancho III de Castilla: *1157–8*
Alfonso VIII de Castilla: *1158–1214*
Fernando II de León: *1157–88*
Alfonso IX de León: *1188–1230*
Enrique I de Castilla: *1214–17*

Fernando III de Castilla (1217–52) and León (*1230–52*)
Alfonso X: *1252–84*
Sancho IV: *1284–95*
Fernando IV: *1295–1312*
Alfonso XI: *1312–50*
Pedro I: *1350–69*
Enrique II de Trastámara: *1369–79*
Juan I: *1379–90*
Enrique III: *1390–1406*
Juan II: *1406–1454*
Enrique IV: *1454–74*
Isabel I: *1474–1504*
Juana I and Felipe I (King-Consort): 1506–8

## KINGS OF ARAGÓN

Ramiro I: *1035–63*
Sancho I: *1063–94*
Pedro I: *1094–1104*
Alfonso I: *1104–1134*
Ramiro II: *1134–7*

## KINGS OF ARAGÓN AND COUNTS OF BARCELONA

Petronila I of Aragón and Ramón Berenguer IV of Barcelona: *1137–62*
Alfonso II: *1162–96*
Pedro II: *1196–1213*
Jaime I: *1213–76*
Pedro III: *1276–85*
Alfonso III: *1285–91*
Jaime II: *1291–1327*
Alfonso IV: *1327–36*
Pedro IV: *1336–87*
Juan I: *1387–95*
Martín I: *1395–1410*
Interregnum: *1410–2*
Fernando I de Trastámara: *1412–16*
Alfonso V: *1416–58*
Juan II: *1458–79*
Fernando II and V de Castilla by marriage to Isabel I: *1479–1516*

## Hispanic Rulers

### TRASTÁMARA-BURGUNDIAN-HABSBURG DYNASTY

Carlos I: *1516–1556*
Felipe II: *1556–98*
Felipe III: *1598–1621*
Felipe IV: *1621–65*
Carlos II: *1665–1700*

### BOURBONS

Felipe V: *1701–24*
Luis I: *1724*
Felipe V: *1724–1746*
Fernando VI: *1746–59*
Carlos III: *1759–88*
Carlos IV: *1788–1808*
Fernando VII: *1808*
José I: *1808–1813*
Fernando VII: *1814–1833*
María Cristina, Regent of Spain during Isabel II's minority
Isabel II: *1843–1868*

## 1868: The 'Septembrina' Revolution

### REGENCY AND PROVISIONAL GOVERNMENT

Presidents:
Francisco Serrano (Duque de la Torre): *October 1868 to June 1869*
Juan Prim (Marqués de los Castillejos): *June 1869 to December 1870*
Juan B. Topete (Admiral): *December 1870 to January 1871*

### AMADEO I (31 OCTOBER 1870–11 FEBRUARY 1873)

Heads of Government
Francisco Serrano: *January to July 1871*
Manuel Ruiz Zorrilla: *July to October 1871*
José Malcampo: *October to December 1871*
Práxedes Mateo Sagasta: *December 1871 to May 1872*
Francisco Serrano: *May to June 1872*
Manuel Ruiz Zorrilla: *June 1872 to January 1873*

## FIRST REPUBLIC

Presidents:
Estanislao Figueras: *February to June 1873*
Francisco Pi y Margall: *June to July 1873*
Nicolás Salmerón: *July to September 1873*
Emilio Castelar: *September to December 1873*

## BOURBON REGENCY

Heads of the Provisional Government:
Francisco Serrano: *January to May 1874*
Juan de Zavala: *May to September 1874*
Práxedes Mateo Sagasta: *September to December 1874*

## *Restoration of the Bourbon Monarchy*

Alfonso XII: *29 December 1874–1885*
María Cristina, *Regent: 1885–1902*
Alfonso XIII: *1902–1931*

## HEADS OF GOVERNMENT

Miguel Promode Rivera: *1923–1930*
Dámaso Berenguer: *1930–1931*
Juan Bautista Aznar: *February to April 1931*

## SECOND REPUBLIC

Head of the Provisional Government:
Niceto Alcalá Zamora: *April to October 1931*

Presidents:
Niceto Alcalá Zamora: *December 1931 to April 1936*
Diego Martínez Barrio: *April to May 1936*
Manuel Azaña: *May 1936 to February 1939*

Heads of Government:
Manuel Azaña: *October 1931–September 1933*
Alejandro Lerroux: *September to October 1933*
Diego Martinez Barrio: *October to December 1933*
Alejandro Lerroux: *December 1933–April 1934*
Richardo Samper: *April to October 1934*
Alejandro Lerroux: *October 1934–September 1935*

Joaquín Chapaprieta: *September to December 1935*
Manuel Portela Valladares: *December 1935–February 1936*
Manuel Azaña: *February to May 1936*
Santiago Casares Quiroga: *May to July 1936*
Diego Martínez Barrio: *19–20 July 1936*
José Giral: *July to September 1936*
Francisco Largo Caballero: *September 1936 to May 1937*
Juan Negrín: *May 1937–February 1939*


MILITARY UPRISING (17–18 JULY 1936)

President of the National Defence Council:
General Miguel Cabanellas: *23 July to 30 September 1936*

### General Francisco Franco Bahamonde:
Head of State and Armed Forces: *1 October 1936–20 November 1975*

Presidents of the Council of Ministers:
Generalísimo Franco: *30 January 1938–11 June 1973*
Admiral Luis Carrero Blanco: *8 June to 20 December 1973*
Carlos Arias Navarro: *3 January 1974–20 November 1975*

### King Juan Carlos I of Spain: 22 November 1975–
Heads of Government:
Carlos Arias Navarro: *4 December 1975–June 1976*
Adolfo Suárez González: *3 July 1976–29 January 1981*
Leopoldo Calvo Sotelo (UCD): *21 February 1981–27 October 1982*
Felipe González Marques (PSOE): *28 October 1982–3 March 1996*
José María Aznar (People's Party) *3 March 1996–*

# Chronology of Major Events

## B.C

| | |
|---|---|
| *c.* 1100 | Foundation of Gades (Cádiz) by Phoenicians |
| *c.* 1000 | Arrival of Celts in the Iberian peninsula |
| *c.* 650 | Carthaginians settled in Ebusus (Ibiza) |
| *c.* 600 | Tartessos, west of Gades, important cultural centre in the western Mediterranean |
| 550–500 | Greek traders found Emporion (Empúries) and Hemeroskopeion (Denia) |
| 535 | Destruction of Tartessos |
| 241 | First Punic War |
| 228–7 | Hadrubal founds Carthago Nova (Cartagena) |
| 219 | Sacking of Saguntum by Hannibal |
| 206 | Roman victory over Carthaginians at Ilipa (Alcalá del Río). Roman legions found Italica (Sevilla) |
| 202 | Roman victory over Carthaginians at Zama (Carthage) |

## Roman Hispania

| | |
|---|---|
| 197–5 | Hispania Citerior and Ulterior |
| 149–6 | Third and Last Punic War. Destruction of Carthage |
| 147–39 | Celtiberian Viriathus' uprising against Rome |
| 133 | Fall of Numantia: the last bastion of Celtiberian opposition to Roman rule |
| 27 | Further division of Hispania into three provinces: Baetica, Lusitania and Tarraconensis |
| 26–24 | Foundation of Caesar Augusta (Zaragoza) and Emerita Augusta (Mérida), capital of Lusitania, by Emperor Octavius |

## A.D

| | |
|---|---|
| 98 | Trajan (98–117), first Spanish-born Roman emperor |
| 170–3 | Lusitanian rebellion against Rome; general disruption throughout Roman Empire |
| 235–97 | Collapse of Roman authority; Hispania for herself in the face of growing pressure from Germanic tribes (Franks) in the Tarraconensis |
| 284 | Division of Roman Empire into east and west |
| 305 | First Christian Bishops' Conference at Iliberris (Granada) |
| 312 | Western emperor Constantine embraces Christianity as the state religion of Rome |
| 370 | The Huns make their first appearance in the west |

## Hispania Gothica

| | |
|---|---|
| 409 | Hispania invaded by Vandals, Suebi and Alans |
| 419 | Establishment of the Visigothic Kingdom of Tolosa |
| 429 | Vandals move from southern Spain to Africa |
| 507 | Alaric II defeated and killed by Franks at Vouillé. Visigoths reduced to the Iberian Peninsula |
| 549–621 | Byzantium occupies south-eastern Spain and Balearic Islands for the Eastern Roman Empire |
| 554 | Toledo becomes capital of the Visigothic Kingdom of Spain |
| 585 | The Suebi reduced to the north-west |
| 587–9 | Reccared's conversion to Roman Catholicism as the state religion of the Visigoths |
| 654 | Recceswinth's *Forum iudiciorum* |
| 681 | *Codex Euricus* |

## al-Andalus (Muslim Spain)

| | |
|---|---|
| 711–13 | Muslims defeat Roderic, 'the last Goth', and occupy Spain. Córdoba, their first capital from 716 |
| 756 | Establishment of the Emirate of Córdoba |
| 785 | Start of the building of the Mosque |
| 929 | Abd al-Rahman III proclaims himself Caliph of Córdoba |
| 1002 | Death of al-Mansur: the end of Muslim hegemony in the Iberian Peninsula |
| 1031 | The Caliphate of Córdoba breaks up into Taifa Kingdoms |
| 1049 | Building of the Aljafería Palace in Zaragoza |

| 1085 | The Muslim Kingdom of Toledo falls to the Christians |
| 1086 | Almoravids reassert Muslim military rule in central and eastern Spain |
| 1147 | End of Almoravid rule and new break-up of al-Andalus into Taifa kingdoms |
| 1147–1212 | The Almohads restore political unity to al-Andalus |
| 1195 | Defeat of Alfonso VIII of Castilla at Alarcos |
| 1212 | Las Navas de Tolosa: crushing defeat of the Almohads |
| 1223 | Third break-up of al-Andalus |
| 1238 | Abu-Abdallah Muhammad I establishes the Nasrid Kingdom of Granada. Construction of La Alhambra |
| 1274–1344 | The Marinids, new power in Marrakesh, to the help of the Nasrids of Granada in their struggle for survival |
| | Battle for the Straits of Gibraltar |
| 1492 | Fall of the Muslim Kingdom of Granada |

## Northern Principalities (Christian Spain)

| 722 | Covadonga (Asturias): First sign of resistance to Islam |
| 732 | Muslim advance in France stopped at Poitiers |
| c. 830 | First mention of the relics of Apostle St James and Santiago de Compostela as the leading pilgrimage centre of Christian Europe |
| 946 | Emergence of the Kingdom of Castilla |
| 1037 | Fernando I unites Castilla and León under his rule |
| 1085 | Castilian Conquest of Toledo |
| 1118 | Conquest of Zaragoza by Alfonso I of Aragón and introduction of the Military Order of the Templars |
| 1137 | Dynastic union of Catalunya and Aragón |
| 1139–43 | Portugal becomes a separate kingdom |
| 1212–64 | Victory over al-Andalus at Las Navas de Tolosa. |
| | Christian expansion to Andalucía |
| 1244 | Treaty of Almizra defines southern boundaries between Castilla and Aragón |
| 1258 | Castilian foundation of the Military Order of Calatrava |
| 1267 | Treaty of Limits between Portugal and Castilla |
| 1311 | Aragonese expansion in the eastern Mediterranean: Foundation of the Duchies of Athens and Neopatria |
| 1340–4 | Defeat of the Marinid Muslims at the Battle of El Salado; Algeciras for Castilla |
| 1348–51 | Black Death and first anti-Jewish pogroms |
| 1369 | The beginning of Trastámara rule in Castilla |

| 1391 | Pogroms and mass conversions of Jews (*conversos*) |
| 1412 | Trastámara succession to the Crown of Aragón |
| 1415 | The Portuguese take Ceuta |
| 1442–3 | Alfonso V of Aragón conquers Naples |
| 1449–76 | Civil wars, peasant revolts and *converso* massacres throughout Christian Spain |
| 1479 | Dynastic Union of Castilla and Aragón |
| 1481 | Establishment of the Holy Inquisition in Castilla |
| 1492 | Castilla occupies the Muslim Kingdom of Granada. Expulsion of Jews who refused to become Christians. Cristóbal Colón discovers the Indies. Elio Antonio de Nebrija publishes the first Castilian Grammar. |
| 1493 | Treaty of Barcelona: return of Rousillon and Cerdagne to the Crown of Aragón |
| 1494 | Treaty of Tordesillas between Castilla and Aragón sharing out areas of influence overseas |
| 1497 | Conquest of Melilla |
| 1499–1506 | Moorish rebellions in Granada (Albaicín, Alpujarras). Victories in Italy. Casa de Contratación de Sevilla (1503). Death of Isabel I (1504). Succession problems, food shortages and plague |
| 1508 | Foundation of the University of Alcalá de Henares |
| 1512 | Annexation of Navarra to Castilla |
| 1516 | Death of Fernando II of Aragón. Carlos of Ghent declared of age in Brussels to succeed to the joint Crowns of Castilla and Aragón. |

### Monarchia Hispanica: Imperial Spain

| 1517 | Arrival of Carlos I in Tordesillas (Valladolid) |
| 1519 | Charles V elected Holy Roman Emperor. Magellan's voyage of circumnavigation of the globe. Hernón Cortés arrives in México |
| 1520–1 | Civil wars and constitutional clashes. Villalar. French invasion of Navarra. |
| 1525 | Pavia: Victory over France in Italy |
| 1532–3 | Conquest of Perú by Pizarro and Almagro |
| 1534 | Ignatius Loyola founds the Jesuit Order |
| 1535 | Expedition against Tunis and Algiers. Foundation of Buenos Aires |
| 1545–1564 | Church Council of Trent. Discovery of silver mines in Potosí (Bolivia), Zacatecas (México) and Huancavélica (quicksilver) |

| | |
|---|---|
| 1547 | Undecisive victory over Lutherans at Muhlberg. 'Purity of Blood': Statute of Toledo Cathedral |
| 1553 | Charles V's miserable and humiliating retreat before Metz |
| 1555 | Peace of Augsburg with the Lutheran Princes. Abdication of the Emperor. |
| 1557 | San Quintín: Crushing defeat on the French. Peace of Cateau-Cambrésis (1559) |
| 1559–1562 | Spectacular *autos de fé* in Sevilla and Valladolid against Protestantism. |
| 1561 | First rumblings of opposition to Spanish rule in the Netherlands |
| 1568–1571 | Morisco uprising and their expulsion from Granada. Lepanto: Naval victory against the Ottoman Turks |
| 1580 | Incorporation of Portugal to the Castilian Crown |
| 1581–1676 | Years of intermittent drought, famine and plague |
| 1585 | Break of diplomatic relations with England |
| 1588 | Failure of the *Armada Invencible* |
| 1600 | Martín González de Cellorigo's memorial on the state of the Hispanic Monarchy |
| 1605 | Publication of Cervantes' *Don Quijote*, Part I |
| 1609 | Truce in Flanders. Moriscos expelled from Spain |
| 1626 | Publication of Quevedo's *El Buscón* |
| 1631–68 | Internal disturbances and separatist wars (Vizcaya, Catalunya, Aragón, Andalucía, Portugal, Sicily and Naples) |
| 1639–1640 | Naval disasters in the Channel and Brazil |
| 1643 | French decisive victory over the Army of Flanders |
| 1648 | Spain forced to recognise Dutch Independence. End of Thirty Years War |
| 1656–1668 | End of Spanish Hegemony in Western Europe. Treaty of the Pyrenees ratifies the victory of Louis XIV. Ten years unsuccessful war of attrition to keep Portugal under Spanish rule. |

## Spanish Bourbons

| | |
|---|---|
| 1700 | Carlos II dies without issue, naming Philip of Anjou (nephew of Louis XIV) as his heir |
| 1701–1714 | Felipe V arrives in Madrid. The Emperor, England and the United Provinces reject French succession to the Spanish throne |
| 1714 | Peace of Utrecht recognises Felipe V's succession in return for further territorial and commercial concessions to the members of the 'Grand Alliance' |

| | |
|---|---|
| 1707–1716 | Administrative and political reforms. Abolition of regional charters (*Decreto de Nueva Planta*) |
| 1763 | Peace of Paris to conclude Seven Years War with colonial losses to Spain and failure to regain Gibraltar and Menorca |
| 1766 | Bread Riots. Expulsion of the Jesuits (1767) |
| 1778 | Free Trade Act for the American Colonies |
| 1783 | Colonial gains in the Peace Treaty of Paris after the Thirteen Colonies' War of Independence. Menorca recovered but failure to take Gibraltar in 1782 |
| 1789–93 | Serious food crises in the north. Reactionary backlash which brings Spain into war against the French Revolution when Louis XVI was executed |
| 1795–1807 | Forced to make peace with the French, Spain now sides with France against Britain and Portugal. Naval disasters: Cape San Vicente (1797) and Trafalgar (1805) |
| 1808 | French military occupation of Spain. Popular rising against Napoleonic troops (2 May). Carlos IV and Fernando VII resign the Spanish Crown to Napoleon who appoints his brother José I as King of Spain |
| 1812 | Cortes assembled in Cádiz draft the first liberal constitutional charter. |
| 1813 | French withdrawal after the victory at Vitoria of Anglo-Portuguese-Spanish combined forces |
| 1814 | Fernando VII restores Royal Absolutism. War devastation and ensuing economic recession |
| 1820 | Riego's Army revolt forces Fernando VII to accept the 1812 Constitution |
| 1823 | French military intervention to restore Fernando VII's absolutist rule |
| 1824 | Independence of the American Colonies |
| 1833–9 | Death of Fernando VII without male issue. First Carlist War. Convention of Vergara enhances position of the Army |
| 1837 | First disentailing legislation |
| 1841 | Re-statement of Navarra's Foral Pact |
| 1842–9 | The Matiners' War in Catalunya |
| 1848 | First railway (Mataró-Barcelona) |
| 1855–6 | Madoz's Disentailing Legislation. Railway, Banking and Finance Acts |
| 1868–74 | Isabel II's fall, Serrano's Regency. Amadeo de Savoy. First Republic. Carlist revolt, Cuban insurrection and Cantonalist rising in Cartagena |

## Restoration of the Bourbon Monarchy

| | |
|---|---|
| 1875–6 | Army restoration of Alfonso XII as King of Spain |
| 1881–1912 | Growing militancy in country and town. Political assassinations. Workers' organisations. PSOE obtains its first parliamentary seat in 1910 |
| 1885–92 | Maria Cristina's Regency |
| 1898 | Loss of all remaining possessions overseas (naval disaster before US Navy off Santiago de Cuba) |
| 1909 | Tragic Week in Barcelona |
| 1912 | Spain acquires Protectorate over western Morocco. |
| 1917 | General Strike. Collapse of the Restoration political system. Military unrest. Economic crisis |
| 1921–2 | Military disasters in the Moroccan Protectorate |
| 1923–30 | Rise and fall of Don Miguel Primo de Rivera |

## Spain's Second Republic

| | |
|---|---|
| 1931 | Municipal Elections, Alfonso XIII leaves Spain. |
| 1932 | General Sanjurjo's Conspiracy. Agrarian Reform Bill and Statute of Autonomy for Cataunya |
| 1933 | Social unrest; growing unemployment. Victory of the Right in the General Election of 19 November |
| 1934 | Repressive and regressive policies from an increasingly reactionary administration. Wave of strikes and Asturian Insurrection (4 October) |
| 1936 | Republican Electoral Victory. Descent to violence |

## Military rising at Melilla (Morocco): 17 July 1936

| | |
|---|---|
| 1936 | General Francisco Franco Bahamonde. Head of State and Chief of the Armed Forces (1 October). Battle for Madrid. Civil War |
| 1937 | The Battle of El Jarama (February): international volunteers fighting for the Republic. Political Unification of the 'nationalist movement' (April) |
| 1939 | Fall of Barcelona (25 January). France and Britain recognised Franco as the ledgitimate government of Spain (27 February). Fall of Madrid on 28 March and Victory Day for *Generalisimo* Franco on 1 April |
| 1939–1951 | Political repression and severe economic recession. |

| 1941 | Death of Alfonso XIII. Don Juan, his son and heir |
| 1942 | Monarchical opposition to Franco. Anglo-American offensive in North Africa. Don Juan's anti-Franco Manifesto |
| 1945 | Bill of Rights as signal to the 'democratic' world |
| 1946 | United Nations' diplomatic boycott |
| 1947 | Franco declares Spain to be a kingdom |
| 1948 | France re-opens frontier with Spain. Agreement for Juan Carlos (Don Juan's son and heir) to be educated under Franco's supervision as his successor |
| 1953 | Treaty with USA and Concordat with Rome |
| 1955 | UN rescind their 1946 Resolution |
| 1957–9 | On the brink of bankruptcy. Industrial unrest and feuding among political families. New style of government: Opus Dei. Stabilization Plan |
| 1964 | First Economic Development Plan. |
| 1969 | Juan Carlos officially designated to succeed Franco in the fullness of time. State of emergency. Matesa Affair |
| 1970 | Burgos Trial (ETA). Preferential Trade Agreement (EEC) |
| 1973 | Economic Difficulties. Prime Minister Carrero Blanco assassinated (20 December) |
| 1974 | Carlos Arias Navarro, first civilian head of government under Franco. First signs of political reform. Execution of Catalan anarchist Salvador Puig |
| 1975 | 20 November: Franco's death. |

### King Juan Carlos I de Bourbón: 22 November 1975

| 1976 | Visit to the USA in June. Adolfo Suárez invited to form government on 3 July. Political Reform Act and legalisation of political parties (December) |
| 1977 | Escalation of political violence. Electoral Decree (18 March). Legalisation of the Spanish Communist Party (April). Don Juan abdicates on his son, Juan Carlos I (May). First democratic elections for a constituent parliament (June). UCD: the new party of government. |
| 1978 | Free trade union elections (February). Constitutional Charter endorsed by the nation on 12 December and sanctioned by Juan Carlos I. |
| 1979 | General Election (March). Municipal Elections (April). Autonomy for Catalunya and Euskadi (December) |
| 1980 | Catalan and Basque Regional Elections |
| 1981 | Tejero's abortive 'pronunciamiento' (*23–February*). LOAPA |

|      | (September). Elections in Galicia (October) |
|------|---------------------------------------------|
| 1982 | Spain's accession to NATO and Andalusian regional election (May). General Elections of 28 October. Victory of Partido Socialista Obrero Español (PSOE) |
| 1983 | Autonomy for Castilla and León (February). Local and Regional Elections (May) |
| 1984 | Elections in Euskadi (February) and Catalunya (April) |
| 1985 | Elections in Galicia (November) |
| 1986 | Spain joins the EEC. Andalusian and General Elections (June) and Elections in Euskady (November). PSOE renewed, but weakened, mandate |
| 1987 | Municipal Elections. Accession to the Single European Act |
| 1988 | General Strike of 14 December |
| 1989 | Spain's Presidency of the European Community and her first European Elections. Accession to the European Monetary System. General Election of 29 October |
| 1991 | Regional and Municipal Elections. In October Madrid plays host to the Middle East Peace Conference |
| 1992 | Catalan Elections. The Treaty of Maastricht: European Project for further economic and monetary unification. Quincentenary of the encounter with the West Indies in 1492. Olympic Games in Barcelona. Madrid, cultural capital of Europe |
| 1993 | General Election on 6 June. Ruling party returned to Parliament with diminished majority amid serious criticism about economic mismanagement, growing unemployment, corruption and imcompetence in high circles |
| 1994 | General Strike on January 27. Regional Elections in Andalucía and Euskadi. European Elections' |
| 1995 | Municipal Elections (May) and Regional Election in Catalunya (November). Second Spanish Presidency of the European Union in the second half of the year culminating in the European Summit held in Madrid in mid-December |
| 1996 | General Election: March 3 |
| 1997 | Kidnap and execution of Miguel Angel Blanco by ETA |
| 1998 | ETA declares an indefinite truce (Sept) |
| 1999 | Spain joins the new European currency: the Euro (1 January) |

# Further Reading

FERNÁNDEZ CASTRO, M.C. (1995) *Iberia in Prehistory* London: Basil Blackwell

KEAY, S.J. (1988) *Roman Spain* London: British Museum Publications

COLLINS, R. (1995) *Early Medieval Spain: Unity uin Diversity, 400–1000* London: Macmillan

GLICK, THOMAS F. (1995) *From Muslim fortress to Christian castle* Manchester and New York: Manchester University Press

MACKAY, A. (1977) *Spain in the Middle Ages* London: Macmillan

KAMEN, H. (1983) *Spain 1469–1714* London: Longman

YUN CASALILLA, B & I.A.A. THOMPSON *The Castilian Crisis of the Seventeenth Century* Cambridge University Press

LYNCH, J. (1989) *Bourbon Spain 1700–1808* London: Basil Blackwell

CARR, R. (1982) *Spain 1808–1975* Oxford University Press

HOOPER, J. (1995) *The New Spaniards* Harmondsworth: Penguin

SALMÓN, K.G. (1995) *The modern Spanish economy: transformation and integration into Europe* London: Pinter

HOLMAN, O. (1996) *Integrating Southern Europe.* EC Expansion and the Transnationalization of Spain London and New York: Routledge

# Historical Gazetteer

Numbers in bold refer to the main text

*Al-Andalus* was the Arabic name for the Iberian Peninsula. Its derivative Andalucía refers only to the South, the most Arabised region. 'Andalusí' is used for the inhabitants and culture of al-Andalus. The term 'hispano–musulmán' or 'islámico' normally describes their arts and crafts, **22, 25, 42–4, 54**

*Alarcos* (Ciudad Real) was the scene of the crushing defeat inflicted by the Almohads on the Christian troops of Alfonso VIII of Castilla in 1195. **44, 47**

*Albacete* (Arabic: 'the plain'), capital of the province of the same name, lies in the centre of the wine-growing region of La Mancha; it has always been renowned for the quality of its knives and daggers. From the nineteenth century it has been the centre of a prosperous saffron trade and more recently in 1936–7 became famous as the recruiting and training centre of the International Brigaders who rallied to defend Republican Spain. **5, 187**

*Alcalá de Henares* 'fortress' on the northern bank of the Henares River built by the Arabs, was Complutum to the Romans. Alfonso XI of Castilla promulgated there his famous legal code (*Ordenamiento de Alcalá*) and in 1508 Cardinal Cisneros founded a university, the 'complutense', which competed with Salamanca for the intellectual leadership of the country. After a long decline it was transferred to Madrid in 1836, still retaining the name of 'complutense'. Alcalá's university status has been restored recently with a new foundation. It was also the birthplace of the author of *Don Quijote de la Mancha*. **62, 109**

*Alcántara* takes its Arabic name from the famous Roman 'bridge' over the Tagus built in 105 A.D., and was once the headquarters of the knightly Order of Alcántara created to defend the western frontier against Muslim attack; similarly the Order of Calatrava was designed for the defence of the middle frontier and Santiago for the defence of Cáceres. **9, 52, 61**

*Algeciras* the 'green island' of the early Muslim invaders, lies to the north-east of Tarifa, the southernmost tip of the Iberian Peninsula. For nearly a hundred years it was the scene of the embattled struggle between Christian and Muslim for control of the Straits of Gibraltar until its destruction by Muhammad V of

Granada in 1368. The town came back to life in the eighteenth century and is now the main Spanish port of call to and from North Africa. Not far from Algeçiras, the ruins of the ancient city of Carteia, which the Romans rebuilt in 171 B.C. as a colony (their first) for retired legionaries and their Iberian wives, may still be seen from the promontory of San Roque. *Alicante* was known as 'al-Lucant' to the Arabs and as 'Lucentum' to the Romans before them. In the Middle Ages it was one of the strongest fortresses south of Valencia. It was there that José Antonio Primo de Rivera was executed on 20 November 1936 and the last Republican town to surrender to Franco's nationalist troops on 30 March 1939. Since then it has become one of the leading tourist centres (Costa Blanca) and a prosperous agricultural market. The salt work at Torrevieja date back to Roman times. **5, 12**

**Almadén** ('the quicksilver mine' of the Arabs) is the richest mercury deposit in Europe, exploited in the past by Greeks, Romans (who called it Sisapo) and Muslims. In the sixteenth century mercury was crucial to the amalgam process of silver extraction in the Indies. Still in production it has been the property of the State since 1921. **10, 88**

*Almería* ('mirror of the sea') is the easternmost provincial capital of the Costa del Sol, the most Muslim-like in customs and architecture and the driest part of Spain with a semi-desert hinterland. The Romans called it 'Campus Spartarius' (the land of esparto grass). The town was an important port under the Romans and a prosperous Muslim city in the eleventh century. As part of the Nasrid Kingdom of Granada it retained its prosperity until its fall to the Catholic Monarchs in 1488, when most of its inhabitants were forced to leave. In recent years it has managed to build up a considerable trade of mining exports from the interior, early fruit and vegetable crops and tourism (Mojácar), despite water shortages and general impoverishment of the soil. **3, 153, 228**

*Almuñécar* (Sexi for the early Phoenician traders) is a well-known holiday resort, near Nerja, where Abd al-Rahman I landed in 756 in his flight from the Abbasids to found the independent Umayyad Emirate of Córdoba. **4, 27, 28**

*Avila de los Caballeros* ('of the knights'), like most other 'walled population centres' (see Segovia) at the heart of Castilla's struggle for expansion against the Muslims of al-Andalus, is particularly noted for the impressive circuit of fortifications and Romanesque churches. An ancient tradition ascribes its foundation to Hercules himself. The fortifications we so admire today were initiated by Alfonso VI, the conqueror of Toledo, in 1090 and so was its early Gothic Cathedral started in 1091 and completed in the thirteenth century. Its claim to fame was reinforced by the presence there in the sixteenth century of one of the leading mystics and writers of Castilian Reformation, Teresa de Cepeda y Ahumada (1515–1532), known as Santa Teresa de Avila. After the expulsion of the

Moriscos in the early seventeenth century the town declined until quite recently, when pilgrims and tourists in ever increasing numbers crowd the streets of the once most-famed city in the Kingdom of Castilla. **79, 104, 129**
*Ayacucho* was the last battle in 1824, which sealed the independence of the American colonies from metropolitan Spain.

*Badajoz* on the left bank of the Guadiana River has endured over the ages more than a fair share of fighting and destruction as a frontier town between Roman and Lusitanian, Christian and Muslim, Portuguese and Spaniard, French and British. In August 1936 it was again the scene of mass executions when Franco's nationalist forces entered the city. With Cáceres, the other province of Extremadura, Badajoz is still one of the poles of the 'frontier of under-development' (along the Portuguese border) which, despite certain attempts to improve agricultural conditions through irrigation, continues to ease out a large number of migrants from the land as in the early sixteenth century when it provided conquistadores, explorers and sea-farers to the American enterprise. **136**
*Bailén* (Battle of) was the first Spanish victory over Napoleon's invading forces in the Spanish War of Independence (1908).

*Barcelona* is perhaps the most prosperous and interesting of all Spanish cities. Its origin stretches back to the Iberian name of Barcino, founded by Carthaginian Hamilcar Barca in 230 B.C.. The Romans renamed it Julia Faventia as the capital of Laietania, a district of Hispania Tarraconensis. It was destroyed by the Franks in 263 A.D. and rebuilt and fortified by the Romans with a great wall. King Ataulf of the Visigoths made it his capital in 415 which explains, perhaps, the name Catalunya ('land of the Goths'. Or is it 'the land of castláns – Castellans – not unlike Castilla?). For close to a century it was a Muslim city until a son of Charlemagne pushed the Muslims back and set up the Spanish March as a county. In 874 Count Wilfred obtained his independence from the Carolingian, Charles the Bald. For years it was to live in the shadow of the great Caliphate of Córdoba. It was sacked by al-Mansur in 985 and again by his son in 1003. Marriage in 1137 brought Catalunya and Aragón together as a federation of equals and thereafter as the capital of the Crown of Aragón it expanded as far as Murcia and Languedoc and overseas to the Balearic Islands, Sardinia, Sicily and Greece, to become in the thirteenth and fourteenth centuries the foremost commercial and military power in the Mediterranean as testified by the magnificent buildings of the period and the maritime laws, which served as a model to other Mediterranean states. Following the Black Death of the mid-fourteenth century, succession problems and civil wars in the fifteenth, the dynastic unification of Castilla and Aragón in 1479 in the context of the ensuing shift of political and commercial hegemony to the Atlantic seaboard left Barcelona struggling behind until the end of the sixteenth century. From then on a slow, but steady recovery brought her to a prime position from the eighteenth century to the present time, notwithstanding a constant tug of war to maintain its identity and autonomy against repeated pressure and attacks from the French and the Castilian centre, and social and political conflicts in the nineteenth and twentieth centuries. Architect Antonio Gaudí (1852–1926) is perhaps the outstanding example of Catalunya's cultural and economic endeavour at the turn of the nineteenth century for the extent and originality of his work, most of which may be admired in Barcelona itself. It was the capital and last bastion of Republican Spain until its fall in January 1939 and yet again had to endure the odium and repression of the Castilian masters. Its staying power has not been blunted, and, once more, Barcelona as the capital of the Principality of Catalunya is now enjoying a greater degree of administrative and political autonomy and played a great role as the world capital of sport in 1992. **11, 14, 32, 39, 55, 114, 153, 156, 158, 160–1, 165–6, 168, 173, 180, 191–2, 205, 210, 213, 231–4, 240**

**Bilbao** was founded by Don Diego López de Haro in 1300. For a long time the surrounding area was a wild backwater sparsely populated by Vascones, speakers of a language totally different from those common in the Mediterranean at the time who had remained quite impervious to Roman, Muslim and Christian influence. The prosperous woollen trade of the fifteenth and sixteenth century was conducted mainly through Santander, Laredo and Bilbao, and there was an incipient industry, iron foundries, and a long tradition of shipping and sailing from the fourteenth century which contributed to its growing prosperity. The French plundered the town in 1808 and it was besieged in both Carlist wars and again in 1937 (hence the name 'ciudad de los sitios'). Modernisation and industrialisation came in the form of huge profits for productive investment from export of iron ores, mainly to Britain, from the last part of the nineteenth century. Since then it has developed as the heavyweight of Spanish industry. In recent years internal political strife and social unrest have put a premium on further development, all the more difficult to promote in the context of serious differences, between the 'devolved' government of Euskadi in Vitoria (Alava) and the Spanish State. **10, 125, 155, 156, 158, 205, 210, 231**

**Burgos** was founded in 822 as a fortified enclave on the bank of the Arlanzón, a tributary of the Tagus. As the balance of power shifted to the Christian principalities, it became the capital of the Kingdom of Castilla closely associated with the three centuries of war against al-Andalus and competing with Toledo for precedence as the centre of the struggle against Islam. With its strategic position at the crossroads of the *Camino de Santiago* and the chief routes between the northern ports and the main lines of expansion to the Muslim south, between the thirteenth and sixteenth century Burgos was one of the leading trading, financial and cultural centres of Castilla la Vieja.

Since then the old fortified city (the original castle was blown up by the French on their retreat to Vitoria in 1813) declined steadily until the Civil War when it was for a while the capital of Franco's Spain. In the 1960s and the 1970s the city has known a considerable amount of growth, due to its political pre-eminence and its key position between the industrial north and Salamanca, Valladolid and Madrid. **53, 68, 75, 80, 214**

*Cádiz* (Gadir: 'an enclosure'): Gades or Gadeira as the Greeks knew it dates back to 1100 B.C.; the oldest recorded town in the Iberian Peninsula, and probably in Europe, was settled by Phoenician traders as an important market for tin, silver and amber. Carthaginians occupied it for several hundred years and under the Romans it had the monopoly of the salt-fish trade with the imperial capital. After the fall of Rome it nearly disappeared. When Alfonso X of Castilla entered the town in 1264, it was almost depopulated. The discovery of the Americas brought wealth and prosperity to these shores in the form of trade and silver fleets, especially after 1640 when Cádiz started to replace Sevilla as the port of call for the riches from America. The last great cathedral was built there in the seventeenth century with the proceeds from the Indies. Its population grew from 8000 in 1600 to 80,000 by the end of the eighteenth century. It played a crucial role in shaping Spanish liberalism and constitutional theory at the start of the nineteenth century but then it receded again into the distance when the American colonies severed their

political connection with Spain in 1824. Recently some recovery may be assumed from a great deal of construction along the isthmus linking the small peninsula, which houses the old city and the port, with the mainland. The poor state of repair of its walls, ancient buildings and highly attractive nineteenth-century, housing stock belie the popular notion of Cádiz as *una tazita de plata* ('silver bowl') but then, like so many other Spanish towns and cities, it has been at the sharp end of plunders, sieges and even an earthquake. **4, 8, 11, 53, 61, 76, 88, 129, 132–4, 136**

*Cartagena* (Nova Carthago) was founded by Hasdrubal Barca in 227 B.C. Well secured by two forts guarding a deeply indented bay, it was a leading administrative and mining centre, commercial port and naval base under Carthage, Rome and Byzantium. Under Visigoths, Muslims and Christians it played a diminished role and was sacked in 1585 by Francis Drake. In 1873 it set up a cantonalist revolt against Spain's First Republic suffering then, and later in the Civil War, from heavy bombardment and subsequent repression. The city is still Spain's principal naval establishment, arsenal and shipyard, and the first location of oil refining activities since the 1940s (Escombreras). Its water sport and recreational facilities all the year round (Mazarrón, La Manga) have improved the economic prospects of the area. **4, 7, 10, 17, 24, 53, 148, 158**

*Ceriñola* (1503: Battle of) opened a series of brilliant victories in northern Italy which finally wrested the neighbouring peninsula from French competing territorial claims. **73**

***Ciudad Real*** ('Villareal' originally) typified the pattern of occupation imposed upon al-Andalus by the conquering north between the Tagus and Sierrra Morena. It was founded in 1262 by Alfonso X of Castilla to consolidate territorial acquisitions from al-Andalus and to oversee and supervise land distribution among the nobility, the new Military Order of Calatrava established in 1258 and the town itself. Its special status was embodied in the municipal charter of 1420. It is the capital city of La Mancha (Don Quijote's birthplace and field of adventure) with important mining resources, the best pasture grounds for migratory sheep and largest wine-producing area of Spain. **53**

***Córdoba*** was an important Iberian centre on a plain sloping gently down

to the Baetis (Guadalquivir: the 'mighty river' of al-Andalus) and the capital of the Roman province of Hispania Ulterior, alternating with Hispalis (Sevilla) and Italica (north of Sevilla) its prime position in the Baetica. Abd al-Rahman I raised the city to a period of unparalleled splendour, starting in 785 with the building of the Great Mosque. The centuries of unprecedented wealth and prosperity came to an abrupt end when Fernando III entered the city in 1236. Many of its inhabitants fled and the city declined until quite recently when visitors from all over the world help to revive the economy of the city, which still offers the most exciting view of Islam civilisation at its best. The city in recent democratic times has also had the distinction of returning to the Town Hall the first Communist mayor, fully appreciative of the implications of a positive and sympathetic interpretation of Spain's, and most particularly Córdoba's, Islamic past. **9, 23, 25, 27, 30, 32, 34, 53, 61**

***Covadonga*** (Battle of): this Christian victory in 722 in the fastnesses of the Picos de Europa (Asturias) was the first sign of resistance to Muslim advance from the old Hispano-Gothic population. For that reason it has been a pilgrimage centre and a symbol of Castilian nationalism ever since, as Roncesvalles is to the Navarrese, San Juan de la Peña (Huesca) is to the Aragonese or Montserrat is to the Catalans. It is also a holiday resort and one of the highest points of the recently-declared Parque Nacional for the preservation of the local species of flora and fauna. **36, 38**

**Cuenca** a picturesque medieval town famous for its 'hanging houses' and the 'enchanted city' (a natural labyrinth of rocks looking like a ruined city), is situated halfway between Madrid and Valencia, and was once the headquarters of the knightly Order of Santiago and the provider in the fifteenth and sixteenth centuries of the best quality wool in Europe. Since then, the provincial capital has suffered at the hands of the French in 1808, the Carlists (who sacked it in 1873) and more recently during the Civil War in 1937. **28, 44**

**Ebro** (Treaty of): Carthage and Rome set the river as the boundary for their spheres of influence in the Iberian Peninsula (226). **1–3, 6, 8**

**Elche** in the province of Alicante was a leading centre of Celtiberian culture in the fourth and third centuries B.C. as shown by the discovery there of the first of a series of striking sculptures known as 'The Lady of Elche'. **5**

**El Escorial** (The Monastery of St Lawrence of), was built by Juan Bautista de Toledo and Juan de Herrera between 1563 and 1598 for Felipe II as a burial place for his father Carlos I and a summer residence to commemorate San Quintín, the victory over the French on St Lawrence's Day (10 August 1557). It represents the zenith of Castilla's Imperial Supremacy and the typical architectural style of the period. **95, 97, 98**

**Empúries** (Ampurias), one of the large holiday resorts of the Costa Brava, was founded in the sixth century B.C. by Greeks as a trading station ('Emporion': market). In the early days of Rome it was the main base of military operations in the Iberian Peninsula and Charlemagne made it the capital of the Maritime March of the Empire. **8**

**Estella** was the capital of the kings of Navarra and a very important staging point for pilgrims on the road to Santiago de Compostela, which explains a number of fine buildings, royal palaces, aristocratic residences and churches of the twelfth and thirteenth centuries. It was also the headquarters of the Carlists in the 1830s and 1870s. **82, 138**

**Granada** was an Iberian settlement which the Romans named Illiberis (whence Elvira). Under Roman rule it must have been an early Christian centre as the first Bishops' Council in 305 A.D., preceding Constantine's conversion took place there. It remained relatively forgotten from the mainstream of peninsular history until the collapse of the Umayyad Caliphate of Córdoba in 1031. When al-Andalus fell to the Christian conquerors after Las Navas de Tolosa, Muslim 'Gharnatha' under Muhammad I, the founder of the Nasrid dynasty, emerged from obscurity to become the wealthiest and most splendid kingdom in the West. It was its first ruler who initiated the construction of La Alhambra ('the red one'), the highest expression of Islamic art in the Iberian Peninsula. The Nasrid Kingdom of Granada, with its capital perched on the southern slopes of Sierra Nevada, stretched from Almería to Cádiz and Jaén, quite impregnable to attacks, bribes and entreaties from the northern neighbours until 1492.

After much unrest and rebellion, intolerance and repression the new Christian masters found a final solution in the total expulsion of Muslims and *moriscos* from the territory. The pinnacle of Islamic civilisation in the Iberian Peninsula has not recovered from the ensuing decline until the twentieth century with the introduction of further irrigation works, new crops and, of course, tourism as it is beautifully situated between the winter resorts of Sierra Nevada and the summer attractions of the Costa del Sol. **14, 23, 25, 34, 35, 43, 54, 61–2, 66, 70–1, 84**

*Gudalajara* (Arabic: 'river of stones') was a minor frontier post on the main route of Muslim invasions and raids from Toledo along the Henares River to the Ebro Valley. In the sixteenth century it knew a period of cultural splendour through the artistic patronage of one of the leading families of the country, the Mendozas (Duques del Infantado). The town gained some notoriety as the one pitched battle resoundingly won by Loyalist troops against the combined forces of Franco's Insurrectionists and Mussolini's expeditionary corps. **96**

*Guadalete* (711: Battle of) this is supposed to be the name of the river on whose banks the fatal victory of Muslim invaders over the Visigothic King Roderic took place. The issue of its exact location has been the subject of heated debate but we are still a long way from a satisfactory account of one of the most popular myths of Spanish history.

*Huelva* (Onuba for the Romans), on the southernmost border with Portugal, may well have been the site of the legendary emporium of Tartessos. From very early times it has channelled a large trade of mineral exports from the interior (Tharsis and Río Tinto), tunny and sardine fisheries and, more recently, early strawberries and oil products from the new refineries built near the Monastery of La Rábida (Arabic: 'watch-tower'), where a despairing Cristóbal Colón found in 1491 a powerful advocate in Isabel I of Castilla for his cause of discovery and exploration. **4, 151**

*Ilipa* (Alcalá del Río, ten miles north of Sevilla) was the scene of the famous battle against the Carthaginians in 206 B.C. which opened up the whole of Baetica to Rome. **8**

*Jaén* was known to the Romans, who exploited its rich silver mines. Lying north of the capital city of the province is Linares, near the site of the Iberian settlement of Castulo, with lead and copper mines partly exploited by the English. The importance of the province and its capital city is due to its key position as the door to Andalucía from Castilla la Nueva, through the narrow gorges of Despeñaperros ('The Pass of the Overthrow of the Dogs', that is, 'the Moors'). From Valdepeñas (Ciudad Real), famous for its wines, to Jaén there runs the 'battle Highway', the scene of fierce fighting between Muslims and Christians for close to two centuries. When Fernando III conquered Jaén in 1245 after several long and costly sieges, the land was distributed among the military Orders of Calatrava and Santiago, and the See of Toledo. It has declined ever since, seemingly condemned to one of the lowest places in Spain's regional wealth distribution table as a landscape dominated by large plantations of olive-trees. The failure of such a drop could bring devastation to the area as in 1930, and in the 1950s (together with Toledo) Jaén ('latifundista y proletaria') topped the illiteracy rate for Spain and continued in the 1960s contributing a large share of the migrant population escaping from the hardness and ingratitude of the land. **4, 53, 61, 154, 175**

*Jerez de la Frontera*  in the southernmost province of Cádiz is now a large and prosperous town famous for its wines (sherries), which were exported to England from Henry VII's times (its best known *bodegas*  still owned by descendants of English and Irish families) and horses of Arab stock, both celebrated in the splendid festivals of May and September. Its name Zeres derives from the Arabic spelling of the old Roman foundation, with the additional 'de la frontera' reminiscent of its role as the advancing line of Castilian expansion to the Straits of Gibraltar in the middle of the thirteenth century. Alfonso X seized it from the Muslims in 1264.

**Las Navas de Tolosa**  (Battle of), on the 'Battle Highway' between Valdepeñas and Jaén, was the scene in 1212 of a decisive victory of the combined Christian army over the Almohads, which enabled Castilla and Aragón to launch their final bid for the fabled wealth and prosperity of al-Andalus. **35, 47–8, 52**

*León*  owes its name to the Seventh Legion which was quartered there to police a highly sensitive area on the border of Roman rule (south of the Astures and Galicians) with rich cereal-producing plains (*Tierra de Campos*) and silver and gold mines. It led a fairly uneventful existence under the Visigoths and Suebi but rose to international importance from the tenth to the twelfth century as the capital of the kingdom of the same name and staging point on the road to Santiago de Compostela, the main route of culture and trade from western Europe. The array of magnificent buildings of the period, from Romanesque to Gothic, bears witness to the prominent part played by the city. When the frontier with al-Andalus was pushed southwards in the thirteenth century, León lost a great deal of its former glory as one of the main cultural centres of Christendom. **4, 9, 11, 32, 35, 39–42, 45, 48, 50–5**

**Lepanto**  (1571: Battle of) naval victory over the Ottoman Turks in the narrow straits from the Gulf of Corinth which reasserted Hispanic supremacy in Mediterranean waters.

*Madrid*  (Arabic: 'Magerit') was a fortress built by Muhammad I in the second half of the ninth century as a military outpost dominating the main route of access along the Henares, through Alcalá and Guadalajara to the middle Ebro. It was a small village with a formidable fortress which Juan II and Enrique IV used as their regular residence in the fifteenth century. Also Carlos I on the few occasions he was in Spain for any length of time, seemed to have preferred the keen air from the Sierra de Guadarrama. Madrid is the highest capital city in

Europe, and Felipe II made it his regular and 'única corte' in 1561, a position which it has retained (except under Felipe III) to the present day. It has no other claim to special status than its location at the very centre of the Iberian Peninsula and only in the last thirty years has it managed to slightly reduce its almost exclusively bureaucratic and patrimonial characteristics under severe demographic pressure from internal migration. It is said that such an artificial creation as the centre of the Spanish Empire has contributed to the depopulation and decay of the surrounding countryside and of towns like Toledo, Avila and Segovia, and now that it has to share its functions with seventeen seats of autonomous governments ('autonomías') it may be even more difficult to retain its capital status in anything other than name. As the capital city of the nation it has amassed a considerable wealth of civic buildings, royal and noble residences, museums and art galleries. Carlos III's patronage during one of the significant periods of urban development in the eighteenth century and his mantle as the 'best mayor of Madrid' fell in more democratic times on Don Enrique Tierno Galván who more than anybody else in the twentieth century seemed determined to turn the capital city into a civilised and urbane centre of modern living. **121, 122, 127, 134, 156, 158–61, 166, 186–9, 192**

*Málaga* like all important ports in southern Spain, has known a long and chequered career through its long history from its Phoenician foundation as a trading post in salt fish (hence

its name from 'malac'=to salt), minerals and vegetable produce, to its present status as the capital of Costa del Sol. Carthaginians, Romans and Byzantines held the town and maintained a thriving trade. It then became the principal port of the Nasrid Kingdom of Granada. The Muslims regarded it as 'a paradise on earth' and there will be many today who would readily agree with their verdict. There are important remains of the passing civilisations, including a Roman theatre, Muslim fortifications, a lighthouse (Gibralfaro) and one of the last great Cathedrals, built on the site of an earlier mosque. **4, 11, 17, 25, 28, 34, 92, 95, 178**

*Mérida* (near Badajoz) is the richest Spanish town in Roman remains. It was founded in 25 B.C. as Augusta Emerita, capital of Lusitania. **11**

*Montiel* (Battle of: 1369), on the 'Battle Highway', was the encampment where Enrique de Trastámara defeated and killed his half-brother Pedro I, thus initiating the long rule of the Trastámara dynasty in Castilla and Aragón. **63**

*Moriscos* after the fall of Granada in 1492 the local Muslim population of Spain were sooner or later forced to abandon their customs and religion or leave their country; the converts were known as 'moriscos' (as those of Jewish origin were called 'conversos') and were despite their conversion expelled from the the Christian kingdoms in 1609.) **71, 81, 105, 110**

*Mozárabes* ('Muslim-like', 'Arabicised') was the name given by the Christian northerners to their brethren in al-Andalus. From early on they were 'liberated' by Christian raiders or moved to the lands occupied by the warriors of the Cross, taking with them skills and techniques so overwhelmingly evident in the early Hispano-Christian culture and architecture of León, Zaragoza, Tierra de Campos and, above all, Toledo. **25, 43, 46, 50, 60**

**Mudéjares** were local Muslims who, as the Christians moved deeper into al-Andalus, chose through conversion or were allowed to remain in their land. As with the 'mozárabes', their skills and techniques in ceramics, wood, iron and building work in general are again eminently obvious, specially along the eastern regions and the provinces of Teruel and Zaragoza. **55, 61**

**Murcia** is the name of the region, which includes also Albacete and Cartagena (the community's port), and the capital of the autonomous community. The city is situated on the bank of the Segura river in the middle of a fertile vega of fruit and vegetable gardens, canning factories and a large export trade. Mazarrón and La Manga del Mar Menor contribute the profits of winter and summer tourism. Little is known of the city before the Muslims rebuilt it in the early part of the eighth century. After Las Navas de Tolosa Murcia became a separate Muslim Kingdom, easy prey for Castilians and Aragonese who disputed its conquest and annexation. Eventually this frontier territory was annexed to the Crown of Castilla but the Catalans of the Crown of Aragón had by then substantially repopulated the area. As in the region of Granada, after its con-

quest by the Christians there were serious conflicts, heavy repression, shifts of population and skills (the moriscos from Granada and Alpujarras took the silk trade with them to Murcia) and the final expulsion of 1609, which severely affected agricultural production throughout the Levant. **5, 28, 44, 53, 56**

**Numancia** (near modern Soria) was the capital of the Arevaci, Celtiberian people whose fight to a finish against the Roman legions in 134–133 B.C. has been one of the inspiring landmarks of Spanish nationalism. **6, 15, 19**

**Palencia** (see Segovia) situated on the banks of the River Carrión south of the fertile, corn-growing region of Tierra de Campos, was the old Iberian settlement of the Vaccaei, Pallantia. The Visigoths settled mainly in that area, which explains the name 'Campi Gotici' of medieval writers and the relative abundance of first names of Germanic origin. It was the royal residence of the Kings of Castilla in the twelfth and thirteenth century and the site of the first Castilian university foundation by Alfonso VIII in 1208, which was transferred to Salamanca in 1239. Its fine late Gothic Cathedral was started in 1331 and completed in 1516. Palencia was one of the old Castilian towns most severely punished by Carlos I for its participation in the Comunero Revolt of 1520–1. It is still the capital of one of the main grain-producing areas of Spain, now part of the 'Autonomous Community' of Castilla y León. **18**

**Pamplona** was a settlement of the Vascones rebuilt by Pompey's sons as Pompaelo in 68 B.C. It was taken by the Goths and held by the Muslims who called it Pampilona. By the end of the ninth century it was a separate county seeking to assert its independence from Charlemagne whose rearguard army they defeated at Roncesvalles in 778 in collaboration with the Banu Qasi of Zaragoza. In the early eleventh century as the capital of the Kingdom of Navarra it occupied a prime position in Christian Iberia as the guard of the Pyrenean passes and staging post of foreign cultures and pilgrims on their way to Santiago. With the expansion of Castilla and Aragón, Navarra was squeezed into the political orbit north of the Pyrenees until its annexation to Castilla by the Duke of Alba in 1512. Its distinctiveness and administrative and legal autonomy have been retained despite its strategic position, or perhaps because of it, as the point of entry for French territorial ambitions on the Iberian Peninsula from the sixteenth to the nineteenth century, and the two Carlist wars of the nineteenth century and the civil war of 1936–9. The prominent role played by the region as the most Catholic and conservative part of Spain in the last war enabled Navarra to retain and even enhance its separateness. Unlike large parts of Spain where nineteenth-century disentailment put paid to municipal and communal lands, Navarra managed to hold on to collective ownership of great tracts of land which in the 1950s offered the prerequisites for agricultural and industrial development. The region has grown and prospered economically and culturally and is now facing pressures and entreaties from Euskadi to compliment them in a large and diversified 'nacionalidad' within the Spanish State. **38, 39, 82, 127, 205**

***Pavia*** (Battle of) was the scene of a formidable victory over the French in 1525 which finally placed Italian territories under the rule of Castilla. **84**

***Rocroy*** (Battle of) in northern France was the first serious defeat of the Army of Flanders in 1643 which presaged the end of Spanish supremacy in the Low Countries and in central Europe. **99**

***Ronda*** is one of the most visited towns in southern Spain on account of its spectacular position perched above the deep gorge ('tajo') of the River Guadelivín (Guadiaro) which divides the old site of Roman Arunda from the new town founded by the Catholic Monarchs. Thanks to its impregnable position it remained as an isolated and independent Muslim Kingdom until 1485. Its proximity to Gibraltar and salubrious summer weather has made it very popular among British officials and officers, and their families, from the colony.

***Sagunto*** (near Valencia) is celebrated in Spanish history books (like Numancia) for its obstinate defence against the Carthaginians in 219 B.C. As Saguntum was an ally of the Romans, who as it happened did not come to the rescue, Hannibal Barca's provocative action was deemed as a declaration of war on the Empire. The ensuing war brought Carthaginian domination of the peninsula to an end. The town fell into decay and the Muslims renamed it Murbiter (from

'muri veteres': old walls) and then Murviedro, a name in use until 1868. Sagunto today, dominated by the imposing ruins of the old fortress of Saguntum, benefits from market gardening and heavy industry (Altos Hornos), and has witnessed in the very recent past some of the worst disruption and industrial strife in the wake of the so-called 'racionalización'. **8, 147**

**Salamanca** on the banks of the Tormes, was first captured by Carthaginian Hannibal Barca in 217 B.C. and later built by the Romans as a station of the Vía de la Plata (Silver Road) from Mérida to Astorga. Its claim to international fame came with the foundation of the university in 1230 by Alfonso IX, King of León, on the basis of the earlier one established by Alfonso VIII of Castilla in Palencia. Historically it is one of the most important cities in Spain, attracting large numbers of students to its university cloisters and visitors from all over the world to admire magnificent buildings covering the whole range of late medieval and early modern architectural endeavour. Because of its strategic position close to the Portu-

guese border it suffered considerably at the hands of French and English during the Napoleonic Wars. Strongly traditionalist it played a very prominent role in helping to shape Franco's nationalist movement in the early months of the military uprising of 1936. **95, 97**

**Segovia** (Roman Segóbriga), like Palencia, Avila, Cuenca or Burgos, typifies the fluctuations of Spain's history from the early Iberian settlements; it stands proudly on the banks of a tributary of the River Duero as a fortified enclave to protect the locals from Muslim raids and, when the tide turned, to launch their territorial ambitions beyond the River Tajo. The Alcázar was built on Roman and Arab foundations. Apart from the towers, it was seriously damaged by fire in 1862. What we see today is the result of an extensive restoration started in 1882. Like those early medieval towns it offers a range of defensive works, churches, royal and aristocratic residences as well as the famous Roman aqueduct built in the reign of Trajan. Not far from Segovia lie the ruins of the ancient town of

Coca or Cauca, where Roman Emperor Theodosius was born of an Iberian mother (Thermantia) in 346 A.D. Segovia entered the sixteenth century as a highly reputed producer of cloth (an industry probably introduced by the Muslims in the eighth century) from the highly regarded merino wool. As a manufacturing centre, jealous of its administrative privileges and constitutional charter, Segovia was at the forefront of the abortive attempt to withstand the heavy burden to be imposed upon Castilla la Vieja by Carlos I's succession to the Holy Roman Empire in 1519. **68, 104, 129**

***Sevilla*** is the fourth city of Spain today but in the past it has occupied more than once a foremost position as the cultural, political and commercial capital of the Iberian Peninsula. Situated on the left flank of the Guadalquivir, in the middle of a flat and fertile land (Tierra de María Santísima), its early Iberian inhabitants were already praised by ancient geographers as a civilised and highly structured society. Roman Hispalis was the leading urban centre of the province Baetica, and it continued to hold that leading position from the fifth century for its material prosperity and as a seat of learning, rivalling Toledo, the capital of the Visigothic kingdom. Muslim Ishbiliya rivalled Córdoba under the Umayyads and surpassed it in size and splendour under the Almohads from the mid-twelfth century. The Christian conquest and occupation of the city in 1248 initiated a marked decline though still retaining its attractiveness,

for its captor (Fernando III) made it his residence as did Pedro I in the mid-fourteenth century. The pinnacle of its glory came with the discovery of America and the establishment of the city at the centre of the Atlantic trade. By the middle of the seventeenth century Sevilla's centrality was giving way to Cádiz and its harbour as capable of accommodating bigger ships. In the eighteenth century certain river improvements brought overseas trade back to Sevilla, but the maritime conflicts of the turn of the century and the breakaway of the American colonies set the scene of decline and deprivation so characteristic of the Deep South. The splendid remains of those brilliant civilisations are an important source of income as visitors flock to admire palaces, churches or to dwell in the past at the Archivo de Indias, the national repository of all records pertaining to the overseas empire, but not sufficient to finance a more caring attitude for those jewels. An Andalucian historian wrote not long ago that Sevilla must hold the record for urban vandalism. In 1992 it enjoyed the opportunity of the commemorative celebrations of the quincentenary of the discovery of America; at least some of the wealth brought from the Indies should go towards repairing and refurbishing the buildings whose construction it initially paid for. As the capital of the 'comunidad autónoma' of Andalucía, Sevilla is once again in charge of its own destiny and may even be able to count on the favourable disposition of an Andalusian administration in the central seat of government. **22, 23, 32, 43, 61, 68, 88–9, 97, 185**

*Simancas* was the scene of one of the early triumphs of Christian against Muslim in 939. There is now a formidable castle, high above the River Pisuerga, between Valladolid and Tordesillas, which houses the national records of imperial Spain, the Archivo General de Simancas. **37**

*Tamarón* (Battle of: 1037) is the name of the valley in the province of Burgos where Fernando I of Castilla by defeating Vermudo III of León brought about the union of the two kingdoms under his rulership. **41**

*Tarragona* (Tarraco), together with Mérida in Extremadura, was the leading city of Roman Hispania and has a considerable number of Roman remains in and around the city, like the impressive aqueduct of Las Ferreras or the victory arch of Bará. Since then it has been under the sword time after time, practically deserted for three centuries, and severely repressed after the Catalan rebellion of 1640 and sacked by the French in 1811. **11, 13**

*Toledo* perched upon the middle course of the River Tajo and washed on three sides by the waters running down the narrow gorges, certainly is the most spectacular of Castilian cities beautifully positioned as a natural fortress and strategically situated on the main vertical axis of Castilla la Nueva. Historically, too, it has played a central role from Visigothic times as the capital of the country and the Primate See of all Spains. As part of al-Andalus it was a prosperous trade centre, a crossroads of the three Mediterranean cultures, Jewish, Islamic and Christian,

and the conveyor-belt of classical antiquity to the west. This conclave of peoples and ideas coexisted relatively peacefully well beyond its Christian capture in 1085. Its new ruler, Alfonso VI of Castilla and León styled himself 'Emperor of the Three Religions'. From the critical years of hunger and disease in the mid fourteenth century to the social and political strife of the fifteenth and sixteenth centuries, Toledo continued to hold its prime position. Its diminishing role in Castilian imperialism may explain its intolerant and intransigent attitude towards the ethnic and religious variety that had been the hallmark of Toledo's past. With the expulsion of Jews, the repression of *conversos* and expulsion of *moriscos*, Toledo began its long decline until it recovered some military and political strength in the early months of Spain's internecine war (September 1936). In the 1950s Toledo, together with Jaén, represented the highest illiteracy rate in southern Spain. More recently, though, the city of the Tajo has become alive with visitors of many different tongues who throng the narrow and winding streets of Toledo in search of a past which the city, like no other, can illustrate its past handsomely. **4, 17, 20, 25, 28, 29, 35, 42–5, 48, 50, 51, 78–9, 81, 88, 108, 175, 177, 210**

*Tordesillas* situated on a hill above the Duero River, was the venue where Castilla and Portugal, after arbitration by Pope Alexander VI, agreed in 1494 to a demarcation line for their respective spheres of influence overseas. Queen Juana, Carlos I's mother, was confined there after her husband's death and the Holy League of the Comuneros set up their headquarters there in the hope of obtaining support from Juana for their rebellion against the Emperor in 1520.

***Trafalgar*** (Battle of: 1805) the Franco-Spanish fleet under Villeneuve and Gravina was badly beaten off the Coast of Galicia by the British Navy under Nelson, who had already inflicted a serious defeat on the Spanish Navy off Cape San Vicente in 1797 under Admiral Jarvis. **127**

***Valencia*** is the third largest city of Spain and one of the most prosperous because of its position as an easily accessible harbour on the western Mediterranean seaboard and a large and fertile hinterland. As in the case of other coastal areas of eastern and southern Spain, Romans and Muslims exploited and developed its agricultural potential with irrigation works and water tribunals. A popular saying describes the city as 'a piece of heaven fallen on earth'. When in 1253 Jaime I of Catalunya and Aragón occupied and repopulated the region, mainly with Catalans, he too commented admiringly on the terraced and carefully tended *huertas* (market gardens) of the Valencian plains. The Muslim population responsible for the excellent husbandry of the land were for the most part allowed to stay on. But their expulsion in 1609 caused the area to decline for a couple of centuries until in the nineteenth centuries it returned to its former position as the main exporter of agricultural produce, ceramics and leather work. Capital of Republican

Spain during the Civil War, it is now from 1982 the seat of the regional government (Generalitat) of the 'Valencian autonomous community' which comprises the three coastal provinces of Castellón, Valencia and Alicante. **53, 55, 56, 104, 81–2, 110, 115, 187, 191**

***Valladolid*** apart from Madrid itself, is the fastest-growing city in central Spain as the main car manufacturer in the country, the centre of the wheat-producing plains of Castilla la Vieja and the producer of some of the best Spanish wines. It was a favourite residence of Castilian rulers in the late medieval period and replaced Burgos as the capital until the early seventeenth century. There are some fine buildings and the famous Plaza Mayor rebuilt in 1631 after the fire of 1619, celebrating the status of the city at the start of Castilla's imperial expansion, and a large selection of religious sculpture, which Napoleon's troops must have left behind when they plundered the town in the early nineteenth century. **77, 80, 83, 96**

***Villalar*** (Battle of: 1521) this village not far from Tordesillas was the scene of the final battle which crushed the revolt of the Comuneros. **82**

***Zaragoza*** on the right bank of the river, is the economic and political centre of the middle Ebro and its extremely fertile valley, and one of the fastest-growing cities in Spain today, both demographically and economically. It has always been at the crossroads of the main arteries of movement and change from the Pyrenees to Castilla and from Catalunya to the Basque Provinces. Salduba was an early settlement renamed Caesar-augusta by Emperor Octavius and corrupted later to 'Sarakosta' from which the present name derives. It was in the tenth and eleventh century a semi-independent Muslim Kingdom under the Banu Qasis competing in prosperity and splendour with the great Andalusian cities. From its capture by Alfonso I in 1118 it was the capital of the Kingdom of Aragón. After the dynastic union of Castilla and Aragón in 1479 apart from certain differences with Felipe II, feuds among the nobility and its support for the Austrian claimant in the Succession War of 1702–14, it played a minor role until it gained its title of 'always heroic and immortal' for its refusal to surrender in 1808–1809 to Napoleon's seasoned troops until more than half of the population of the city had been killed. The Carlists inflicted also considerable damage when they captured it in 1838. **4, 28, 39, 46, 77, 136, 185**

# Index

Abbasids 28–9
Abd al-Aziz 22–4
Abd Allah 31
Abd al-Malik 32
Abd al-Rahman I 27–30, 33
Abd al-Rahman II 30
Abd al-Rahman III 27, 31–3, 37
Abd-el-Krim 167, 169
Abril Martorell, Fernando 223
Adrian of Utrecht (Pope Adrian VI) 78, 80, 82, 84
*agermanats* 81–2
agriculture 4, 11–12, 27, 59–60, 75, 91–2, 105, 112–5, 125, 136–44, 152–6, 175–7, 200–2, 209–10
al-Andalus 22, 25, 36, 42–4, 54, 60
Alarcos 44, 47
Alaric I 15
Alaric II 17
Alava 185, 230
Albacete 5, 187
Alba, Duke of 74, 83, 97
Albareda Herrera, José María 206
Alcalá de Henares 62, 93, 109
Alcalá-Zamora, Don Niceto 171, 174, 180
Alcántara 9; Order of 52, 61, 84
Alcarria 27
Alfaro 11
Alfonso I of Aragon 45–6, 52, 55
Alfonso I of Portugal 45
Alfonso III of Portugal 45

Alfonso IX of León 48
Alfonso VI of Castilla 35, 41–3, 45
Alfonso VII of Castilla 40, 45
Alfonso VIII of Castilla 44, 45, 47
Alfonso X of Castilla-León 45, 52, 53, 56, 62
Alfonxo XI of Castilla 62
Alfonso XII 147, 148, 170
Alfonso XIII 146, 148, 152, 165, 167, 170, 217; in exile 170, 173; death 196
Algeçiras 34
al-Hakam I 29–30, 33
al-Hakam II 27, 32
Alhucemas Bay 169
*Alianza Popular* 221, 228–9
Alicante 5, 12, 24, 56
Almadén 10, 88
al-Mamun 42
al-Mansur 27, 28, 32–4, 53
Almería 3, 34, 92, 153
Almizra, treaty of 54
Almohads 35, 44–5, 47, 51–2, 60
Almoravids 35, 43–5, 47, 51, 60
al-Muktadir 34
Almuñécar 4, 27, 28
al-Mutamid of Sevilla 43
al-Mutamid of Toledo 42
Alpujarras 71
Amadeo I 147
America 85–95; Spanish conquest and occupation 85–8, 99; Sevilla

and Atlantic trade 88–9, the Royal Fifth 89; lands of opportunity and plenty 91; rise of new service class 92–3; relations with Britain over Thirteen Colonies 119–20; independence of colonies 136; loss of last overseas possessions 154, 156

Amiens, peace of (1802) 127

Ampurias (Empúries) 8, 11

anarchist movement 162–3, 166, 178

Anarcho-Syndicalist Confederation (CNT) 168–9

Andalucía (Baetica) 3–13, 16, 22, 60–1, 72, 99, 166, 175, 227, 232

Annaeus 12

Annual 167

Añoveros, Monsignor 216

Antwerp 91

Arab-Berbers 22–6, 28, 33, 35

Aragón 38, 40; population and land occupation 55–8; economic and demographic decline 58–9; fifteenth-century crisis 59–60

Aranda, Don Pedro 123, 124, 126

Aranjuez 132

Araquistáin, Luis 198

Arburúa, Manuel 204

architecture 50, 57, 96, 97

Arcos de la Frontera 61

Arfe (sculptors) 97

Arias Navarro, Carlos 215–19

Armada 99

army 26, 33, 37, 48–9, 54, 67, 70, 83, 94–5, 103, 137–8, 145–7, 165–7, 178, 220, 227–8

*Arte de la lengua castellana* 73, 94

Asturias 9, 17, 35, 155, 159; miners' revolt 181–2; in Civil War 188

Astur-Leónese monarchy 36–7

Atahualpa 91

Atapuerca 41

Athanagild 24

Augustus, Emperor 10

autonomy 224–34

Avila 79, 104, 129

Ayacucho 136

Azaña, Manuel 174, 176, 178, 181–192

Aznar, Admiral Juan Bautista 170

Aznar, José María 238, 240

Badajoz 23, 35, 41, 43, 45, 126, 136, 210

Bailén 128

Bakunin, Mikhail 160–2

Balearic Islands 7, 17, 28, 34, 44, 53, 55; Black Death 58

banking and finance 90–2

Barbate *see* Guadalete 102–9, 114, 149–50, 155, 201

Barcelona, sacked in 985 and 1003 32; conquered by Charlemagne (801) 37; industrial unrest 160, 165, 168, 205; population growth 156, 158; in Civil War 191, 192; Olympic Games 237

Barcelona, treaty of (1493) 73

Basque autonomy 180, 187, 189, 213–14, 224, 230–2, 236, 239

Basque language 7, 216

Bayonne 127, 132

Benedictine monks 50

Berenguer, General Damaso 170

Berenguer, Ramón 46, 55

Berrugete, Alonso 97

Besteiro, Professor Julián 163

Biar, Castle of 54

Bilbao 10, 126, 155, 156, 158, 205, 210, 230, 240

Blanco, Miguel Angel 239

*Buen Retiro, El* 96, 97, 136

Burgos 53, 68, 75, 80, 214

Byzantine Empire 17, 24

Caballero, Largo 168, 178, 179

Cáceres 52, 97
Cádiz 4, 8, 11, 53, 61, 76, 88, 129, 132–4, 136
Calahorra 12, 50, 95; castle of 97
Calatayud 12
Calatrava, Order of 52, 53, 61
Calderón de la Barca, Pedro 94
Calvo Sotelo, Don José 184
Calvo Sotelo, Leopoldo 228
Cambó 156, 164–6
Campomanes, Don Pedro 123, 124, 138
Cano, Alonso 97
Cánovas del Castillo, Don Antonio 148, 153, 157, 164
Carlism 137–42, 148, 185, 189
Carlist war 137–8
Carlos Hugo de Borbón-Parma 222
Carlos I of Spain and Charles V, Emperor of the Holy Roman Empire 75–85
Carlos II 101, 104, 112
Carlos III 113, 117–8, 120–5, 124, 125
Carlos IV 121, 125–7, 137, 142
Carrero Blanco, Admiral 215
Carrillo, Don Santiago 220
Cartagena (Carthago Nova) 4, 7, 10, 17, 24, 53, 148, 158
Carthage 4, 6–8; 10
Casas Viejas, massacre of 178
Castilian language 27
Castilla, rise of Christian Spain 35–40; early Christian settlements 40–2; population and resettlement 54, 60–1; monarchical power 62–4; Castilian Fisc 64–5, 113; financial straits of nobility 65–7; social and racial conflicts 67–9; union with Aragón 69–73; revolt of *comuneros* 78–81; population growth and decline 104–5; wealth from America 88
Castilla la Nueva 45, 60
Castilla y León, the last autonomous community 54, 229
*castros* 6
Catalan counties 37, 58
Catalunya, expansion 56–7; Black Death and fifteenth-century crises 58–60; rebellion in 1640 99; economic growth 115, 119; industrialisation 155–6, 158–9; autonomy 173, 176, 213, 222, 230–3; industrial unrest 161–6, 205; in Civil War 189, 192
Catholic Monarchs 69–75, 84, 85, 93, 104, 106
Cavestany, Rafael 204
CCOO (Communist trade union) 235
Cellorigo, Don Martín González 106, 109
Celtiberians 6, 15, 18
Celts 6–7
Cerdenya 59, 73, 100
Cerignola 73
Cervantes, Miguel de 94, 108
Ceuta 32
Charlemagne 37–9
Charles of Habsburg, Archduke 101
Charles VI, Emperor 101, 102
Charles VIII of France 73
Church 14–15, 19, 35–40, 42–3, 46, 50–3, 61, 67, 70–1, 84, 95–7, 108, 122–4; disentailment 141–2; Second Republic 173–4; in Civil War 189, 194; recent changes 221, 228
Churchill, Winston 197
Cid, el 47
Cisneros, Cardinal 75, 76
Ciudad Real 53
Civil War and its sequels (1936–1945), Spanish 183–97
Columbus, Christopher (Cristóbal Colón) 72–3

commerce 4, 12, 28, 49, 56–8, 80, 91–2, 114–9, 129, 135, 138–9, 154, 164–5, 206–12, 222

communications 9–10, 28, 39–40, 49, 89, 116, 135–6, 149–50, 155–6

Communist Party (PCE) 168, 219, 220, 235

*comuneros* 78–81

*Confederación Española de Derechas Autonomas* (CEDA) 179–81, 183, 198

Constantine I, Emperor 14, 15

Constitution of 1978 217–18, 224–30

Constitutional Tribunal 228, 230, 232

Constitution of Cádiz (1812) 132–6

Convention of Vergara (1839) 142

Córdoba 9, 12; Muslim capital 23, 25–30, 32, 34, 38; taken by Fernando III (1236) 53, 61

Cortés, Hernán 85

Covadonga 36, 38

Cuba 85, 148, 154, 163

Cuenca 7, 28, 44

Dali, Salvador 187

Davídiz, Count Sisnando 42, 43

demographic changes 10, 13, 49–50, 57, 94–5, 104–5, 125, 144, 151, 157–63, 168, 201–2, 210–11

Denin 34, 40

Diocletian, Emperor 14

disentailment laws 141

Domingo, Marcelino 179

Duero, River 3, 35, 36, 49

Dunkirk 100

Ebro, River 1–3, 6–8, 35, 40, 82, 202

education 26–7, 34, 93–4, 122–30, 176–7, 193, 194, 212

Egilona 22

Elche, Lady of 5

Escorial, El 95–8

Enrique (Trastámara) of Castilla 62–3

Enrique III of Castilla 63

Enrique IV of Castilla 59, 63, 64, 66, 68, 70

Erwigian Code 20

Esparter, General 142, 146

Estella 82, 138

ETA (Basque separatist movement) 214, 222–3, 230–1, 239–40

European Economic Community (EEC) 208, 232, 236, 240

Euskadi 222, 223, 229–232

Expo '92 237

Extremadura 61, 97, 180

Falange 189, 190, 193–7

Falkland Islands (Malvinas) 119

Fatimid Caliphate 32–4

Felipe II 85, 95–7, 99, 102, 104, 105, 108

Felipe III 105

Felipe IV 96–8, 100, 102

Felipe V 101, 112–17, 137

Fernández de Córdoba, Don Gonzalo 73

Fernández, Gregorio 97

Fernando I of Castilla 41, 50

Fernando II of Aragón 59, 69–75, 82, 84

Fernando II of Castilla 40

Fernando II of León 45, 52

Fernando III of Castilla-León 35, 48, 53, 61, 62, 195

Fernando VI 113, 117, 118

Fernando VII 125, 133–8, 140, 142, 202

Figuerola, Don Laureano 157

First International 161

Flanders 76, 90

Florez Estrada, Alvaro 143

Florida 117, 120

Floridablanca, Count 124–6, 132
foreign capital 150–2, 168–9, 204–5, 236
Fortú Garcés of Pamplona 32
Fraga, Don Manuel 229
France 101–2
Francis I of France 78, 84
Franco, General Francisco, service in Morocco 181, 195; takes command of insurgents 188, 189; offensive against Catalunya 192; proclaims himself *Caudillo* 195–6; declares Spain a kingdom 199, 217; in World War II 197–9; control of army 200; economic policies 200–5; last decade 213–16; death 216
Frankish counties 37–8
FRAP 220
French Revolution 121, 125–6
Fuenterraía 83

Galba 9
Galicia 4, 6, 35, 67, 68, 78, 92, 222, 223; in Civil War 188
Galindo, Aznar, first count of Aragón 38
Gallaecia 9, 16, 17
Gallienus 13
García III of Navarra 41, 42, 50
García Lorca, Federico 177, 193
García Ramírez 40
Garcilaso de la Vega 94
general strike of December 1988, 234–6
geographical mobility 94, 157–60
Gerona 37
Gibraltar 4, 102, 117, 120, 186
Gil Robles, José María 179–81
Giménez Fernández, Manuel 181
Giralda 34
Girón, Don Pedro 83

Godoy, Don Manuel 126, 127, 129, 135
Góngora, Luis de 94
González, Felipe 228, 235, 236, 239
González, Julio 187
Goya, Francisco 127–8, 129
Gracián, Baltasar 94
grain 4
Granada 14, 23, 25, 34, 35, 43, 54, 61–2, 66, 69, 84; conquest of Muslim kingdom 70–1
GRAPO 220
Greeks 4–6
Guadalajara 6, 96
Guadalete 22
Guadalquivir, River 2–4, 6, 10, 61
Guadiana, River 3, 4, 45
*guardia civil* 147, 153, 178
Guardiola, Juan Cristóbal de 108
Guernica 187
Guggenheim Museum, Bilbao 240
*guerrileros* 128–9, 146
Guijarro, Juan Martínez de 108
Guzmán, Leonor de 62

Hadrian, Emperor 12
Hannibal 8
Henry II of France 96
Henry VIII of England 78
Herrera, Angel 179, 198
Herrera, Juan de 97, 98
*hidalgos* 44, 50, 107
Hisham I 29
Hisham II 32, 33, 34
Hisham III 34
Hispania Romana 7–15
Hispania Gothica 15–21
Hitler, Adolf 191, 197, 199
Honduras 117, 120
Hontañón, Gilde 97
Huelva 4, 151
Huesca 39
Hundred Years War 54, 65

Hurtado de Mendoza, Don Diego 81
Ibáñez Martín, José 198, 206
Ibarruri, Dolores (*la pasionara*) 187
Iberian Anarchist Federation (FAI)
    178
Iberians 1, 5
Ibiza 28
Ibn Hafsun 30
Ibn Hayyan 37
Ibn Tumart 44
Ifriqiya 22, 23
Iglesias, Pablo 162–3
Ilipa 8
Independence, War of 128–34
industrialisation 149–57, 160, 163
Innocent VIII, Pope 84
Inquisition 69, 71, 123, 132, 135
intendant system 113
International Brigades 187
Isabel, Empress 84–5
Isabel I of Castilla 64–6, 69–75, 77
Isabel II 137, 138, 142, 144, 147, 148
Islam 17, 22, 23–5; *see also* Muslim
    conquest
Italy 17, 73, 191

Jaca 38, 50
Jaén 4, 48, 53, 61, 154, 175, 177, 210
Jaime I of Aragon-Catalunya 48, 53,
    55, 56
Jaime II 56
Játiva 53
Jesuits 93, 122–3, 174
Jews 19–20, 24–6, 54, 56, 60–1, 64;
    *conversos* 68; expulsion 71–2;
    persecution 67–9
José I 127, 129
Joseph, Emperor 101
Juana I 65, 66, 70, 74, 76, 77, 79
Juan Carlos I de Borbón, succeeds to
    throne 199, 215, 216–19, 222–3;
    constitutional monarchy 224–5;
    foils army coup 228

Juan de Borbón, Don 196–9, 216,
    221
Juan de la Cruz, San 94
Juan II of Aragón 70
Juan II of Castilla 59, 63, 64
Julius Caesar 10
Juni, Juan de 97
*juros v censos* 109–10
Justinian, Emperor 17

Kairouan 34
Kindelán, General 188

La Coruña 78
Lafargue, Paul 161
La Granja (Segovia) 117
land distribution 160, 178
Las Casas, Bartolomé de 94
Las Navas de Tolosa, battle of 35,
    47–8, 52
Leguina, Joaquín 230
León (Legio) 4, 9, 11, 32, 35, 39–42,
    45, 48, 50–5
León, Fray Luis de 94
Leovigild, King 20
Lérida 16
Lerroux, Alejandro 174, 180, 183
liberalism 138–9
Limits, treaty of (1778) 120
Líster, Enrique 222
literacy 93, 160, 177
literature ('Golden Age') 94
Lobregat, River 3
LOAPA ('Law on the Harmonisation
    of the Autonomy Process') 227,
    229
Logroño 82
Lopez de Gomara, Francisco 91
Los Arapiles, battle of 134
Los Ríos, Don Fernando de 173, 179
Louix XI of France 59
Louis XIV of France 100, 101, 112
Louis XVI of France 121, 126

Luna, Don Alvaro de 64–6

Machado, Antonio 193
Madoz 142, 143
Madrid 10, 84, 97, 112, 117–18, 121, 122, 127, 134, 149, 199; population growth 156, 158, 159; industrial unrest 160–1, 166; in Civil War 186–9, 192; recent events 234, 240
Málaga 4, 11, 17, 25, 28, 34, 92, 95, 178
Mallorca 28, 56, 59, 81
manorial system 37, 62, 63, 115, 138
Manrique, Jorge 67
Manuel I of Portugal 74
Maragall, Pasqual 231
Marca Hispanica 37
María Cristina, Princess 137, 144
Maroto General 142, 146
Marrakesh 44
Martial 12
Martín Artajo, Alberto 198
Mataró 149
Maura, Don Miguel 166, 171, 174
Medina Azahara 27
Mela 12
Melilla 32, 167
Mendizábal 139, 141–3
Menorca 102, 117, 120, 127
Mérida 9, 11
Mesa, Juan de 97
mineral resources 4, 6, 7, 8, 9, 12, 28, 34, 72–3, 85, 88, 90, 150–1, 155, 157, 159
Miranda de Ebro 126
Miró, Joan 187
Molina, Tirso de 94
monarchical power 38, 60, 62–9, 84, 104, 125–6, 139–41, 171, 196, 199, 217–9, 224
Moncloa Pacts 222
Montañés, Juan Martínez 97
Montiel, battle of 63, 65

Montseny, Federica 222
*moriscos* 71, 81, 104–5, 110
Morocco 164, 167, 169, 184, 195
Mosquito Shore 120
*mozárabes* 25, 36, 43, 50–7, 60
*mudéjares* 55, 61
Muhammad I 30, 35
Muhammad II 33
Mulhacen 3
Murat, Marshal 127
Murcia 5, 23–4, 28, 44, 53, 56
Murillo, Bartolomé Esteban 97
Musa 22, 23
Muslim conquest of Spanish peninsula 22–3; Umayyad dynasty 27, 28–35; end of Umayyad dynasty 33–5; fall of Toledo (1085) 35, 42–3; country life 27–8; social integration 23–6; town life 26–7
Muslim revivalism 43–5
Mussolini, Benito 190, 191

Naples 73, 74, 116
Napoleon 127, 128, 132–5
National Federation of Landworkers (FNTT) 178, 181
NATO 229
Navarra 38–40, 54, 74, 82–3, 113, 222, 227; special status under Foral Pact 142; in Civil War 185, 188, 194
Nebrija, Elio Antonio de 73
Negrín 191, 192
Niebla 61
nobility 65–7, 80–5, 106–11, 140–1, 146, 173, 196, 201
North, Lord 120
Numancia 6, 11, 15

Ocaña 132
Olavide, Don Pablo de 123, 124
Olmedo, battle of 64
Olympic Games, Barcelona 237

'Operación Galaxia' 223
Opus Dei 206
Orihuela 24, 81
Ortega y Gasset, José 174, 176
Ottoman Empire 84, 90

Pacheco, Francisco 97
Padilla, Juan de 79
Palencia 18, 92
Pamplona 11, 32, 38, 39, 82, 127, 205
Paris International Exhibition (1937) 186
Patiño, Don José de 116
Pavia 84
Pedro I of Castilla 62–5, 68
Pedro II of Aragón 47
Pelayo 36
Pellicer, Faraga 160, 161
Perú 85
Petronila of Aragón 46, 55, 60
Philip of Anjou 101
Phillippine Islands 89, 154, 163
Phoenicians 4, 6, 10
Picasso, Pablo 187
Piñar, Blas 217
Pizarro, Francisco 85, 91
Plá i Deniel, Cardinal 198
Plate, River 120
Pliny 9
Political Reform Act of 18 November 1976 220
Portugal 4, 45, 54, 72, 99–101, 117, 127
Pradera, Javier 190
Prieto, Indalecio 163, 198
Primo de Rivera, Don Miguel 167–70, 184
Prim y Prats, Juan 147, 157
protectionism 156–7
Puerto Rico 154, 163
Puig Antich, Salvador 216
Pujol, Jordi 230
Punic Wars 7

Pyrenees, treaty of 100

Quevedo, Francisco de 94, 106, 108
Quintilian 12

railways 149–50, 155, 156
Ramón Berenguer IV of Barcelona 46, 55, 60
Ramón Borrell I 38
Raymond of Burgundy 45
Reccared, King 15, 19
Recceswinth, King 15, 16
Republicanism 147, 163, 171
Restoration 148, 164, 165, 170, 217
Ribalta, Francisco 97
Ribera, José 97
Río Tinto 4, 10, 151
Rocroi 99
Roderic, King 20, 22, 23, 36
Rojas, Fernando de 94
Roman conquest of Spanish peninsula 7–15; life under Roman rule 10–13; Romanisation 10–13; break-up of Western Roman Empire 13–15
Romulus Augustulus, Emperor 16
Roncesvalles 37–9
Ronda 34
Roussillon 59, 73, 100
Royal Fifth 89
Ruiz Giménez, Joaquín 198
Russia 186, 191
Russian Revolution 164

Sacramento 120
Sagrajas (or Zalaca), battle of 35, 43
Sagunto (Saguntum) 8, 147
Salamanca 97
Salazar, Alonso 181
Sancho I of Aragon 40, 46
Sancho II of Navarra 33
Sancho III of Navarra 38, 39, 41, 50
Sancho IV of Navarra 41, 42

Sancho VII of Navarra 47
Sanchuelo 32–4
Sanjurjo, General 176, 184
San Martín de Albelda 39
San Martín de Frómista 50
San Miguel de Escalada 36
San Millán de la Cogolla 39
San Sebastián 134, 136
Santa Fé 71
Santa María la, Real de Nájera 50
Santiago, Order of 52, 61
Santiago de Compostela 32, 37, 39, 40, 49, 53, 78
Santo Domingo 85, 126
Sardá Dexeus, Joan 204
Scipio, Cnaeus Cornelius 8
SEAT 237
Second Republic 171–82
Segovia 14, 68, 104, 129
Seguí, Salvador 166
Segura, Cardinal 173
Seneca 12
Sentence of Guadalupe 60
Serrano, General Francisco 147
Serrano, Súñer, Ramón 190, 197
Seven Years War 117, 120
Sevilla 22, 23, 32, 34–5, 41, 43, 61; architecture 84, 97; taken by Fernando III (1246) 53; Atlantic trade 88–90, 92, 95, 97, 114; Jews 68; in Civil War 185; 1492 anniversary 237
'Siliceo', Martinez de, Archbishop of Toledo 108
Silvestre, General 167
Simancas 37
Socialist Party (PSOE) 162–3, 178, 181, 183, 221, 228, 235–6, 239
Soult, Marshal 129
'Spanish' flu 158
Spanish Succession, War of the 101–2, 112
Stabilisation Plan (1959) 207–9

Strabo 1, 6, 10
strikes 162, 165, 169, 205
Suárez, Adolfo 219, 221
Suebi 15, 16
Sulayman 23

*taifa* rulers 34, 43, 44
Tajo, River 3, 6, 9, 18, 42, 49, 52
Talavera 22
Tamarón, battle of 41
Tarifa 1, 16
Tariq 22, 23
Tarragona (Tarraco) 9, 11, 13
Tartessos (Tarshish) 4
Tejero, Colonel 223, 228
Templars 46, 52
Teresa de Avila, Santa 94
textile industry 12, 129, 145, 160
Theodomir 24
Theodosius, Count 14
Theodosius I, Emperor 15
Thirty Years War 102, 110
Toledo 4, 17–8, 20–1, 22, 25, 28, 29, 36, 39, 44–5, 88, 108, 175, 177, 210; fall of (1085) 35, 40–5, 48, 50, 55, 61; revolt against Carlos I 78–9, 81; Church 50–3; Visigothic kingdom 17, 20
Toledo, Juan Bautista de 97
Tordesillas 76, 78–81
Tordessilas, treaty of 65
Toro, battle of 70
tourism 210, 211, 235
towns 49–50
trade 76, 80, 91–2, 107, 115–116
trade-balance deficit 205, 206
trade unions 162–3, 168, 177, 194
Trafalgar 127
'tragic week' 161–2, 164
Trajan, Emperor 12
transhumance 28
Trastámara family 69–70, 74
Trinidad 127

Umayyad dynasty *see* Muslim conquest
Unamuno, Miguel de 174, 176
*Unión del Centro Democrático* (UCD) 228
*Unión General de Trabajadores* (UGT) 162, 163, 168, 169, 178, 181, 235–7
United Left 236
United Nations 199, 205
United Provinces 99, 101–2
United States of America 163, 164, 196, 199, 200, 202; economic and financial aid to Spain 204–5, 211
Urraca of Castilla-León 45
Utrecht, treaty of 102

Valdés Leal, Juan de 97
Valencay 134, 135
Valencia 11, 23, 47, 53, 55, 56, 58–60, 104, 113–5, 154–5, 158, 209; revolt of *agermanats* 81–2; expulsion of *moriscos* 110; in Civil War 187, 191
Valentian I, Emperor 14
Valentian II, Emperor 15
Valladolid 77, 80, 83, 93, 96, 97
Vandals 15–17
Vascones 38–40
Vázquez, Lorenzo 96

Vega, Lope de 94
Veláquez, Diego Silva de 97, 108
Vález 81, 83
Vermudo III 41
Vespasian 9
Vieques Island 119
Vikings 25
Villalar 82
viniculture 4, 115, 144, 152, 154, 161–2, 180
Visigoths 14–20, 23, 35
Vitoria, battle 128
Vitoria, Francisco de 94

Ward, Bernard 118
Wellington, Duke of 128, 133–5
World Bank 208, 212
World War I 163–6
World War II 196–9

Yusuf 11 47
Yusuf Ibn Tashunin 43–4

Zalaca *see* Sagrajas
Zaragoza 4, 11, 28, 34, 37, 39, 40–1, 53, 77, 136; in Civil War 185; conquered by Alfonso I (1118) 46
Zurbarán, Francisco 97